ALDHELM
THE PROSE WORKS

TRANSLATED BY MICHAEL LAPIDGE
AND MICHAEL HERREN

D. S. BREWER · ROWMAN & LITTLEFIELD

Published by D. S. Brewer Ltd., PO Box 24, Ipswich IP1 1JJ
and 240 Hills Road, Cambridge
and Rowman & Littlefield, 81 Adams Drive,
Totowa, New Jersey 07512, U.S.A.

First published 1979

British Library Cataloguing in Publication Data

Aldhelm, *Saint*
  Aldhelm the prose works
  1. English texts
  I. Title II. Lapidge, Michael
  III. Herren, Michael
  878'.02'08   PA8246

ISBN 0 85991-041-5

Photoset by Benham & Company Limited, Sheepen Place,
Colchester, Essex CO3 3LH and printed in Great Britain by
Redwood Burn Limited, Trowbridge & Esher

TABLE OF CONTENTS

PREFACE

The present translation was conceived and planned jointly, but each translator has been responsible for various aspects of its execution. Michael Lapidge translated the *De Virginitate* and wrote the Introduction to that work; Michael Herren translated the Letters and the selections from the *Epistola ad Acircium*, and wrote the Introductions to those works. The General Introduction and the section on The Writings of Aldhelm were written by Michael Lapidge. The section on Aldhelm's Life and the Translators' Notes were written in collaboration. The Bibliography and Index of Names were compiled by Michael Lapidge. We have benefited from the advice and criticism of several colleagues, and wish to acknowledge their help. Michael Winterbottom helped to clarify a number of textual obscurities. David Dumville answered many questions about Aldhelm's historical background. Simon Keynes advised us concerning the authenticity of the two 'Aldhelmian' charters printed in Appendix II. Peter Godman and Vivien Law helped to eliminate many errors from the translation of the *De Virginitate*. Jill Mann read meticulously—*membratim et particulatim*, as Aldhelm would say—through the translation of the *De Virginitate*, catching more errors than it is flattering to recall and clarifying the English at every turn. But Aldhelm is not an easy author to translate, and errors will no doubt remain. If future readers of Aldhelm are able to understand something more of his work than previous readers, unguided by a translation, have done, then these errors will have been committed in a worthwhile cause.

M.L.
M.H.
Cambridge and Toronto, January, 1978

GENERAL INTRODUCTION

Aldhelm may justifiably be called the first English man of letters. By any reckoning he was one of the most learned and influential English scholars of the Anglo-Saxon period. To his younger contemporary, Bede, he appeared a man 'most learned in every respect', and Bede went on to observe that Aldhelm was 'both resplendent in his style and also noteworthy for his erudition in classical as well as patristic writings'.[1] After some 1300 years we are still able to appreciate the accuracy of Bede's assessment. Aldhelm left a considerable corpus of Latin writing both in prose and verse (metrical and rhythmical), and these writings reveal a breadth of learning that was hardly excelled by Bede himself. Furthermore, because of their impressive erudition and sophistication, Aldhelm's writings exerted a vast influence on his contemporaries and on the generation which succeeded him. Nearly every facet of his literary output found an English imitator. Aldhelm's rhythmical verse,[2] for example, was imitated by a circle of his students that included the otherwise unknown Æthilwald;[3] the form of this rhythmic verse—rhyming octosyllables—became very popular among English writers of the eighth century,[4] no doubt as a result of Aldhelm's prestige. Similarly, Aldhelm's dedicatory verses on various churches and altars (the so-called *Carmina Ecclesiastica*[5]) served as models for less proficient Anglo-Latin poets of the eighth century.[6] Aldhelm's collection of poetic *Enigmata*—'mysteries' we should say, rather than 'riddles'—was widely influential in the eighth century, and was imitated by Tatwine (archbishop of Canterbury, 731–4), 'Eusebius' (possibly the Hwætberht who became abbot of Wearmouth/Jarrow in 716), Boniface, and the anonymous authors of the Berne and Lorsch riddle collections.[7] Several of Aldhelm's *enigmata* were translated at an early stage into Old English (both Northumbrian and West Saxon dialects), and it is probable that Aldhelm's collection was the model for the collection of nearly one hundred Old English riddles which survive in the Exeter Book.[8] Even more influential than Aldhelm's poetry was his prose (incredible as this may seem to modern taste!), particularly the long and stylistically convoluted treatise *De Virginitate*. This work was a stylistic model not only for Boniface himself but also for the wide circle of English correspondents whom Boniface addressed and whose letters have been preserved—Eadburg (abbess of Thanet), Ecgburg, Daniel (bishop of Winchester) and Leobgyth among others.[9] Lul, who became Boniface's successor as bishop of Mainz and who earlier had been a student at Malmesbury (a decade or so after Aldhelm's death), wrote Latin prose that is heavily indebted to a study of Aldhelm.[10] The prose of Felix, author of the *Vita S. Guthlaci*[11] (composed *c.* 716 × 730), is profoundly Aldhelmian in its use of grecisms and convoluted periods, as is the prose of the Englishman Willibald (who wrote a *Vita S. Bonifatii*[12] sometime shortly after Boniface's martyrdom in 754), as well as that of Hygeburg, a nun of Heidenheim who composed a *Vita Willibaldi et Wynnebaldi*[13] to celebrate two English brothers who were prominent in the mission in Germany. From this list of examples—and it is by no means complete—one may surmise that all of Aldhelm's writings enjoyed a wide and immediate circulation among English audiences in the eighth century.

Nor was Aldhelm's influence limited to England and to the eighth century. The Anglo-Saxon missionaries to Germany were well acquainted with his writings, and it is not surprising that Aldhelm's works should subsequently have been studied in continental centres, particularly those associated with the Anglo-Saxon mission. In fact the earliest surviving manuscript of Aldhelm's Letters (the Codex Vindobonensis 751, s. ix[med]) was copied at Mainz, and the earliest copy of the prose *De Virginitate*, a ninth-century manuscript written at Würzburg in Caroline script but containing Insular (English) additions, may possibly have been copied from a manuscript sent by Dealwine in England to Lul in Germany.[14] In the tenth century, when English learning was re-established through the energy of the Benedictine reform movement, Aldhelm's Latin writings once again received the careful attention of English monastic audiences. At this time many manuscripts of Aldhelm's works were imported into England from the continent.[15] Aldhelm became one of the principal authors on the English curriculum. The great majority of surviving manuscripts of the prose *De Virginitate* was copied in England in the tenth and eleventh centuries. That these manuscripts were attentively studied may be appreciated from the vast number of glosses, both Latin and Old English, which were entered in them.[16] One manuscript of the prose *De Virginitate* from Abingdon (Oxford, Bodleian Library,

2

MS Digby 146) contains more than 5500 glosses! Not only Aldhelm's vocabulary but also his syntax was studied with care, as may be observed from the syntactical markings which often accompany a manuscript copy of his work.[17] The intensive study of Aldhelm in the tenth and eleventh centuries is reflected in virtually all the Latin literature produced in England at that time: there is scarcely a Latin work which does not display one or more features of what may be called the 'hermeneutic' style[18]—either grecisms or archaisms exhumed from glossaries or neologisms coined in an effort to ornament the work in hand. Only with the advent of Norman ecclesiastical administration and learning in the late eleventh century does Aldhelm's importance as a curriculum author begin to wane.

And yet, in spite of Aldhelm's immense prestige and immeasurable influence on the Latin culture of preconquest Anglo-Saxon England, he has been virtually ignored by modern scholarship. The lament of William of Malmesbury in the early twelfth century is pertinent today: 'adeo, praeter illud quod de illo (*scil.* Aldhelmo) Beda in Gestis Anglorum tangit, semper infra meritum iacuit, semper, desidia civium agente, inhonorus latuit'.[19] Nowadays one can point only to two monographs written at the turn of this century (one of which is more concerned with the archaeological remains of churches which Aldhelm may have built than with his literary estate),[20] to a few commemorative lectures,[21] to a rather fanciful biography,[22] and to an account in the standard history of Anglo-Latin literature that contains many errors.[23] The neglect of Aldhelm is more forcibly emphasized when one compares the huge amount of scholarly energy which has been devoted to Bede this century. It may well be that, after all, Bede is the more interesting of the two authors; but to the Anglo-Saxon reading public Aldhelm was the pre-eminent author, not Bede; and given that twentieth-century scholarship has concerned itself so fully with the exploration of Anglo-Saxon culture, it is more than a little surprising that Aldhelm should be so widely ignored. All the more so, when one considers that Aldhelm's Letters and portions of the *Epistola ad Acircium* provide the *only* contemporary witness for certain important ecclesiastical developments and for the history of education in England in the last quarter of the seventh century.

Bede's corpus of writing is still far from being available in modern critical editions, whereas the works of Aldhelm can be read in the excellent edition of Rudolf Ehwald in the *Auctores Antiquissimi* series of the *Monumenta Germaniae Historica*[24]—an edition which in every way may be described as monumental. Ehwald made available for students of Aldhelm virtually all the information which they conceivably could require—meticulous reporting of the results of extensive collation of

3

surviving manuscripts, exhaustive documentation of Aldhelm's sources and of parallels to Aldhelmian passages in contemporary Anglo-Latin literature, indices as comprehensive as any which have ever been lavished on a medieval author, and an account of Aldhelm's life, work, and influence as accurate as any which has yet been written. Sadly, this great treasury of scholarship has been too seldom consulted, and accounts of Anglo-Saxon literary culture customarily by-pass Aldhelm in a few sentences.

Perhaps there are obvious reasons for the neglect of Aldhelm's work by students of Anglo-Saxon culture. Aldhelm's Latin is extremely difficult, and sometimes impenetrable. His sentences are tediously long and complicated; his vocabulary is often bizarre and arcane, sometimes inscrutable. Indeed, Aldhelm's love of verbiage for its own sake—he calls it 'verbose garrulity or garrulous verbosity'—must often exasperate the well-intentioned reader who, having penetrated the lexical and syntactical obscurities of a two-page long sentence, finds that he is left with a trivial apophthegm of the merest banality. Moreover, the subjects of Aldhelm's works are not, for modern readers, compelling ones. But in spite of these difficulties, there is much in Aldhelm which must be considered to be of direct importance to the study of Anglo-Saxon culture.

Aldhelm's prose works have never been translated, as far as we are aware, into any modern language. It seems to us, therefore, that a translation into modern English of these prose works would make Aldhelm accessible to a scholarly public which might otherwise continue to ignore him. Such a translation might ideally be used as a stepping-stone to Ehwald's edition, and it is as a 'crib' to Ehwald's text of Aldhelm's prose works that we have intended the present volume. If it serves as a guide to only a handful of readers who would otherwise be lost in what Aldhelm proudly refers to as his *densa Latinitatis silva*, it will have amply rewarded its translators' efforts.

4

ALDHELM'S LIFE

Very little can now be known about Aldhelm's life. There is almost no contemporary or near-contemporary witness. Bede includes a brief account of Aldhelm in the fifth book of his *Historia Ecclesiastica* (V.18), but, except for noting that Aldhelm became bishop of the western sector of the West Saxon see on Hæddi's death and held that bishopric for four years, Bede tells us very little about Aldhelm himself, and Bede's account of Aldhelm's writings contains some inaccuracy (see below p. 141). The *Anglo-Saxon Chronicle* records Aldhelm's death against the year 709,[1] but this information almost certainly derives from Bede. Bede's brief notice can be supplemented with biographical details contained in Aldhelm's own writings. However, it should be stressed at once that these details are extremely elusive and must be interpreted with extreme caution. Finally, there are two later medieval lives of Aldhelm (see Bibliography, Section C, below). The earliest of these was written by Faricius, probably between 1080 and 1100.[2] Faricius (*ob.* 1117) was an Italian from Arezzo who spent some years at Malmesbury before he was appointed abbot of Abingdon by King Henry I in 1100. The second, and more reliable, life of Aldhelm was written by William of Malmesbury (*c.*1090–1143); it constitutes Book V of William's *Gesta Pontificum*[3] and was composed in approximately 1125. Both Faricius and William provide a good deal of information about Aldhelm's life, but this information too must be treated with extreme caution. On one hand, they had access to works concerning Aldhelm which we no longer possess—for example, King Alfred's *Handboc* (which, since it was written in Old English, was of little use to Faricius: William criticizes Faricius on several occasions for misinterpreting Old English words). On the other hand, we possess works by Aldhelm which were not available to these two biographers (for example, the Letters to Geraint and Heahfrith, Nos. IV and V). Furthermore, William accepted uncritically certain charters relating to

5

Aldhelm as genuine which are today regarded as spurious. And since a period of some 400 years separated Aldhelm from Faricius and William, many of the traditional anecdotes concerning Aldhelm which they relate must be treated with scepticism.[4] In short, we are faced with an embarrassing paucity of information about Aldhelm's life. Faced with this paucity, certain modern scholars have embraced fiction—on the principle, no doubt, that nature abhors a vacuum. Unfortunately, many so-called 'facts' about Aldhelm's life which were in origin no more than conjectures or inspired guesses, have become embedded in textbooks and are repeated uncritically. One would very much welcome a fresh and thorough study of the sources for Aldhelm's life. For the time being, it may be salutary to stress the tenuous nature of the available evidence.

We do not know where or when Aldhelm was born. It is commonly stated that he was born in 639 or 640. This date has been deduced from a statement in William of Malmesbury (p. 332) that Aldhelm was 'not less than a septuagenarian when he died' (*non minor decedens septuagenario*): and 70 subtracted from 709 (the date of his death given by the *Anglo-Saxon Chronicle*) leaves 639. If any trust can be placed in William's statement, any date between 630 and 640 would not be wide of the mark. However, William's statement is manifestly a conjecture, and he states elsewhere that he had no accurate information before him.[5] It is commonly assumed that Aldhelm was born in Wessex; but again, this is no more than a guess, for which some people have sought confirmation in the story, reported by both Faricius and William, that Aldhelm was the son of Kenten,[6] an otherwise unknown brother of the West Saxon king Ine (*c.*688–*c.*726). However, William himself notes that this statement is more a matter of 'transitory opinion than of historical truth' (p. 322). Modern scholarship would do well to follow William's scepticism on this point.

Much opinion has been expressed on Aldhelm's early training. Our knowledge here is not securely based. We have a letter from an anonymous student to Aldhelm (No. VI) in which the writer remarks that Aldhelm has been 'nourished by a certain holy man of our race'. The nationality of this student cannot be determined with certainty. The writer's remark that Aldhelm had been to Rome may possibly suggest that he was Italian; the 'man of our race' would then presumably be Hadrian, who was African in origin, but who lived most of his life in Italy.[7] On the other hand, Ehwald and others have held that the student was Irish; by implication, Aldhelm's 'nourisher' must also have been Irish (see discussion below, p. 146). In the event, Aldhelm himself is silent on the subject of training at the hands of an Irish master. However, William of Malmesbury reports nearly five centuries later that Aldhelm's early training took place at Malmesbury with one Máeldub, whom William describes as an 'Irishman by birth, a philosopher by erudition, and a monk by profession' (pp. 333–4), who left Ireland in pursuit of the solitary life. Except for what William says, we know nothing of this Máeldub.[8] The name occurs several times in Irish annals and martyrologies,[9] but none can be identified conclusively with the Máeldub of William's account. (Therefore Browne's conjectures[10] about Máeldub's origins in Lismore can be discounted.) In short, we cannot be entirely certain that Aldhelm studied under an Irish teacher; we are even less certain that the name of that teacher was Máeldub. What Aldhelm studied before he went to Canterbury is almost entirely a matter of speculation.[11]

Our ignorance of Aldhelm's early education needs to be emphasised in view of the frequently-repeated statements about the 'Celtic' or 'Hisperic' aspect of Aldhelm's education, and specifically, of his Latin prose style. As Michael Winterbottom has recently shown, Aldhelm's stylistic connections are with the continent, not with Ireland.[12] The common assumption that Aldhelm's style is 'Hisperic' is untenable.[13] Whereas the syntax of the *Hisperica Famina* is straightforward, that of Aldhelm is extraordinarily complex, even tortuous. Despite a handful of rare words in common, Aldhelm's vocabulary is far richer than that of the *Famina*. On the other hand, Aldhelm was familiar with works of Irish provenance: he cited a line from Virgilius Maro Grammaticus;[14] he drew the first section of the *Epistola ad Acircium* from the *Liber Numerorum*—a work transmitted from, if not composed in, Ireland (see below, p. 32); and he may have known the Irish *Liber de Ordine Creaturarum*.[15] A case has been made for his knowledge of the *Hisperica Famina*.[16] Furthermore, he was aware of the sort of training available in an Irish school, as his letters to Wihtfrith and Heahfrith (Nos. III and V) show. But familiarity with Irish teaching and with a few Hiberno-Latin texts does not prove that Aldhelm's literary culture was predominantly Irish. In view of this, it is well to avoid speculation about what Aldhelm might have studied before his arrival in Canterbury, save to note two indisputable facts: (1) that Aldhelm in his letter to Leuthere (No. I) stresses the inadequacy of his earlier training in computus; and (2) judging from his remarkable command of Latin, his early training in the rudiments of that language must have been thorough.

We are on firmer ground concerning the subsequent stage of Aldhelm's education. In 669 Theodore, a Greek originally from Tarsus,[17] arrived in England to become archbishop of Canterbury; some time shortly thereafter Theodore's colleague Hadrian arrived to become abbot of the monastery of SS Peter and Paul (later St Augustine's) in Canterbury. From Aldhelm's second letter, addressed to Hadrian, it is clear that Aldhelm had studied with Hadrian on two separate occasions in Canterbury; and since Aldhelm himself was abbot of Malmesbury probably by 673 or 674 (see below, p. 9), it is a reasonable inference that the tutelage under Hadrian took place between (say) c.670, the probable date of Hadrian's arrival, and the date of Aldhelm's election to the abbacy. Aldhelm makes reference to the subjects of his study under Hadrian (Letter I), and these included jurisprudence, metrics, computus, and astronomy. However, this precisely defined curriculum does not indicate the full extent of Aldhelm's extraordinary learning. A cursory glance at Ehwald's list of authorities[18] quoted by Aldhelm will suggest that, by any standard, Aldhelm's reading was vast, and embraced classical as well as patristic authors. The extent of his learning rivalled, if it did not surpass, that of Bede. It is difficult to assess how much of Aldhelm's education was acquired at Canterbury. As far as we can tell, Aldhelm only spent a period of a few years at Canterbury, and even that period was interrupted. It is impossible at this remove to estimate accurately the learning of Hadrian and Theodore: no writings of Hadrian, and very few of Theodore,[19] survive. Bede makes reference to the school of Theodore and Hadrian at Canterbury, and notes that their curriculum included metrics, astronomy and computus;[20] Bede further notes that certain students acquired a sound knowledge of Greek as well as of Latin (*HE* IV.2). Again, it is not easy to judge whether Aldhelm was one of the 'certain students' who acquired a knowledge of Greek. Despite his fondness for Greek and Greek-derived words,[21] we possess no unambiguous evidence that he was able to construe a sentence in that language. He is addressed by an unknown student (Letter VI) as 'distinguished in native ability and for (his) Roman eloquence, and for various flowers of letters, even those in the Greek fashion'. But the phrase *Graecorum more* might indicate no more than that Aldhelm adorned his vocabulary with Greek words. On the other hand, Aldhelm at one point in the *Epistola ad Acircium* cites the Greek names of six *pathē* which are found in hexameters; since these six *pathē* are found only in Hephaestion,[22] a Greek writer on metrics, and not in any Latin grammarian, there is some possibility that Aldhelm may have known the Greek text of Hephaestion. However, as Ehwald observes, Aldhelm could well have found the terms in a Latin treatise which is no longer extant. Similarly, it has been suggested that a Latin verse translation of a Greek acrostic poem was made by Aldhelm (who cites the translation on several occasions), but this suggestion cannot be affirmed (see below, p. 19). In short, the

8

question of Aldhelm's knowledge of Greek must remain in suspense until further research has been undertaken. Finally, there is no support whatsoever in Aldhelm's writings for Faricius's assertion that he knew Hebrew.[23]

We know very little of Aldhelm's subsequent career save that he became abbot of Malmesbury and later bishop of Sherborne. Scholars, following William of Malmesbury,[24] have put the date of Aldhelm's election to the abbacy at 675 and have further assumed both that Máeldub was his predecessor as abbot and that Máeldub died in the same year. Knowledge of the latter's very existence depends solely on the witness of William; and William is silent on the subject of Máeldub's abbacy (he simply refers to him as a hermit) and the date of his death. The date of Aldhelm's election assigned by William may be in need of revision. It seems likely that Aldhelm attended the Council of Hertford, in September 672, and that there he was instructed to write to Geraint concerning the issues of this council. In his letter to Geraint (No. IV) Aldhelm refers to himself as abbot. It is probable that his letter followed soon after the council, and therefore that he was abbot by 673 or 674 (see below, pp. 141–2).

From his own writings we know that Aldhelm's career as abbot was a busy one. He apologizes at the end of his prose De Virginitate (c. LIX) that the work has been delayed because he has been 'weighed down with the burden of pastoral care' and 'because the demanding responsibilities of ecclesiastical administration did not allow any space of undisturbed peace'.[25] Similarly, in his Epistola ad Acircium (c. CXLII) he describes himself as weighed down by 'such great tumultuous uproars in secular affairs' and by 'the ecclesiastical concerns of the pastoral care'. It is a fair assumption that part of Aldhelm's ecclesiastical responsibilities involved the construction of churches in the territory which was later to become his diocese. William tells us (p. 345) that he rebuilt a church at Malmesbury, which was dedicated to the apostles Peter and Paul, and that he built two monasteries: one next to the river Frome[26] and one at Bradford-on-Avon.[27] Three at least of Aldhelm's Carmina Ecclesiastica probably refer to churches which he himself built (see below, p. 11).

There is sound evidence that Aldhelm made one trip to Rome, since reference is made to such a journey in a contemporary letter by an anonymous student (Letter VI): 'because you were a visitor at Rome'. However, the date, duration, or purpose of the visit cannot be determined. It has been assumed that Aldhelm went to Rome during the papacy of Sergius I (687–701), but this assumption derives from a papal bull (preserved by William, pp. 367–70) that is a confirmation of privileges by Pope Sergius to the monastery at Malmesbury.

However, this bull is almost certainly spurious.[28] Nevertheless, the mere fact of the journey is consonant with Aldhelm's defence of the Roman position on the Easter reckoning and tonsure (Letter IV) and with his support for the exiled Wilfrid (Letter XII; see discussion below, pp. 150–1).

According to Bede (*HE* V. 18), the West Saxon see was divided on the death of bishop Hæddi, and Aldhelm became bishop of the western sector of that diocese. Bede tells us in the same place that Hæddi died 'at the beginning of the reign of Osred', the young son of Aldfrith. The date of Osred's accession presents difficulties, because it is clear that Bede did not know the precise date, day and year of either Aldfrith's death or Osred's accession.[29] However, we know from other sources (the D and E versions of the *Anglo-Saxon Chronicle*) that Aldfrith died on 14 December 705, and it is probable that there was a two-month interregnum between Aldfrith and Osred; that is, the first year of Osred's reign began early in 706. Presumably, then, Hæddi also died in 706. Aldhelm, therefore, could not have become bishop before 706 (and so the usual date assigned to Aldhelm's bishopric—705—must be abandoned). In any case, as Bede tells us, 'Aldhelm presided over this diocese energetically' (*HE* V. 18). The seat of his diocese, according to William (p. 375), was Sherborne, where, according to the same source, Aldhelm constructed 'a magnificent cathedral', which was still standing in William's day.[30]

Bede tells us (V. 18) that Aldhelm was bishop for four years. It would therefore be safe to conclude that Aldhelm died late in 709[31] or early in 710. According to William (p. 382), he died at Doulting in Somerset.

THE WRITINGS OF ALDHELM

The following Latin writings of Aldhelm are extant:

(a) the *Carmina Ecclesiastica*. This is the title given by Ehwald to a collection of five short poems which have been transmitted under Aldhelm's name separately in continental rather than English manuscripts. The poems dedicate churches or altars. The first of these (Ehwald's No. I) dedicates an unspecified church in honour of SS Peter and Paul. We know from William of Malmesbury (p. 345) that Aldhelm's own church in Malmesbury was so dedicated, and the poem is probably the dedication of this church. If this identification is correct, we may perhaps follow William in assuming that Aldhelm built his church soon after he became abbot (673 or 674?—see above, p. 9), and so assign a date of *c*.675 to the poem. But even this approximate dating is based on a series of unverifiable conjectures. The second poem dedicates a church to the Virgin Mary; William again tells us (p. 361) of a second church built at Malmesbury by Aldhelm and dedicated to the Virgin Mary. The poem perhaps commemorates this later church, but neither the church nor the poem may be dated exactly (in spite of Ehwald's efforts, p. 7). The third poem dedicates a church built by Bugga, a daughter of the West Saxon king Centwine (676–685), probably at Withington, Gloucestershire, not far from Malmesbury. The poem mentions the death of King Cædwalla (*ob*.689) and hence may be dated to about 690. The next poem (Ehwald's No. IV), a series of dedications of twelve altars in honour of the apostles, possibly commemorates altars which were found within Aldhelm's earlier church at Malmesbury. It may perhaps date to the same period as the first of the *carmina ecclesiastica* (*c*.675?), and this early date would then be confirmed by the fact that one line of the fourth poem (IV. i. 2) is quoted in Aldhelm's letter to Geraint (Letter IV), which is to be dated slightly earlier than 675 (see below, p. 141). The fifth and last of the dedicatory poems commemorates a church built in honour of St Matthew; the church has never been identified and the poem cannot be dated.

Aldhelm's industry as a builder of churches in Wessex has been mentioned earlier. It is interesting to notice that his literary activity as occasional poet, dedicating churches and altars, corresponds fairly with this industry as church-builder. It is also worth noting that the composition of such dedicatory verse was apparently a normal function of the literate Anglo-Saxon ecclesiastic: Bede, too, composed dedicatory epigrams for churches built in Lindsey and Hexham,[1] and Alcuin composed dozens of dedications to altars in the Frankish kingdom.[2]

(b) the *Epistola ad Acircium*. This immense and composite work was addressed to King Aldfrith of Northumbria (685–705); on the identification of 'Acircius' with Aldfrith, see below, p. 32. Aldfrith was an enlightened monarch who had studied at Iona with Adomnán and who could speak Irish; Bede tells us of his deep interest in books and learning (*HE* IV.26, V.15). Aldhelm relates in the *exordium* that, twenty years earlier, he and Aldfrith had 'made the unbreakable pledge of a binding agreement' (below, p. 34). This 'binding agreement' would seem to imply that Aldhelm was Aldfrith's godfather: as Aldhelm goes on to say, 'In the era of our young manhood (*pubertatis nostrae*) . . . I acquired the name of "father" . . . you received the appellations of your adoptive station'. However it be interpreted, *pubertas* would seem best to refer to an age from the late teens to the early thirties. If we begin with the dates traditionally assigned to Aldhelm's birth (630 × 640; see above p. 6), then add the highest possible age to which *pubertas* could refer—say, 35—and add finally the twenty years of which Aldhelm speaks, we arrive at a date of approximately 685 × 695, where 695 must represent the outer possible limit. That is to say, the composition of the *Epistola ad Acircium* probably fell within the earlier rather than the later part of Aldfrith's reign; but this is at best a guess, based on two unverifiable assumptions: that the date of Aldhelm's birth can even approximately be known, and that the word *pubertas* can safely be interpreted.

The *Epistola ad Acircium* consists in several parts. It begins, after prefatory remarks to Aldfrith, with a long discussion of the significance of the number 7. This part of the work is discussed and translated below, pp. 35–45. The large part of the work, however, is a treatise on metre. Aldhelm discussed the varieties of metrical feet, giving long lists of examples of words which are naturally trochees, anapests, and so on, and citing many examples of classical hexameters to illustrate his discussion of these various feet. This metrical treatise should perhaps be considered a compilation rather than an original composition, since it is drawn largely from similar treatises by the Late Latin grammarians Audax, Diomedes, Servius and Victorinus. But one should not underestimate its utility for an Anglo-Saxon audience of the late seventh century: Aldhelm was one of the earliest Latin poets—and certainly the first in England—to be faced with the problem of extensive metrical composition who was not a native speaker of Latin.[3] Clearly the Late Latin metrical treatises, which were designed for Latin-speaking readership, required some adaptation if they were to be used successfully by non-Latin speakers. Aldhelm's metrical treatise should be understood as a pioneering effort in this field and as the first of several such treatises by Anglo-Saxon authors,[4] notably Boniface's brief *De Caesuris*[5] and the *De Arte Metrica* by Bede.[6]

Into the middle of his metrical treatise Aldhelm inserted a collection of 100 poetical *enigmata*—'riddles', or as Aldhelm himself describes them, 'mysteries'.[7] Aldhelm ostensibly introduced these *enigmata* into the treatise in order to illustrate the various metrical principles he had been enunciating. But it is clear that they are only loosely connected with the preceding and following discussion, and they may easily be considered a separate work; in fact they often circulated independently of the *Epistola* in medieval manuscripts. One suspects that Aldhelm had composed them somewhat earlier than the metrical treatise itself, but here as elsewhere, it is not possible to ascertain when.

(c) the *De Virginitate*. This is Aldhelm's largest work. It consists in two parts, one in prose (some 60 chapters of varying length), the other in verse (about 3,000 hexameters). Only the prose part is translated here (below pp. 59–132); the poetic part has never been translated.[8] The *De Virginitate* was known to Bede, who described the entire work as an *opus geminatum* or 'double work' (*HE* V.18). The model which Aldhelm followed in composing his *De Virginitate* as an *opus geminatum* was Caelius Sedulius, a fifth-century Italian poet who produced a verse epic on the life and miracles of Christ seen typologically against events in the Old Testament, and then subsequently produced a prose translation of the same material; the prose work is known as the *Opus Paschale*.[9] Aldhelm certainly had Sedulius's combined work in mind while writing the *De Virginitate*, although, unlike Sedulius, he wrote the prose part first. The two parts of Sedulius's work are fairly closely related, but Aldhelm handled the two-part structure with somewhat more freedom. For example, there is no introduction on the subject of virginity in the poetic part to correspond to the first nineteen chapters of the prose work, whereas the final section of the poem—entitled *De Octo Vitiis Principalibus* in some manuscripts—has no correlate in the

13

prose. The catalogues of male and female virgins are found in both parts (with only a few exceptions),[10] but the treatment is often strikingly different: the prose part usually provides a literal account of an event, whereas the poetic part often gives a figural interpretation of the same event. In short, it is insufficient to assume that the one part is a simple versification of the other, and we would do better to think of the separate parts as two panels of the one diptych. At all events, Aldhelm's combined *De Virginitate* became in its turn a model for subsequent Anglo-Latin *opera geminata*: Bede's two lives of St Cuthbert[11] are in some sense an *opus geminatum*, as is Alcuin's *Vita S. Willibrordi.*[12]

The *De Virginitate* is the most difficult of Aldhelm's works to date. In its very first chapter Aldhelm remarks that he had received letters from the nuns at Barking while he was 'proceeding to an episcopal convention' (below p. 59). This might suggest at once that the work dated from the period of Aldhelm's episcopacy (706 × 709 or 710); however, he need not have been a bishop to attend an episcopal synod. In fact we know that he attended at least one such synod—possibly that at Hertford in 672—at a much earlier stage in his career (cf. below, p. 141). If the synod mentioned in c.I is indeed that held at Hertford in 672, an approximate date could be assigned to the *De Virginitate*: Aldhelm states that he had attended the synod 'some time ago' (*iamdudum*), and we could therefore date the *De Virginitate* after 675, perhaps after 680, depending on how we might wish to interpret *iamdudum*.

However, an active abbot and a disciple of the archbishop might well have attended many such synods; and Theodore, at the same synod at Hertford, made some attempt to ensure that synods would be convoked each subsequent year on August 1 at a place called *Clofeshoh*. One is therefore obliged to seek some other control for dating the *De Virginitate*. In a letter to Aldhelm from Cellanus of Péronne (Letter IX), Aldhelm is addressed as 'abbot' (*archimandrita*); and Cellanus notes that he has read Aldhelm's 'books (*fastos*) which were painted with the charms of various flowers' (below p. 167). Now Aldhelm himself describes the composition of his prose *De Virginitate* as 'plucking crimson flowers of modesty from the meadow of holy books' (c.XIX). Furthermore, Aldhelm describes the prose part of his *De Virginitate* by the glossary word *fastus* (= 'book') in the later poetic part of the same work (line 21), and this is the same word which Cellanus used in the plural to describe the works of Aldhelm which he had read; it is probable, therefore, that the *fasti* which Cellanus had read were the two parts of Aldhelm's *De Virginitate*. Unfortunately—once again—it is impossible to date the letter of Cellanus exactly. But we know that Cellanus wrote before 706 (since Aldhelm was still abbot), and we must allow some lapse of time—how much is difficult to say—for the works to have been circulated and read in northern France. All that Cellanus's reference to the two books of the *De Virginitate* can safely establish is that they were written somewhat before the period of Aldhelm's bishopric.

One other fact needs to be considered. In his letter to Heahfrith (No. V), Aldhelm quotes four lines which are also found in the poetic *De Virginitate* (although they do not occur consecutively there).[13] If these lines were indeed repeated from the poetic *De Virginitate*, the date of the letter could establish a *terminus ante* for both parts of the *De Virginitate*. The letter describes Theodore as alive and as actively engaged in teaching. The letter must therefore have been written before 690 at the latest (the date of Theodore's death), and it was probably written a good deal earlier, perhaps by about 675 (see below, p.144). The citation of lines from the poetic *De Virginitate* would thus appear to confirm an early date for the composite work. The problem is that Aldhelm may well have re-cycled in his *De Virginitate* four lines which he had earlier composed for inclusion in his letter to Heahfrith. In that case, the date of the letter could not be a reliable *terminus ante* for the composition of the *De Virginitate*.

Attempts by earlier scholars to establish a date for the *De Virginitate* are not trustworthy. Ehwald's arguments (p. 229) for a date after 685 are not acceptable. Ehwald argued that, since Cuthburg was the queen of Aldfrith of Northumbria (685–705), and since she was already installed at Barking when Aldhelm was writing the *De Virginitate*, the date of the work must be later than 685. Unfortunately, we have no contemporary evidence concerning Cuthburg, and no source of any date tells us when she married Aldfrith or when she left him. It must remain at least a possibility that she had married and left him before he acceded to the Northumbrian throne. In these difficulties, perhaps a passage from the epilogue to the *Epistola ad Acircium* may be of avail. Aldhelm there (below p. 47) would appear to be comparing Aldfrith to the emperor Theodosius, whom Aldhelm describes as married (*maritabatur*), and this may well suggest that Aldfrith was married (to Cuthburg?) at the time he was writing the *Epistola ad Acircium*. And this in turn might suggest that Cuthburg abandoned Aldfrith after the *Epistola ad Acircium* was written, and therefore that the *De Virginitate* was later than the *Epistola ad Acircium*. But in view of the insubstantial nature of all this evidence, it is impossible to ascertain a date for the *De Virginitate*.

(d) *Epistolae*. Aldhelm wrote a number of letters, some of which survive separately in various manuscripts, some of which are only preserved by William of Malmesbury. All Aldhelm's correspondence (including a few letters addressed to him) is translated and discussed in detail below, pp. 136–70.

(e) *Carmina Rhythmica*. There is dependable contemporary evidence that Aldhelm composed rhythmical verse. The English missionary Lul (bishop of Mainz, 755–86) wrote from the continent to one Dealwine somewhere in England requesting 'some works of Aldhelm, either in prose or metre or rhythmical verse'.[14] Lul had studied at Malmesbury, and may be presumed to have been familiar with Aldhelm's corpus of Latin writings. In the ninth-century Vienna manuscript (Codex Vindobonensis 751), which preserves part of Aldhelm's correspondence, are found five poems of varying length in rhythmical octosyllables; these poems are printed by Ehwald as *Carmina Rhythmica* in his edition of Aldhelm (pp. 519–37). However, Ehwald did not believe that any of the five poems was by Aldhelm himself, even though the first of them bears the subscription *finit carmen Aldhelmi*. Ehwald's opinion has been accepted uncritically by modern scholarship.[15] On this point modern scholarship is seriously in need of revision.

When the unique manuscript of an Insular work is of a relatively early date and, as seems probable, has been copied from an Insular exemplar,[16] and when such a manuscript bears an attribution of authorship, strong and convincing reasons must be advanced for spurning this attribution. As mentioned above, Codex Vindobonensis 751 attributed the first (in Ehwald's numbering) of the five rhythmical poems to Aldhelm: *finit carmen Aldhelmi*. What convincing reasons did Ehwald and others advance for spurning this testimony?

The received argument runs roughly as follows: (1) four of the rhythmical poems begin with the heading *incipit carmen AL*. Ehwald notes (p. 520) that this must mean 'here begins a poem of Aldhelm'; he next reminds us that, in the case of the *carmina ecclesiastica*, one St Gall manuscript had passed off Aldhelm's poems under the name of Venantius Fortunatus, and therefore, that manuscript attributions must be treated with circumspection. (No doubt there are countless false attributions in medieval manuscripts: there are also countless correct ones.) However, the fifth of the rhythmical poems cannot be by Aldhelm: it names its author (line 8) as Æthilwald. And in a letter from (presumably this same) Æthilwald to Aldhelm (No. VII), Æthilwald had noted that he was sending Aldhelm *inter alia* an epistolary poem in octosyllables, together with another one dedicated to one Wihtfrith and describing a transmarine journey. It has long been noted that the fourth rhythmical poem is dedicated to Aldhelm: it announces as much in line 59, and in line 15 plays on Aldhelm's name by calling him *cassem priscum* (*priscus* = OE *eald, casses* = OE *helm*, hence 'old helmet' or Aldhelm). Apparently, then, this poem is iden-

16

tical with that mentioned by Æthilwald in Letter VII; similarly, the second of the rhythmical poems describes a voyage to Rome, and it too is no doubt identical with the poem dedicated to Wihtfrith and dealing with a transmarine journey. In short, three of the rhythmical poems (Nos. II, IV and V) are almost certainly by Æthilwald, not Aldhelm. Therefore the scribe who wrote *incipit carmen AL*—'here begins Aldhelm's poem'— four times, was plainly mistaken. He may therefore be presumed to be in error, so the argument runs, when he writes *finit carmen Aldhelmi* after the first poem. (*Exeunt* bath-water and baby). (2) This argument from probability is bolstered by another: in the fourth rhythmic poem Aldhelm is addressed as *cassem priscum*. Now the first poem contains a similar verbal play: it begins 'Lector, *casses catholice*/atque *obses* anthletice'. Once again, so the argument runs, Aldhelm is being addressed in a word play; and if the poem is *addressed to* Aldhelm, it cannot very well be *by* him. Ehwald is thus led to the following position: none of the five poems is by Aldhelm himself; four of the five (Nos. II–V) are almost certainly by Æthilwald; the first, attributed erroneously by the scribe to Aldhelm, is stylistically quite different from the other four (p. 522); it is probably by an author other than Æthilwald—an anonymous poet perhaps of Aldhelm's circle at Malmesbury (p. 524). Ehwald is followed by most modern scholars except Bradley,[17] who could see no stylistic differences between the first poem and the other four, and accordingly attributed them all to Æthilwald.

Ehwald's sensitivity to the stylistic differences between the first poem and the others should have served to warn him; uncharacteristically, for once, his wits deserted him.[18] Unlike the other four poems, the first is resonant with Aldhelmian phrases—as Ehwald's apparatus shows, nearly every line of the poem reproduces a phrase from somewhere or other in Aldhelm's corpus. If the poem is by an imitator, this imitator was immensely diligent. In view of this, let us examine the above arguments more closely. First, the interpretation of *incipit carmen AL*. Scholars have made unnecessarily heavy weather of these three little words. The most simple and straightforward way of reading them would be to expand *AL* as *aliter*; thus *incipit carmen AL* repeated at the beginnings of various poems means 'here begins a poem once again'.[19] That is to say, *AL* has nothing whatsoever to do with Aldhelm. By preferring this *lectio facilior* we may exonerate the scribe: he was not attempting to identify the author of each poem, but rather to indicate where it began.

What, then, of the scribe's note at the end of the first poem: *finit carmen Aldhelmi*? The second argument is now advanced: since the poem is allegedly addressed *to* Aldhelm, it cannot be *by* him. It is true that *priscum* + *cassem* in the fourth poem is equivalent to *Eald* + *helm*. It is not true that *casses* + *obses* in the first poem is equivalent to *Eald* + *helm*. *Casses* + *obses* is equivalent, as Bradley noted long ago,[20] to *helm* + *gisl* (= 'hostage'), a well-attested Old English name.[21] The poem, therefore, is addressed not to Aldhelm but to one *Helmgisl* or *Helmgils* (with customary metathesis).[22] The final obstacle to trusting the scribe's attribution falls away: the first rhythmical poem is by Aldhelm and is addressed to someone called Helmgils.[23] This apparently simple conclusion squares well with other evidence: that the poem resounds with Aldhelmian phrases and that it is stylistically more accomplished than the other four poems, which are works by Aldhelm's disciple Æthilwald. It also squares with the opinion of Unterkircher (following Tangl)[24] that, from the point in the manuscript where the poems occur onwards (f.40ʳ ff.), the scribe was copying directly from a collection of materials in Mainz which almost certainly was made by Lul himself. It is not improbable to see the first rhythmical poem as one of the *opuscula rithmica* of Aldhelm sent by Dealwine to Lul at Lul's request. In short, we have the scribe's attribution *finit carmen Aldhelmi* on the highest authority. Given that no reasonable objections have so far been advanced against this attribution, the first of the rhythmical poems printed by Ehwald (pp. 523–8) should henceforth be included among Aldhelm's works.

(f) *Chartae.* William of Malmesbury preserves two charters in favour of the monastery at Malmesbury: one, a donation by bishop Leuthere of Winchester of land at Malmesbury itself, the other, a grant by Cenfrith (*comes* of the Mercians) to Aldhelm of land at Wootton Bassett in Wiltshire; these two charters are printed by Ehwald (pp. 507–10) together with three other charters which are tenuously linked with Aldhelm. It has been argued, on the basis of the unusual language of the first two charters, that they were drafted by Aldhelm himself.[25] However, although each of these charters may possibly preserve a basis that is genuine,[26] most modern scholars of Anglo-Saxon diplomatic would regard the charters in the form preserved by William of Malmesbury as spurious.[27] We have not, therefore, included these charters among the prose writings of Aldhelm; but since, for stylistic reasons, they might be of interest to students of Aldhelm, we have translated them in Appendix II (pp. 173–5 below).

The above-mentioned works constitute Aldhelm's extant corpus. How many more works have not survived cannot easily be judged. At some time before 706, for example, Cellanus of Péronne wrote to

18

Aldhelm (Letter IX) requesting a copy of his *sermones*, which appear to have been 'discourses' or possibly even 'homilies', but these have not survived. William of Malmesbury (p. 344) mentions them among Aldhelm's works, but does not seem to have known them apart from the reference in Cellanus's letter. More interesting, perhaps, is the question of verse composed by Aldhelm in Old English. William of Malmesbury (p. 336) reports the testimony of King Alfred's *Handboc* to the effect that Aldhelm had no equal as a poet in his native language. It is a matter of great regret that Alfred's *Handboc* has not survived, and we are obliged to accept William's account of it. According to William, King Alfred attested that one of the best-known Old English poems—which was still being sung in Alfred's time—had been composed by Aldhelm, and Alfred then proceeded to relate the now-famous anecdote about Aldhelm chanting profane poetry interspersed with biblical phrases at the bridge in Malmesbury for the behoof of his congregation. Aldhelm's Old English verse has apparently not survived, and there have been no successful attempts to discover it among the body of surviving Old English poetry. In any case, Aldhelm's attempts to combine biblical narrative with traditional native verse mark him as a pioneer in this endeavour, since he is at least contemporary with if not earlier than Cædmon, whose similar attempts to combine biblical and traditional verse are recorded at some length by Bede (*HE* IV. 24).

Finally, mention may be made of works tentatively attributed to Aldhelm by modern scholarship. Walter Bulst suggested that an acrostic poem in Latin on the Day of Judgment (which is a close translation of a similar Greek poem) might be ascribed to Aldhelm or at least to Theodore's and Hadrian's school at Canterbury, inasmuch as the earliest citations from the poem are found in Aldhelm's *Epistola ad Acircium*.[28] More recently, it has been suggested that the anonymous *Liber Monstrorum*,[29] which shares many topics and sources with Aldhelm's *Enigmata*, might be by Aldhelm himself.[30]

TRANSLATORS' NOTES

As mentioned earlier, the present translation is intended primarily as an aid to Ehwald's edition of the Latin prose works of Aldhelm. We have therefore attempted to provide a literal translation of the Latin, so that the reader may follow the text with some ease. To this end we have given references to pages of Ehwald's edition (in slant brackets) throughout, and have arranged the separate works in the same order as that followed by Ehwald. In general we have tried to make a sentence in the English translation correspond to a sentence in Aldhelm's Latin. Another translator might well wish to break up Aldhelm's long sentences into shorter and more manageable units; but Aldhelm's sentences are long even by Late Latin standards, and we hope that a reader with no Latin training will, through our long English sentences, acquire some impression of the complexities of Aldhelm's prose.

Other salient features of Aldhelm's Latin prose style, however, cannot always be reproduced in English. These features have been discussed recently by Michael Winterbottom.[1] They include: alliteration (see in particular the beginning of Letter V—but alliteration of a less pronounced kind occurs *passim*); assonantal (and sometimes rhyming) cadences; parallelism of clauses; chiasmus (e.g. *brumosis circionis insulae climatibus*); interlaced word-order of various sorts (e.g. *nullo torridae obstaculo siccitatis obtinente*); and *hypallage* or transferred epithet[2] (e.g. *in glarigeris sablonum litoribus*, where what is meant is 'in the gravelly sands of the shore'). Each of these features defies the translator's efforts, particularly when he is aiming at literal accuracy. In addition, Aldhelm uses a great variety of unusual words, often drawn from glossaries, often of Greek origin, which give his Latin a peculiar flavour; but if these rare words were translated by correspondingly rare English words, Aldhelm's works would continue to be impenetrable. Similarly, Aldhelm often employs groups of synonymous words (e.g. *arenosis*

20

sablonum glareis) which cannot be rendered directly into English without some violation to the pleonasm.

We have attempted to keep our annotation of the translation to a bare minimum in the hope that readers will wish to consult Ehwald's more extensive documentation. Usually we add a footnote only when a passage would be otherwise incomprehensible, or when we depart from Ehwald's interpretation of a particular passage. In cases where Aldhelm quotes *verbatim* from a classical or patristic author, we have given the source in square brackets following the quotation itself. But when Aldhelm is indebted for a notion or an example to a patristic author (in the lists of male and female virgins in the *De Virginitate*,[3] for instance) we have not usually given these sources, since they may readily be consulted in Ehwald's edition. Quotations from the Vulgate are given from the Douay-Rheims translation of 1582–1609; we have noted Aldhelm's deviations from the Vulgate. Words included in parentheses are not present in Latin but have been added in English for the sake of coherency. Finally, we have on rare occasions made alterations to Ehwald's text; a list of these alterations is found in Appendix I.

ALDHELM BIBLIOGRAPHY

A. EDITIONS OF ALDHELM'S WORKS

R. Ehwald, *Aldhelmi Opera Omnia*. Monumenta Germaniae Historica.
Auctores Antiquissimi XV (Berlin, 1919).
[a veritably monumental edition which entirely supersedes
earlier editions]

J. A. Giles, *Sancti Aldhelmi Opera* (Oxford, 1844), reprinted by Migne,
Patrologia Latina, vol. LXXXIX, cols. 87–314.
[even by Giles's deplorable standards, his edition of Aldhelm
is poor. It should not be consulted.]

J. H. Pitman, *The Riddles of Aldhelm*. Yale Studies in English LXVII
(New Haven, 1925; repr. Hamden, Conn.: Archon Books, 1970).
[Ehwald's text of the *Enigmata* with facing English translation]

F. Glorie, *Collectiones Aenigmatum Merovingicae Aetatis*. Corpus
Christianorum, Series Latina CXXXIII–CXXXIIIA. 2 vols.
(Turnhout, 1968), I, 359–540.
[reprints Ehwald's text of the *Enigmata* together with Pitman's
translation]

G. van Langenhove, *Aldhelm's de Laudibus Virginitatis* (Bruges, 1941)
[a facsimile edition of Brussels, Royal Library, MS. 1650]

*Sancti Bonifacii Epistolae. Codex Vindobonensis 751 der österreichischen
Nationalbibliothek*, ed. F. Unterkircher. Codices selecti phototypice impressi XXIV (Graz, 1971).
[facsimile of the manuscript which contains some of Aldhelm's
letters and rhythmical poems]

B. GLOSSARIES AND GLOSSES IN ALDHELM MANUSCRIPTS

C. W. Bouterwek, 'Angelsächsische Glossen. (1) Die Ags. Glossen in dem Brüsseler Codex von Aldhelms Schrift *De Virginitate'*, *Zeitschrift für deutsches Altertum* IX (1853), 401–530.

R. Derolez, 'Zu den Brüsseler Aldhelmglossen', *Anglia* LXXIV (1957), 153–80.

—————, 'Aldhelmus Glosatus III', *English Studies* XL (1959), 129–34.

—————, 'Aldhelmus Glosatus IV', *Studia Germanica Gandensia* II (1960), 81–95.

L. Goossens, *The Old English Glosses of MS. Brussels, Royal Library 1650 (Aldhelm's De Laudibus Virginitatis)* (Brussels, 1974).
   [an important new edition, with valuable introduction on glossing in Aldhelm manuscripts]

J. H. Hessels, *A Late Eighth-Century Latin-Anglo-Saxon Glossary Preserved in Leiden* (Cambridge, 1906).

W. M. Lindsay, *The Corpus Glossary* (Cambridge, 1921).

—————, *The Corpus, Epinal, Erfurt and Leyden Glossaries* (Oxford, 1921).
   [on Aldhelm's use of glossaries, see pp. 97–105]

H. Logeman, 'New Aldhelm Glosses', *Anglia* XIII (1891), 27–41.

H. D. Meritt, *Old English Glosses* (New York, 1945).

—————, 'Old English Aldhelm Glosses', *Modern Language Notes* LXVIII (1952), 553–4.

H. Mettke, *Die althochdeutschen Aldhelmglossen* (Jena, 1957).

T. F. Mustanoja, 'Notes on Some Old English Glosses in Aldhelm's *De Laudibus Virginitatis'*, *Neuphilologische Mitteilungen* LI (1950), 49–61.

A. S. Napier, 'Collation der altenglischen Aldhelmglossen des Codex 38 der Kathedralbibliothek zu Salisbury', *Anglia* XV (1893), 204–9.

—————, *Old English Glosses, Chiefly Unpublished* (Oxford, 1900).
   [prints glosses from many Aldhelm manuscripts, including those from Oxford, Bodleian Library, MS. Digby 146]

R. T. Oliphant, *The Harley Latin-Old English Glossary* (The Hague, 1966).
   [see review by R. Derolez, *English Studies* LI (1970), 149–51]

R. I. Page, 'More Aldhelm Glosses from CCCC 326', *English Studies* LVI (1975), 481–90.

J. D. Pheifer, *Old English Glosses in the Epinal-Erfurt Glossary* (Oxford, 1974).
   [the suggestion (p. lvii) that the ancestor of the Epinal–Erfurt glossary was compiled in the school of Aldhelm at Malmesbury]

K. Schiebel, *Die Sprache der altenglischen Glossen zu Aldhelms Schrift De Laude Virginitatis* (Halle, 1907).

23

T. Wright and R. P. Wülcker, *Anglo-Saxon and Old English Vocabularies*. 2 vols. (London, 1884).

C. MEDIEVAL LIVES OF ALDHELM

Faricius, *Vita Aldhelmi*, ed. J. A. Giles, in *Vita Quorundum Anglo-Saxonum* [*sic!*]. Publications of the Caxton Society (London, 1854), 119–56.

[Giles's edition of Faricius is reprinted by Migne, *Patrologia Latina* LXXXIX, cols. 63–84. Another edition of Faricius is printed by the Bollandists, *Acta Sanctorum, Maii*, vol. VI, 84–93]

William of Malmesbury, *Gesta Pontificum*, ed. N. E. S. A. Hamilton. Rolls Series (London, 1870).

[William's *vita* of Aldhelm constitutes Book V of his *Gesta Pontificum*, ed. Hamilton, 330–443. The *Gesta Pontificum* are also printed in Migne's *Patrologia Latina*, CLXXIX; the life of Aldhelm occupies cols. 1617–80]

John Capgrave, *Vita Aldhelmi*, in *Nova Legenda Anglie*, ed. C. Horstmann. 2 vols. (Oxford, 1901), I, pp. 38–40.

[based entirely on William of Malmesbury, but that it borrows the story of St Ecgwine's vision of Aldhelm's death directly from Dominic of Evesham's *Vita S. Ecgwini*]

D. WORKS WHICH CONTAIN SOME DISCUSSION OF ALDHELM

T. Allison, *English Religious Life in the Eighth Century* (London, 1929), 86–9.

W. F. Bolton, *A History of Anglo-Latin Literature I: 597–740* (Princeton, 1967), 68–100.

[general treatment containing much error; useful bibliography]

B. B. Boyer, 'Insular Contribution to Medieval Literary Tradition on the Continent', *Classical Philology* XLII (1947), 209–22.

[on Aldhelm manuscripts]

T. J. Brown, 'An Historical Introduction to the Use of Classical Latin Authors in the British Isles from the Fifth to the Eleventh Century', *Settimane di studio del Centro italiano di studi sull' alto medioevo* XXII (1975), 237–93.

F. Brunhölzl, *Geschichte der lateinischen Literatur des Mittelalters* (Munich, 1975), I, 200–6, 208–9.

W. Bulst, 'Eine anglo-lateinische Übersetzung aus dem Griechischen um 700', *Zeitschrift für deutsches Altertum* LXXV (1938), 105–11.

24

M. Byrne, *The Tradition of the Nun in Medieval England* (Washington, 1932), 25–43.
[on the prose *De Virginitate*]

E. S. Duckett, *Anglo-Saxon Saints and Scholars* (New York, 1947), 3–97.
[a popular biography of Aldhelm which is filled with error and is totally unreliable]

E. von Erhardt-Siebold, *Die lateinischen Rätseln der Angelsachsen*. Anglistische Forschungen LXI (Heidelberg, 1925).

E. Faral, 'La queue de poisson des sirènes', *Romania* LXXIV (1953), 466–70.
[Aldhelm as author of the *Liber Monstrorum*]

J. Godfrey, *The Church in Anglo-Saxon England* (Cambridge, 1962), 201–6.

P. Grosjean, 'Confusa Caligo. Remarques sur les *Hisperica Famina*', *Celtica* III (1956), 35–85.
[Aldhelm's alleged knowledge of the *Hisperica Famina*: pp. 64–7]

H. Hahn, *Bonifaz und Lul* (Leipzig, 1883).
[much interesting discussion of Aldhelm scattered throughout]

M. Herren, *Hisperica Famina I* (Toronto, 1974).

————, 'Some Conjectures on the Origins and Tradition of the Hisperic Poem *Rubisca*', *Ériu* XXV (1974), 70–87.

P. Hunter Blair, *An Introduction to Anglo-Saxon England*. 2nd edn. (Cambridge, 1977), 314–5, 326–7.

C. W. Jones, *Bedae Opera de Temporibus* (Cambridge, Mass., 1943), 100–1.
[Aldhelm's Letter to Geraint and the Easter-question]

M. L. W. Laistner, *Thought and Letters in Western Europe 500–900* (Ithaca, N.Y., 1957), 153–6.

M. Lapidge, 'The Hermeneutic Style in Tenth-Century Anglo-Latin Literature', *Anglo-Saxon England* IV (1975), 67–111.

A. F. Leach, *The Schools of Medieval England* (London, 1915), 31–45.
[sceptical treatment of Aldhelm's debt to Irish learning; much error]

H. R. Loyn, *Anglo-Saxon England and the Norman Conquest* (London, 1962), 269–74.

M. Manitius, *Geschichte der lateinischen Literatur des Mittelalters*. 3 vols. (Munich, 1911–31), I, 134–41.

H. Mayr-Harting, *The Coming of Christianity to Anglo-Saxon England* (London, 1972), 192–219.

C. Plummer, ed., *Venerabilis Baedae Opera Historica*. 2 vols. (Oxford, 1896), II, 308–13.

F. J. E. Raby, *Christian-Latin Poetry* (Oxford, 1953), 142–5.
[a tissue of errors and wrong-headed opinions]

P. Riché, *Education et culture dans l'occident barbare, VIe–VIIIe siècles.* 3rd edn. (Paris, 1962), 419–26.

M. Roger, *L'enseignement des lettres classiques d'Ausone à Alcuin* (Paris, 1905), 288–303.

[still the most detailed and reliable study of Insular Latin culture of Aldhelm's time, though out-dated in some respects]

F. M. Stenton, *Anglo-Saxon England.* 3rd edn. (Oxford, 1971), 180–3.

W. Stubbs, in *A Dictionary of Christian Biography,* ed. W. Smith and H. Wace. 4 vols. (London, 1877–87), I, 78–9 (s.v. 'Aldhelm').

L. G. Whitbread, 'The *Liber Monstrorum* and *Beowulf*', *Mediaeval Studies* XXXVI (1974), 434–71.

[Aldhelm possibly the author of *Liber Monstrorum*: pp. 455–8]

T. Wright, *Biographia Britannica Litteraria.* 2 vols. (London, 1842–6), I, 209–22.

E. WORKS DEVOTED TO ALDHELM

G. K. Anderson, 'Aldhelm and the Leiden Riddle', in *Old English Poetry*, ed. R. P. Creed (Providence, 1967), 167–76.

L. Bönhoff, *Aldhelm von Malmesbury* (Dresden, 1894).

[a standard work, now in need of considerable revision]

G. F. Browne, *St Aldhelm* (London, 1903).

[out-dated in many respects, and containing many inaccuracies, but also contains many fascinating conjectures, particularly with regard to archaeological evidence]

A. S. Cook, 'Aldhelm's Legal Studies', *Journal of English and Germanic Philology* XXIII (1924), 105–13.

————, 'Sources for the Biography of Aldhelm', *Transactions of the Connecticut Academy of Arts and Sciences* XXVIII (1927), 273–93.

————, 'Aldhelm at the Hands of Sharon Turner', *Speculum* II (1927), 201–3.

————, 'Who was the Ehfrid of Aldhelm's Letter', *Speculum* II (1927), 363–73.

————, 'Aldhelm's Rude Infancy', *Philological Quarterly* VII (1928), 115–9.

————, 'A Putative Charter to Aldhelm', in *Studies in English Philology: A Miscellany in Honor of Frederick Klaeber*, ed. K. Malone and M. B. Ruud (Minneapolis, 1929), 254–7.

R. Ehwald, *Aldhelms Gedicht De Virginitate. Programm des herzögliches Gymnasium . . . von Gotha* (Gotha, 1904).

————, 'De aenigmatibus Aldhelmi et acrostichis', in *Festschrift für Albert von Bamberg* (Gotha, 1905), 1–26.

————, 'Aldhelm von Malmesbury', *Jahrbuch der königlichen Akademie gemeinnütziger Wissenschaften in Erfurt* XXXIII (1907), 91–116.

E. von Erhardt-Siebold, 'Aldhelm in Possession of the Secrets of Sericulture', *Anglia* LX (1936), 384–9.

———, 'Aldhelm's Chrismal', *Speculum* X (1935), 276–80.

J. Fowler, *St Aldhelm* (Sherborne, 1947).
[a brief commemorative lecture]

M. R. James, *Two Ancient English Scholars* (Glasgow, 1931).
[a lecture; brief but interesting comments on manuscripts which Aldhelm may have seen at Malmesbury and which William saw after him]

P. F. Jones, 'Aldhelm and the Comitatus-Ideal', *Modern Language Notes* XLVII (1932), 378.

M. Lapidge, 'Aldhelm's Latin Poetry and Old English Verse', *Comparative Literature* XXXI (1979), forthcoming.

F. P. Magoun, 'Aldhelm's Diocese of Sherborne *be westan wuda*', *Harvard Theological Review* XXXII (1939), 103–14.

M. Manitius, 'Zu Aldhelm und Beda', *Sitzungsberichte der österreichischen Akademie der Wissenschaften*, phil.-hist. Kl., CXII (Vienna, 1886), 535–634.
[pp. 535–614 deal with Aldhelm; in need of revision, but still a standard work on the sources of Aldhelm]

J. Marenbon, 'Les sources du vocabulaire d'Aldhelm', *Archivum Latinitatis Medii Aevi (Bulletin du Cange)* XLI (1979), forthcoming.

A. Manser, 'Le temoignage d'Aldhelm de Sherborne sur un particularité du canon grégorien de la messe romaine', *Revue Bénédictine* XXVIII (1911), 90–5.

D. Mazzoni, 'Aldhelmiana: studio critico letterario su Aldhelmo di Sherborne', *Rivista storica benedettina* X (1915), 93–114, 245–50, 402–47.

H. M. Porter, 'Saint Aldhelm and Wareham', *Notes and Queries from Somerset and Dorset* XXX (1975), 142–5.
[Aldhelm born at Wareham; the church at Wareham built by him]

G. Prago, 'La legenda di S. Ilarione a Epidauro in Adelmo scrittore anglosassone', *Archivo storico di Dalmazia* XXV (1938), 83–91.

W. B. Wildman, *The Life of St Ealdhelm* (London, 1905).
[an honest and thoughtful biography, but very much out of date]

M. Winterbottom, 'Aldhelm's Prose Style and its Origins', *Anglo-Saxon England* VI (1977), 39–76.
[an extremely important study of Aldhelm and his intellectual heritage]

EPISTOLA AD ACIRCIUM

TRANSLATED BY MICHAEL HERREN

Introduction to the EPISTOLA AD ACIRCIUM

As mentioned earlier (p. 12), the long work entitled *Epistola ad Acircium* is neither a letter nor a unified treatise, but rather a composite work which consists in: (1) an exordium to 'Acircius'; (2) an essay on the number 7 in biblical typology; (3) a work on Latin metrics gleaned from various sources, dealing mainly with the composition of hexameters; (4) a collection of one hundred *enigmata*, allegedly illustrations of the metrical principles under discussion; (5) an epilogue to the work entitled by one manuscript *allocutio excusativa ad regem*, again addressed to 'Acircius'. The loose structure of the whole would indicate that the 'letter' was not composed at a single interval, but rather that the author seized a particular occasion to dedicate three works, probably composed at different periods, to 'Acircius', adding an introduction, transitional passages, and a conclusion. Interestingly, two of the three works—(3) and (4)—have come down to us in separate manuscript traditions.[1] Moreover, William of Malmesbury was apparently unaware that the *Enigmata* were included in the *Epistola*.[2] Here I have translated parts (1), (2), and (5). Because the metrical treatise (3) is a highly technical account of the quantities of Latin syllables and the metrical patterns of individual words, it would have little meaning in English and has therefore been omitted from the present translation of Aldhelm's prose works. Finally, the *Enigmata* (4) are available separately with accompanying English translation.[3]

Apart from the introductory section dealing with numerology in the Bible, the treatise is intended mainly as a manual for young poets writing in Latin. Here Aldhelm spells out fully what he learned at Canterbury (compare the Letter to Leuthere, No. I), though undoubtedly adding much from sources that he read at a later time. In the *De Metris* Aldhelm shows considerable knowledge of the late Roman writers on metre: Priscian, Audax, Donatus, Servius, Sergius, Pompeius, Maximus Victorinus, Diomedes, Nonius, and Julian of

Toledo. Thus from the *De Metris* we derive a good impression of what grammatical works were available in England at the end of the seventh century.

The treatise on the number 7 is based primarily on the Isidorian or pseudo-Isidorian[4] *Liber Numerorum*.[5] (This work is not to be confused with the *Liber de Numeris*[6]). It is true, as Ehwald notes (p. xix), that Aldhelm occasionally differs from his source and often introduces material from other writers, notably Jerome. This, however, does not vitiate the close structural similarities, and it would be fairer to say that Aldhelm's work was an elaboration of the *Liber Numerorum* than it would be to call it a composite work drawing on the *Liber Numerorum* as one of its sources. The *Liber Numerorum* probably reached England through Irish hands.[7]

The recipient of the work, 'Acircius', can be none other than Aldfrith, king of Northumbria, 685–705. Even if William of Malmesbury had not told us of the identity of 'Acircius' (p. 344), it could easily have been deduced from the name itself and from the accompanying epithet *Aquilonis*, both meaning 'of the north' (i.e. Northumbria, presumably), and from the fact that Aldfrith was the only Northumbrian king contemporary with Aldhelm whose literary talents and interests are well attested (Bede, *HE* IV. 26 and V. 15).[8] We learn from the introduction to the 'letter' (p. 34) that Aldhelm and Aldfrith were linked in a close spiritual relationship, almost certainly that of godfather and godson—a relationship that had begun twenty years before the compilation of the *Epistola*. Towards the end of the treatise on the number 7 (p. 44), we learn that the two men had drifted apart, so that the author puts forward a plea for the resumption of their friendship. The breaking-off of relations between the two men need not imply hostile attitudes on either side, but may be explained simply by loss of contact. According to various traditions, Aldfrith spent some time in the *regionibus Scottorum* in pursuit of learning.[9] Bede refers to him as 'an exile for the sake of learning',[10] although in fact the exile may have been enforced during the rule of Ecgfrith. One can only speculate on the occasion that prompted Aldhelm to compose his *epistola*. Aldfrith's assumption of the throne may itself have provided the opportunity. Another possibility is Aldfrith's restoration of Wilfrid. As we have seen above, the evidence suggests a time earlier rather than later in Aldfrith's reign.

Aldhelm appears to have been in middle life when he wrote the *Epistola*. He is twenty years past his *pubertas* (p. 34); his writings show improvement over his immature efforts (p. 35); he is weighted down both by secular cares and by ecclesiastical administration (p. 45). Finally, he shows his awareness of his own accomplishment: no one before him 'of a Germanic nation' has equalled his achievement of writing a Latin treatise on metrics (p. 45).

EPISTOLA AD ACIRCIUM

I. *[p. 61]* To the most excellent Lord, illustrious Acircius,[1] who governs the kingdom of the northern empire and dispenses rule over a famous royal realm, laudable above all other ranks of regal dignitaries and joined to me for some time by the bonds of spiritual clientship,[2] Aldhelm, servant of the Catholic Church, (wishes) the imperishable health of eternal salvation.

I do not doubt, most reverent son, but trust, giving rein to deep belief, that the provident heart of your Wisdom may recall that twice-two revolutions of the *lustra* ago [i.e. nearly twenty years ago[3]] we made the unbreakable pledge of a binding agreement, and through the bond *[p. 62]* of spiritual association we established a comradeship of devoted charity. For a long time ago, in the era of our young manhood, when your talented Sagacity was equipped with the septiform munificence of spiritual gifts by the hand of a venerable bishop, I recall that I acquired the name of 'father' and that you received the appellations of your adoptive station together with the privilege of heavenly grace. The word of the prophet (Is.XI.1), explaining the fruit of spiritual increments by means of allegorical mysteries, shows that a bush, after the type of the holy and uncorrupted Mother of God, sprang in fertile shoots from the root of Jesse and brought forth a flower of purple petals, prefiguring with mystical obscuration the Saviour of the fallen world, Who, together with the sevenfold Understanding of Wisdom and the Spirit of the other virtues, fully abrogates the sin of the first men. For truly, the same sevenfold number of sacraments is frequently attested by the sacred oracles of the testaments, (and) pondering with frequent repetition the mystery of which number, I shall endeavour to heap up from the most beautiful garden of the Scriptures, so to speak, certain stalks of the fields or blossoming flowers of meadows (and) gather them into the texture of a single wreath, in order that it might be revealed more clearly and

34

openly and that it might shine more limpidly than light to all who examine with scrutiny from what great spiritual advantages and from what hallowed rituals of our bond (my) first beginnings and yet unripened elementary efforts have advanced, sprouted forth, and flourished by reason of their origin.[4]

II. This sevenfold measure of intervals, I say, came to be sacred from the very first beginning of the new-born world. For not only the entirety of all creation, which the revolving [p. 63] and moving pinnacle of the heavens and the double hemispheres gird, is said to have been brought into being in a multitude of forms in the sevenfold course of a single week, when He who lives in eternity made all things simultaneously in a single stroke, but also the hoped-for rest of future promise and the perennial felicity of the blessed life, which shall be paid to each and every one according to the amount of his merits, is granted to the innocent and those free of the offence of sin only through a sevenfold increment of times, one thousand in number,[5] after the throng of the impious has been separated. The mysteries of the same number are revealed—if I may recall and unfold ancient matters from the beginning—when the terrible irruption of floods, correcting the crimes of mortal men and washing away with avenging waves the obstinacy of sinful life, was slaying all things that enjoyed the alternating breath of corporeal life—up to the point of extinction—except for the offspring required for future propagation, and was sating with cruel slaughter the fearful gluttony of Stygian Pluto with the bloodless shades of the wretched, 'seven and seven' of clean (animals) [Gen. VII. 2] according to their kind are read to have entered the ark—the 'second and third stories' [Gen. VI. 16]—or, as another version has it, 'of two rooms and three rooms'.[6]

Likewise sevenfold is the stock of the children of Job in the beginning of the book [Iob I. 2], which is woven in prose, and from there on, according to the Hebrews,[7] is said to scan in dactyls and spondees, and [p. 64] seven thousand woolly sheep are reported and described, and again, at the end of the book, the same number of sheep, restored twofold to reward (Job's) achievement in illustrious patience [Iob XLIII. 12], is shown to have prefigured the aforesaid secrets of the mysteries. Finally, Isaias, by no means the last in the series of prophets,[8] calls to witness that seven matrons, typifying seven of the churches, 'took hold of one man' [Isaias IV. 1], that is Christ, the reconciler of heavenly and terrestrial concerns. Moreover, to Elias lamenting the crimes of a cruel people and complaining of the sorrowful slaughter of the prophets it was said through divine oracles: 'And I will leave me seven thousand men in Israel whose knees have not been bowed before Baal' [III Reg. XIX. 18]. And he,[9] when he had quickened the child of the bereaved Sunamitess, which had been overcome by the fate of cruel death, by joining members to members and limbs to limbs seven times [IV Reg. IV. 34–5], signifies the Redeemer who revives humankind from the sleep of crime and the disease of sin through the grace of the septiform Spirit. But also the noble offspring of the Macchabean clan [i.e. the seven brethren], who under the tyrannical monarchy of Antiochus spurned pork flesh of sows [II Macc. VII. 1ff.], and on account of the usages of the divine laws and the rituals of their native tradition repudiated the foul practices of the gentiles and the idolatry of a profane people, are not undeservedly known to have prefigured the septiform image of the universal church. How, then? Is not that proverbial building, whose architect and builder is read to have been Wisdom, according to the testimony of Solomon, also sustained and does it not rest upon the support of seven pillars when it is said: 'Wisdom built a home for herself and carved out seven pillars' [Prov. IX. 1]? Did not the curtains of the tabernacle as well, dyed with the purple hues of maroon and scarlet, and sewn by diverse joinings of loops, extend to the quadruplicate calculation of the sevenfold reckoning, that is, twenty-eight cubits [Exod. XXXVI. 2]?

Moreover, we are instructed by sacred authority that the number seven sometimes prefigured the grace of the Spirit, the Paraclete, while sometimes it revealed the image of the ancient law, as in this saying: 'Give a portion to seven' [Eccles. XI. 2]. But also Eleazer, /p. 65/ endowed with the headdress of the highest priesthood, is read to have sprinkled the same tabernacle seven times with the blood of a red heifer, burned as a holocaust according to the usage of the ceremonies, the remains of whose ashes the oracles on high have pledged to be of benefit to the expiation of the people of Israel [Num. XIX. 2–10]. Also the most glorious of kings [i.e. Solomon], who, before he learned of the cradles of the first nativity, by the very word of his own name not undeservedly bore in a figural sense the indications of holy peace,[10] is described as having celebrated for seven days in great throngs the solemn festivity of the temple with the entire crowd of the sons of Israel from the entrance of Emath up to the torrent of Egypt [II Paral. VII. 8], whence the royal sceptre governs the Memphitic kingdoms [i.e. Egypt], according to that which the brief epitome of the Old Testament, that is Paralipomenon, testifies.

But lest I employ only the formula of the ancient law and scrutinize and investigate only the examples of past times, behold, many matters in the New Document, which I think is rightly signified under the heading of the 'Second Law', when set forth plainly, agree in an harmonious and favourable way, because, when the dusky hiding places of darkness and the nocturnal lurkings of shadows grow faint and the dawn breaks, the clear golden splendour of the most bright sun is shed upon all the territories of the earth. For the holy man who reclined upon the Lord's breast [i.e. John the Apostle] and the fourth river of the heavenly paradise,[11] out of which wide streams of living water run downwards in a perennial flow and deluge of moisture, is reported to have written to Smyrna, Pergamum, and Philadelphia, and to the other churches throughout Asia [Apoc. I. 11] in a sevenfold series of discourses. No less did he merit to view in the same vision of the Apocalypse, through his pure heart's most penetrating power of sight—(as it was) removed from all foul stench of vice—the seven signets of the sealed volume [Apoc. V. 1] containing the mysteries of completed prefiguration, which only the lion from the tribe of Judah [i.e. Christ] [Apoc. V. 5], bravest of beasts, fearful at the approach of none, who according to the prophecy of the patriarch [i.e. Moses] is related to 'have gone up to the prey' and 'resting to recline' [Gen. XLIX. 9], having lawfully gained power over things in heaven and on earth and below the earth, /p. 66/ could reveal through the prerogative of the nativity and passion, because he is said to have 'the key of David: he that openeth and no man shutteth; shutteth and no man openeth' [Apoc. III. 7]. For unless one breaks into pieces the stubborn bands[12] of accursed unbelief and trusts with the inmost faith of his heart that he [Christ] has loosed the seals of the aforementioned signets, with closed and blind orbs of pupils and with feeble sight of eyes, as though an epileptic or scotomatic,[13] will he contemplate the secret matters of the law and the opaque (mysteries) of the prophets. And in the same ecstasy of revelation the aforesaid vicar of the Saviour beheld seven golden candlesticks and as many stars [Apoc. I. 12] on the right of one having feet very like the brass of an oven, from whose mouth came forth a two-edged sword [Apoc. I. 15-16]. And I think that that most celebrated candlestick of the Book of Exodus, whose stem, hammered out of pure gold, fashioned skilfully with 'its branches, its cups and bowls' [Exod. XXXVII. 17] like a leafing yew tree or a sprouting plane tree was adorned with charming decoration, in no wise differed from the aforementioned mystery of candlesticks, whose seven torches of lamps flashing with fiery brightness, from which all the lanterns of the churches are illuminated with a clear light, are joined together and bound by golden links. Thus the illustrious vessel of election and wise architect and bearer of the name of Christ, Benjamin, in a figurative sense, 'in the morning eating the prey, and in the evening dividing the spoil' [Gen. XLIV. 27], abundantly moistened the unploughed fields of the seven churches with the dewy waters of holy dogma.

Likewise Zacharias, eleventh in the order of prophets, swept away by the sight of an apparition, and raised to the peak of divine contemplation, merited to behold, with the spiritual and hidden vision of the inner heart and with a pure power of sight, the renowned miracle of the illustrious stone, which is described as equipped in a mystical sense with a sevenfold vision of eyes[Zach. III. 9].The foundations also of the glorious city of God, which the Psalmist relates were built upon holy mountains [Ps. LXXXVI. 1], [p. 67] have amply satisfied the dry and thirsty hearts of the newborn church with the canonical rivulets of seven epistles, and, like the dark water in the clouds of the air, or like trickling drizzle, have bedewed and moistened the open mouths of the faithful. Those ones indeed [i.e. the faithful] in my opinion, imbued with divine teaching and instructed by the example of their tutors, can be said to have ruminated duly and regurgitated regularly to succeeding posterity, that which they (themselves) merited to have received—with the assistance of freely-given-grace—from the very nourisher of their most tender and earliest infancy, so that it might be ruminated and regurgitated by others. For the highest authority in the governance of the Church and the educator of the archetypal and illustrious family [i.e. the Holy Family][14] whom the Seventy-Seventh Psalm, as accords well with the present method of interpreting matters, expressed by calling in a figural sense 'the bread of heaven' and 'bread of angels' [Ps. LXXVII. 24–5], is read according to the narrative of the Gospels to have fed and thoroughly satisfied four thousand men, not counting the multitude of the second sex, with seven pieces of bread [Marc. VIII. 6–7], which increased because of the divine blessing rather than diminished because of the gaping jaws of gluttonous eaters; and when the remainders of the pieces were removed and the crusts of the rolls that were broken into bits were collected, they filled seven baskets or little chests—an amazing spectacle to all. And that famous festivity of the Jubilee commanded by Law [Levit. XXV. 4], celebrated after seven weeks of years are completed [Levit. XXV. 8], when trumpets were sounded with windy blasts during the repose from agricultural work and the cessation of ploughmen and hoes from the disturbance of the soil and the return again of the cycle of the seventh month to the horizon, is declared to have portended future secrets of mysteries in an allegorical (and) figural way. Further, is not the sacrosanct feast of Pentecost known to stipulate quite properly a number of this sort, according to a revolving and returning recurrence of seven weeks, when the Paraclete who is rightly called the 'pledge of our inheritance' [Ephes. I. 14] was sent from the highest citadel of heaven after an interval of ten days and enriched the minds of the Apostles with the grace of spiritual gifts from on high and fecundated them with the speech of

38

seventy tongues covering a wide area, [p. 68] which the seventyfold progeny of warlike Hirobaal, that is Gideon [Iudic. VI. 32], who were slain cruelly, with terrible slaughter unheard of in earlier ages, by the impious Abimelech, who employed tyranny rather than the rightful rule of kingship and broke the laws of brotherhood and the bonds of devoted fraternity upon a craggy peak [Iudic. IX. 4] in the fashion of a mad man, is shown to have prefigured? To whom [i.e. Abimelech], because of his dire parricidal sacrileges and disgraceful and abominable crimes, the thorny shoot of branches [Iudic. IX. 14–5] shall be likened not without effect under the type of the most base and foul anti-Christ according to the parable employed by Joatham, wherein, the flourishing Carian dry fig and likewise the stalk of the branching vine along with the greenish-blue olive refused to under-take the rule of a kingdom they scorned, which also, once the antiquity of the law had become obscured and then removed, attracted the stinking entrails of cattle and the reeking inwards of burnt sacrifices. And our Saviour, in the flashing ray of the New Testament, responded to the key-bearer of heaven—concerning whom the poet [i.e. Aldhelm] (said): 'Aetherial key-bearer, who opens the gateway to the heavens' [*Carm. Eccles.* IV. i.2][15]—when he inquired how many times the bonds of injury should be loosed for transgressors:'Not only seven times, but till seventy times seven times' [Matth. XVIII. 22], that is, fifty times nine and five times eight, which brought together into a single sum are reckoned to be four hundred and ninety.

And the offspring of the seventy-seventh generation, descending from the beginning of the newborn world along a linked chain of fecundity through the revolving alternation of the days, from the moment when unformed matter took on the appearances of form for the first time down to the venerable cradles of the heavenly childbirth, is known to be in harmony with this mystery, as the Physician of Antioch [i.e. Luke], endowed with the purity of uncorrupted virginity, brought to light, beginning his composition with the venerable scion of God [Luc. III. 23ff.], (going) step by step through the generations of grandsons and great-grandsons, reckoning the intervals of grand-fathers and great-grandfathers and recapitulating the genealogical order individually through great-great-grandfathers and thrice-great-grandfathers, set the limit for the first men at a figure of seventy-seven generations traversed; which was prefigured of old by the sacred authority of Genesis speaking in an historical sense: [p. 69] 'Sevenfold vengeance shall be taken for Cain, but for Lamech seventy times sevenfold' [Gen. IV. 24]. After the same number of generations these cruel vindictive punishments afflicting Lamech, who is to be under-stood as the guilt of the whole world, were broken, smashed, ex-tinguished and thrust into Tartarus and the rule of dire death overthrown by the nativity of our Saviour, which was revealed and presignified to the ages. What shall I say of that famous grandson [i.e. Jacob] of the distinguished patriarch [i.e. Abraham]—who returned from his uncle of Mesopotamia in Syria [i.e. Laban] with twice-six offspring of children, and then, after an interval of twice-two *lustra* of time [i.e. about twenty years] had passed, assumed the name of the Israelitic race [Gen. XXXII. 28] after struggling in a wrestling match with an angel [Gen. XXXII. 24]—when the raging madness of his brother came to meet (him) with a throng of soldiers and nearly trampled the laws of all brotherhood, did he not bow down with seven repeated instances of obeisance [Gen. XXXIII. 1–3] in order to mitigate the rancour of the hirsute pettifogger [i.e. Esau] and the fury of old malice?

For the catholic decrees of the Fathers have ordained that the seven-fold calculations of numbers portend mystical allegory not only according to a single and sevenfold course, but also by a tenfold chain of computation, just as the illustrious 'man of desires' [Dan. IX. 23], sub-ject to divine worship though amongst a barbarous people from the very earliest beginnings of his education, (when he was) filled with the spirit of prophecy when Gabriel unlocked the mysteries of history with secret keys, declared:[16] after seventy weeks have been traversed and extended down to the cradles of the leader of Bethlehem, who will rule the people of Israel and the accused nations with a rod of iron, that is, after the cycles of ninety-eight *lustra* have rolled by, which is from the twentieth year of the reign of Artaxerxes who sways the helm of the Persians—it then being the eighty-fourth Olympiad—down to the fifteenth year of Tiberius Caesar, when the long-awaited redemption of the nations is reported to have arrived, four-hundred-seventy-five years are reckoned, that is four-hundred-ninety (years) according to the lunar calculation of the Hebrews,[17] with the addition of quadrants and the increments of intercalations, as Julius Africanus, the writer on (the calculation) of times is shown to have explained.[18]

And did not the prince of the Syrians [i.e. Naaman], whom the ghastly *[p. 70]* filth of leprosy had covered with its virulent corrup-tion member by member rather than bit by bit, when he approached the highly celebrated prophet [i.e. Eliseus] at the behest of a meander-ing servant and prostrated the dreadful figure of his body seven times in the water of the Jordan [IV Reg. V. 1] with kneeling and genuflec-ting, most clearly declare the form of regenerating grace and the privilege of a second birth, which is conferred upon the faithful through the sacrament of baptism from the womb (and) fecund entrails of Holy Church? Then does not the sixth text of the seventh roll[19] declare with the most illustrious and triumphant show and with success not experienced up to this day the sevenfold reckoning related above, which is depicted with the mystical flowers of the sacred canons, when 'the chosen generation' and 'kingly priesthood' and 'purchased people' [I Petr. II. 9], begotten from the root of the patriarchs, with a great phalanx of hosts thoroughly overturned and brought to the ground the famous city [i.e. Jericho], hateful also to the gods, and purified it in the course of a single week, when the seven trumpets of the priests sounded, that is, when the seven horns of the jubilee blared forth with a brief sounding of battle signals [Ios. VI. 24]? This figure of future events, understood anagogically, is shown to portend the terrible end of the collapsing universe and the final conclusion of fleeting life, after the seven revolutions of the ages have been completed.[20] In very truth the adornments of the universal church, according to the decrees of the ancients, are contained in the seven ranks of holy offices, which receive increments of powers distinguished by name from the first rank of the sacrament [i.e. porter][21] through exorcists and acolytes and extend by degrees as far as the helm of the highest pontificate and the spiritual insignia of bishops. Wherefore the *Praxapostolon,* that is the Acts of the Apostles, approves the same number of men performing the office of the diaconate and stewards of the primitive church [Act. VI. 3], regarding whom Arator,[22] employing poetic eloquence, relates *[p. 71]:* 'They established among seven men the duties of the ministry appropriate to the holy altars' [Arat. I. 442 f.]. But alas! Right away at the very outset of the new religion the abominable Nicolaites[23] arose with their gaping canine jaws barking against the orthodox rule of faith; the Apocalypse of angelic revelation clearly manifested [Apoc. II. 6] from what pernicious roots of error their sect sprang and from what poisoned leaves of heretical perversity it grew, which is revealed more clearly in the fifth chapter of 'On Heresies' [i.e. the *De Haeresibus* of St Augustine]. But let me return to my subject.

For the two-fold and two-edged dream of the ruler of the Nile portending and presaging future events, wherein he beheld seven husks of ears (of grain) ripening at the peak of the fertile stalk, and as many bloated cheeks of corpulent thickness grazing upon the lovely pastureland of the banks,[24] in no wise can be understood to oppose the aforementioned species of number. And the second tablet of the Testament [i.e. Deuteronomy] was said to be written according to the tenor of the seven precepts,[25] and the favouring intervention of the Lord's Prayer [Matth. VI. 9-13] and a restoring medicine for the festering wounds of souls is woven in a series of seven sentences,[26] since the diurnal and nocturnal intervals of hours in which, without cease, we fulfil the obligations of prayer—as though a kind of tax to the state and fiscal payment—revolve and rotate according to a heptadic interval between assemblies; whence I think the poet-psalmist sang: 'Seven times a day I have given praise to thee' [Ps. CXVIII. 164]. And elsewhere the holy oracles of speech of the same Psalmist conveyed a thought not dissonant with the aforesaid reckoning, since 'the words of the Lord . . . pure words' [Ps. XI.7] are known to be related by closest comparison to the most pure metal of liquid silver, which through the conflagration of torrid fire, after the foul blight of slag has been extracted, is reported to be purified 'seven times'.

III. The secular and forensic disciplines of the philosophers are also perceived to be reckoned by just so many numerical factors, to wit: arithmetic, geometry, music, astronomy, astrology, mechanics, and medicine.[27] But also, is not the yearly changing of the seasons, which the Psalmist represents as 'the clown of the year of thy goodness' [Ps. LXIV. 12]—enriched with the abundance of divine blessing—*[p. 72]* perpetually turning according to the two and fifty revolutions of weeks and alternating rotation of cycles? Nor is the supernal and celestial creation itself known to want a figure of the same sort of calculation, since the corporeal structure of the visible world is surrounded and girded by the seven orbs of the heavens that incline headlong with the swift impulse of the revolving sphere, although they are retarded by the retrograde courses of the planets.[28] Moreover, the rotundity of the lunar sphere, which in its annual fulfilment of time waxes through fifteen revolutions of days up to the completed cycle of the full moon and wanes (through) just so many alternations of days, as the form of her most beautiful countenance grows faint, varies according to the sevenfold species of numbers, that is, crescent and sectile and the rest, which the statutes of the Fathers have ordained to signify the septiform nature of the Church. Nor do I think we should fail to mention the stars of the Pleiades or Arcturus, regarding which divine oracles from a whirlwind upbraided the man overwhelmed by terrible illness [i.e. Job] in such fashion: 'Shalt thou be able to join together the shining stars of the Pleiades, or canst thou stop the turning about of Arcturus?' [Iob XXXVIII. 31]. For Arcturus, which presides over the Rhiphean mountains and revolves about the boreal hinge of the northern pole, where the Scythian nations cultivate their dreadful barbarism, is distinguished by the septiform star of the Yoke and the Cart,[29] and because it will never set and is always joined to the wintry North on account if its proximity to the axis, not unfittingly prefigures through allegorical mysteries the rigid austerity of the Old Law. What shall I say of the Atlantides, so called from their father's name [i.e. Atlas], which the tradition of the Greeks called *Pleiades* from their plurality, the Latin (tradition) called *Vergiliae* from the vernal season,[30] or from the branch of the intoxicating grape-vine? These forming a half-circle, as they emerge along obliquely-winding paths from the region of the East—where the saffron splendour of the risen sun sheds itself upon the earth—fittingly prefigure the sevenfold distribution of the divine gifts of the universal church [i.e. the sacraments] by the brightness of just so many stars. *[p. 73]* The arrangements of the stars, which in the language of the Argives are called *Hyades*, i.e. 'the Rainers', regarding which the Mantuan poet[i.e. Vergil] is read to have sung: 'of Arcturus, the rainy Hyades and the twin bears' [*Aen.* I. 744 and III. 416], and which the ancient Latinity of Romulus called the *Suculae*, is also shown to be septiform (and) is placed before the forehead of the celestial bull [i.e. Taurus], which is contained within the circle of the zodiac among the twelve constellations, whence the astrologers in their laughable stupidity think they are able to divine or have knowledge of fate, fortune, or birth, or the last threads of the Parcae [i.e. death], regarding which Maro wrote in the *Bucolics*: ' "Ages such as these glide on!" cried to their spindles the Fates, voicing in unison the fixed will of Destiny!' [*Ecl.* IV. 46–7]. And the unequal movement of the plants, which, as we said above [p. 42], moderates the headlong whirling of the universe in the various paths of its course, revolves in a sevenfold circuit of stars,[31] though in differing cycles of years. But also the dusky dens of nocturnal gloom—regarding which it has been cautioned: 'And he made darkness his covert' [Ps. XVII. 12]—which are said to be generated from the loathsome shade of the earth, are divided into seven separate and individual parts, i.e. *conticinium*, 'evening', *intempestatum* 'dead of night', *crepusculum*, 'dusk', etc.[32] The rhythmical rule of the musicians also declares that the lute, resounding in harmonious concord of modulation, consists of seven strings—as Vergil said: 'seven clear notes' [*Aen.* VI. 646]. In like manner the catholic chronicles of our predecessors show more clearly than light that the formulae of the spiritual library and the rules of the divine law are seven.[33] But to me, as the poet [i.e. Vergil] said:

Sooner would heaven close and evening lay the day to rest
and elsewhere, [*Aen.* I. 374]

Sooner, then, shall the nimble stag graze in the air
And the seas leave their fish bare on the strand *[p. 74]*
Sooner, each wandering over the other's frontiers,
Shall the Parthian in exile drink the Avar,
And Germany the Tigris [*Ecl.* I. 59–62],
Than I shall be able to pick all the flowers of the laws
That give examples of the sacred number seven.[34]

IV. But perchance some diligent person, scrutinizing (this) unsophisticated epistle in the private thought of his heart, may search and enquire why the number seven, which I, being compelled by the necessity of explaining events, collated throughout both canons of the testaments, is repeated over and over—sevenfold and sevenfold—in inscrutable recurrence. If he is aroused by a concern of this sort, let him recollect and recall that in the first part of the letter, which I prolonged exceedingly for the sake of examples, my humble self took a root for a future discourse—after the theme of this number had been presented—from which at a later point the stems of a fragile and meagre talent and the delicate shoots of words might grow profusely along spreading branches. Since therefore charity is fettered by so many and such great chains of sacraments through the septiform grace of the Spirit and by such holy bonds of numbers, regarding which [i.e. charity] the egregious preacher [i.e. Paul], who explored the secrets of the third heaven,[35] writing to the Romans in concatenated style—on which the grammarians of the Greeks bestowed the name 'climax'[36]—began thus: 'And patience trial; and trial hope; and hope confoundeth not: because the charity of God is poured forth in our hearts, by the Holy Ghost, who is given to us' [Rom. V. 4–5], it seems worth our pains that a spiritual and eternal relationship is preferred to a bodily and corruptible association, seeing that the evangelical documents narrate that the incarnate Word of God, concerning whom it has been written: 'My heart has uttered a good word' [Ps. XLIV.2] and as the Psalmist sang: 'From the womb before the day star I begot thee' [Ps. CIX. 3], in a certain sense contrary to the laws and ways of nature assumed intimacy with human kin and affection towards an inviolate mother;[37] and although the catholic Fathers who extricate the spiritual marrow of words and scrutinize the sense hidden in letters refer (her) allegorically to the type of the Church, nevertheless they are in no wise known to deny that the person of the sacrosanct mother existed in the historical sense [p. 75]. Therefore we have brought forward these matters by such lengthy verbal circumlocutions, so that the affections of (our) earlier fraternity, which we are known to have united and joined in the unfolding cycles of past years, might be restored in a sense by refreshing the memory, and be rekindled, lest they grow sluggish because of the great duration of wheeling time, or cold because of the long distance between places. For truly, the bond of unbroken charity does not grow weak on account of the length of years or decay on account of spatial intervals between lands; but rather, the heart of perfect charity sometimes pulses the more because of absence than it is gratified by presence, as the famous competitor [i.e. Paul] in the spiritual arena, where the con-

- 879.3 ALD
  Aldhelm, the Prose Works

- 940.1 SAI
Saints, scholars + heroes

-

testants will gain the prize of the heavenly palm, said in a kindly fashion: 'For though I be absent in body, yet in spirit I am with you' [Col. II. 5]. Therefore this relationship, which was pledged by our right hands, should not be terminated or deemed valueless, since the aforesaid preacher joyfully reports that the unbroken 'pillars' of the Churches, that is Peter and James and John, 'gave to me and Barnabas the right hand of fellowship' [Gal. II. 9].

V. Ah, come! My most excellent and most loving son, mindful of (my) earlier paternal role, let the inextricable knot of true affection be tied so much more tightly and tautly with unbroken ropes throughout the succeeding spans of ages for the rest of time, as it is agreed that the glue of close-linked affection sticks more adhesively to (our) very selves because of the sacred and septiform number of mysteries. Thus addressing your venerable highness in friendly fashion with this little preface, employing the boldness of family intimacy,[38] I subjoin my paltry contribution on metres; having been especially challenged by the authority of the ancients, (and) having obtained materials concerning the diverse qualities of things both heavenly and terrestrial, I excerpted (them) in a cursory and summary fashion, considering now the great, now the meagre nature of creatures.

CXLII. Now [p. 201] as the end of (my) discourse approaches, O most reverent son, with anxious and reliant prayers, as though on bended knee, I suppliantly implore that you deign to protect with the unassailable shield of metres and the buckler of the grammarians this little work and the pains of my toil—wherein it is most openly asserted that I am not envious of your sagacious learning and am not consumed with vigorous marshalling against all the catapults of rivals and the venomed darts of the garrulous, which they often strive to shoot from the quiver of sidelong malice; (and) [p. 202] should the ruler of Olympus on high grant (my) prayer, I would wish you to demonstrate your admiration the more earnestly and cherish the more richly the accomplishment of my devout heart—so that (I may enjoy) from it a certain measured portion of recompense and a payment offered in exchange for a weary mind—insofar as it happens that no one born of the offspring of our race and nourished in the cradles of a Germanic people has toiled so mightily in a pursuit of this sort before our humble self and has committed to the structure of letters the statements of earlier minds regarding the discipline of the metrical art, especially one established in the midst of so many and such loud tumultous uproars in secular affairs and weighed down by the ecclesiastical concerns of the pastoral care by which the meticulous and scrupulous mind is constrained as though by the tightest sort of bolt and chains. For I do not believe that I should be wounded by the dreadful shafts of haughtiness for bringing out this (work), nor do I shudder (to think that) I have been pierced by the most cruel missile of swollen pride, if, reliant upon the Lord, I glory for a bit over the free bestowal of a divine gift, which is conferred upon individuals not according to the privilege of previous merits, but according to the munificence of heavenly generosity, since that illustrious one [i.e. Vergil], who said:

> I first, if life but remain, will return to my country, bringing the Muses with me in triumph from the Aonian peak; first I will bring back to thee, Mantua, the palms of Idumaea,

[*Georg.* III. 11–3]

and a little farther on the same poet continued:

> joyous it is to roam o'er the heights, where no forerunner's track turns by a gentle slope down to Castalia,

[*Georg.* III. 292–3]

intended in my view, to signify by it poetically that no one of the Latin (race) before himself had written a *Georgics* for the scions of Romulus, although Hesiod and Homer and other Greeks, trusting to the fluency of (their) eloquence and endowed with the special gift of Argive elegance, produced a fourfold work on agriculture in the Pelasgian tongue.[39]

Finally, /p. 203/ before the last part of my discourse is concluded in fitting measure, compelled by paternal anxiety, which customarily regards the well-being of children, I urge that you in no wise spurn and condemn these things which I, with the greatest outpouring of sweat and toil, as though weighed down by a grave burden, caused to be set down in writing that they might be examined and considered without the grind of sweat and toil; and that you (in no wise) permit the gift of an accomplished mind divinely bestowed upon you—in preference to the rest of your countrymen and contemporaries—to be neglected in the idleness of sluggish leisure. And surely I deem it absurd, if it should be wearisome for you to run through cheerfully and track down and winnow out that which was not wearisome to me to arrange by hard deliberation and compilation, (and absurd), if it should be repugnant to you—as though a snob or an epicure—to chew a bit and ruminate on that which was not repugnant to me, as though doing the job of a pounding baker, to grind thoroughly and cause to rise. Although worn down by the cares of secular administration, as though by the beating of seaweed flowing back and forth against the rocks and by the eddies of roaring waves, may you guide the reins of the

46

people entrusted to you with moderation; yet, (though) shackled on account of (divine) grace in this concern, in no wise should you deem negligible the mellifluous studies of the Holy Scriptures, nor think them unimportant because of some sort of opportune excuse.

For that distinguished Theodosius,[40] as the venerable works of ancient writers report, who, while guiding the government of almost the entire world, was wedded and happily performed the regal duties for a flourishing empire for the course of eleven years, (spurning) the nourishment of daily consumption and the food of bodily sustenance, in which the life of mortals is gratified, at the very peak of his power obtained the wares of a book copyist, preferring to receive the nutriments of fleshly life from the benefit of the written page than to be sated with the useless delicacies of banquets, while languishing in the torpor of idle inactivity. Whence, too, when he set down in writing with the fingers of his own hand the eighteen volumes of the grammarian Priscian, who was called the light of Roman eloquence, and arranged them down to the last line, he promulgated a statement unheard of among his predecessors and outside the experience of emperors of past ages, leaving an example of industry: 'I Theodosius, ruler of the entire world, set down this volume—midst the cares of the palace—with my own hand',[41] etc. Wherefore there sounded the blare of the heavenly trumpet and the blast of the supernal bugle, saying: 'Let not the books of this law depart from thy mouth: but thou shalt meditate on it day and night' [Ios. I. 8]. Therefore, in all your works, reflect on the last things, and you shall not sin unto eternity.

For /p. 204/ what is the prosperity of the perishable world or the felicity of deceitful life? Is it not—to employ the closest comparison—like the dream that vanishes, the smoke that grows faint, or the foam that disappears? 'If riches abound,' said the Psalmist, 'set not your heart upon them' [Ps. LXI. 11]. Would not that the possession of present things be our repayment in the future! Would not that the abundance of perishable things become a dearth of things to follow! Would not that the allurements of the seductive world beget the loss of eternal blessedness! Rather, once the interval of (this) fragile life has been coursed, may there follow, with Christ's assistance, the perpetual rewards of our merits. Which may He, who hung upon the gibbet for our sake, deign to accomplish, living and reigning forever, together with the eternal Father and Holy Spirit forever, world without end. AMEN.

THE PROSE DE VIRGINITATE

TRANSLATED BY MICHAEL LAPIDGE

Introduction to Aldhelm's Prose
DE VIRGINITATE

Aldhelm's prose *De Virginitate* is addressed to abbess Hildelith and a number of her nuns in the monastery at Barking, Essex. According to Bede's account of Barking and its first abbesses (*HE* IV. 6–10), the monastery had been founded by Eorcenwald at some time before he became bishop of London (675–693). Eorcenwald was very probably a member of the Kentish royal house;[1] he established Barking for his (royal) sister Æthelburg, who became its first abbess. Bede does not say when Barking was founded, but a date after 665—when the East Saxons were reconverted to Christianity—and before 675 would seem probable.[2] Hildelith, the dedicatee *inter alias* of the *De Virginitate*, succeeded Æthelburg as the second abbess of Barking, possibly in 675.[3] Hildelith held this position for a long time: she apparently outlived Aldhelm (*ob* 709 or 710), since she is mentioned as living in a letter from Boniface to Eadburg, abbess of Thanet (Kent), that may be dated to approximately 716,[4] and Bede notes that she presided over the monastery until her extreme old age (*HE* IV. 10).

The monastery at Barking under Hildelith's direction was one of many double-houses—that is, monasteries which housed both men and women—in England at this time:[5] we know of other such double-houses at Bardney, Coldingham, Ely, Hartlepool, Much Wenlock, Repton, Thanet, Wimborne and Whitby. The relations between the sexes in these monasteries probably varied considerably: at Wimborne, for example, the segregation was strictly maintained, whereas at Coldingham the inhabitants had slipped into a relaxed intimacy (for which, according to Bede (*HE* IV. 25), they were duly chastized by divine vengeance). Outside the pages of Bede, very little documentary evidence survives regarding these double monasteries, and perhaps Aldhelm's *De Virginitate* will yet yield some useful information about Barking itself to the trained scrutiny of the historian. In any case it would seem that the majority of these monasteries were founded and

governed by rich and noble ladies who for various reasons had abandoned the world in favour of a life of Christian devotion. Hild, who
was a relative of King Edwin of Northumbria (616–633), spent the
first half of her life in secular affairs but thereafter withdrew from the
world to serve Christ alone (*HE* IV.23), becoming in succession abbess
of Hartlepool and then foundress and first abbess of the important
monastery at Whitby, over which she presided until her death in 680.
King Edwin's daughter Eanflæd was married at one stage of her life to
King Oswiu (642–670); she founded the monastery at Gilling to expiate a murder, and later—after the death of Oswiu, apparently—withdrew to the monastery of Whitby which she ruled (as
successor to Hild) conjointly with her daughter Ælfflæd. Æthelthryth,
who was the daughter of King Anna of the East Angles and who had
been married to King Ecgfrith of Northumbria (670–685), withdrew
from him to Coldingham in order to dedicate herself to celibacy
(*c.*672?); she thereafter founded the monastery at Ely. From the *Anglo-
Saxon Chronicle* (*s.a.* 718) we learn that Cuthburg, a sister of King Ine of
Wessex, founded the monastery at Wimborne (Dorset); the same
source notes that Cuthburg 'had been married to Aldfrith, king of the
Northumbrians, and they separated during their lifetime'.[6] Now
among the nuns at Barking to whom Aldhelm's treatise is dedicated is
found one Cuthburg, and scholars have assumed, not unreasonably,
that it is the same Cuthburg who had abandoned her royal husband
and who later became foundress of Wimborne.[7] One may well wonder
if other of the Barking nuns had a similar background. In any case,
Aldhelm addresses his audience with extreme deference and refers
very delicately to their marital (or virginal) status. I would suggest
that much of the doctrine and structure of the *De Virginitate* is determined by this audience of noble ladies-turned-nuns, some at least of
whom had rejected their worldly marriages. In order to understand
something of Aldhelm's doctrine concerning virginity, it is necessary
to consider briefly his relationship to earlier treatments of the
subject.

Aldhelm was by no means the first Christian author to devote a
treatise to the subject of virginity. Virtually every one of the great
Church Fathers had written at least one such treatise: Tertullian,
Cyprian, Jerome, Ambrose and Augustine in prose, and Alcimus
Avitus and Venantius Fortunatus in verse.[8] Of these various works,
Aldhelm was certainly familiar with those by Cyprian, Jerome,
Ambrose and Augustine, since he refers to them throughout and bases
several chapters on long citations from their work. Clearly he felt that
he was writing in a venerable patristic tradition, and much of his dis-
cussion of virginity is traditional.[9] Nevertheless, Aldhelm's teaching

departs in several respects from what might be described as orthodox Christian doctrine.

The orthodox teaching concerning virginity and its relationship to marriage had been set out clearly by St Paul in the seventh chapter of his First Epistle to the Corinthians. Virginity, according to St Paul, was a highly desirable state for those people who were not married; on the other hand, it was no sin to be married (I Cor. VII. 28 and 36). St Paul (cautiously) praised both virginity and marriage.[10] On one point, however, he is absolutely unequivocal: marriages may not be dissolved—even for the sake of virginity—by either marital partner:

> But to them that are married, not I, but the Lord,
> commandeth that the wife depart not from her husband . . .
> And let not the husband put away his wife.
>
> [I Cor. VII. 10–11]

Patristic authors were obliged to endorse this statement of St Paul even when, as in the case of Jerome, their inclinations were plainly otherwise. So Jerome states in his letter to Eustochium that 'it is not to detract from marriage, that virginity be preferable to it'; and therefore he praises marriage (as indeed he must) with a very peculiar slant: 'I praise marriage, I praise conjugality: but because they produce virgins for me.'[11] Augustine, in his treatise *De Sancta Virginitate*, views the question of marriage-versus-virginity with typical and elusive subtlety. For him—possibly replying to Jerome—marriage may not be contrasted simply with virginity: the production of children is not the prerogative of marriage as such, but of nature; on the other hand, virginity is not merely a status conferred by nature, but rather a spiritual state to be achieved by discipline. Augustine stresses the advantages to a Christian society of both marriage and virginity, and firmly states that one may not be abandoned in favour of the other.[12] Ambrose, like Jerome, is obliged to praise and endorse marriage, no matter how much he is inclined to give his exclusive support to virginity. Thus he argues somewhat ironically in one of his treatises on virginity (the *De Virginibus ad Marcellinam*) that he in no way places virginity before marriage: 'Someone might say, "Do you therefore discourage us from marriage?" By no means: I encourage it, and I condemn those who are accustomed to dissuade others from marriage'.[13] Yet in spite of this apparently unequivocal affirmation of marriage, Ambrose proceeds immediately to list the disadvantages of the married state—pregnancy, morning-sickness, breast-feeding, and so on. In short, each of these three great Church Fathers endorsed St Paul's teaching in praise of the marriage state, even when they might otherwise prefer virginity.

Their opinion is unanimous, that marriage is not to be despised and cannot be rejected.

For Aldhelm, writing in southern England some three centuries after these Church Fathers, an entirely different social situation obtained from that of late fourth-century Rome. Among Anglo-Saxon peoples in Aldhelm's time, apparently, it was not unusual for marriages to be dissolved. Several instances from seventh-century England are known: Æthelthryth and Cuthburg, as mentioned above, had abandoned their marriages in favour of the monastic life. Nor was it only women who rejected spouses in favour of Christ. In his sermon on Benedict Biscop, Bede tells us that Benedict, on entering the religious life, had abandoned a wife and children—preferring, as Bede says, to reject his wife on Christ's behalf and to be among the 144,000 virgins of the Apocalypse.[14] Similarly, Dryhthelm, of whom we read in Bede's *Historia Ecclesiastica*, had been nursed back to life from a deathly illness by his loving wife and had thereafter abandoned her in order to enter the monastery at Melrose (V.2).

It is to this seventh-century English milieu that I would assign a charming but fragmentary debate poem preserved in a manuscript from Echternach; the debate consists in dialogue between a man who proposes to enter the monastic life and his wife who begs him to stay with her:[15]

Husband: *I wish to turn to my God,*
          I no longer want my wife.
          My Lord, I ask this of you:
          I wish to serve you now.
                Get away from me, woman!

Wife: *God joined us well together;*
       My heart rejoices at it.
       This were pleasing in God's eyes:
       My husband at my side.
             O my darling husband!

Husband: *You disaster, be gone from me!*
          I do not wish to hear these words.
          If marriage is pleasing to you
          Go find another man.
                Get away from me, woman!

Wife: *Day and night I'm sad*
       And I weep for my sweet husband.
       If God deprives me of you,
       You'll no longer lie beside me.
             O my darling husband!

54

Here the poem breaks off; we do not know if it was ever completed. It was perhaps undertaken as a schematic treatment of the virginity-versus-marriage question: the husband puts the case for monasticism and celibacy, the wife puts the orthodox view of St Paul. Nevertheless the poem has an intimate and personal tone which reflects an entirely different facet of the frequent marital dissolutions of which we read in the impersonal chronicle of seventh-century English history. It may help us respond to the social context in which Aldhelm's *De Virginitate* was conceived.

In any case this social situation—whereby a nobleman or noblewoman could simply reject a spouse on Christ's behalf—was in flat contravention of the words of St Paul on marriage and had no support in the Latin Church Fathers. Faced with the situation, Theodore, the archbishop of Canterbury (669–690) during the period of Aldhelm's maturity, had given some measure of endorsement to the situation as it existed in England; but since, as we have seen, this endorsement could not be affirmed by the testimony of Latin patristic authorities, Theodore was obliged to turn to the Greek Father St Basil of Caesarea (330–379) for support. Thus we find the following promulgation among the ecclesiastical *Canons* attributed to Theodore:

> It is not allowable for a woman to reject her husband, even if he is an adulterer—unless perchance she leaves him to enter a monastery. Basil made this decree.[16]

It is interesting to see how Aldhelm responded to the doctrinal implications of the situation I have described. On one hand, he was sharply aware of the teaching of St Paul as well as the opinions of the Latin Church Fathers—whose successor he perhaps considered himself to be. On the other hand, he cannot but have been aware of Theodore's ruling concerning women who dissolved their marriages in favour of the monastic life: one such woman at least was among his dedicatees at Barking. Aldhelm's response to this dilemma is one of the most novel features of his work. It had been conventional among patristic authors to distinguish three separate states of female chastity: virginity, widowhood, and marriage.[17] Ambrose, Jerome and Augustine had each compared these three states to the hundred-fold, sixty-fold and thirty-fold fruit of the biblical parable (Matth. XIII. 8; Marc. IV. 8).[18] Aldhelm takes over the tripartite distinction, and preserves the comparison with the biblical parable, but he makes a significant alteration to the scheme:[19] in place of widowhood in the patristic scheme, Aldhelm introduces a state which he calls 'chastity', so that for him the tripartite distinction includes 'virginity' (*virginitas*), 'chastity' (*castitas*) and 'conjugality' or 'marriage' (*iugalitas*). He describes these distinctions as follows:

... virginity is (that which), unharmed by any carnal defilement, perseveres pure out of the spontaneous desire for celibacy; and chastity on the other hand (is that) which, having been assigned to marital contracts, has scorned the commerce of matrimony for the sake of the heavenly kingdom; or conjugality (is that) which, for propagating the progeny of posterity and for the sake of procreating children, is bound by the legal ties of marriage.

[*De Virg.*, c. XIX; below, p. 75]

The new feature is 'chastity', the state attained by someone who has once been married but who has rejected this marriage for the religious life. This newly devised category allowed Aldhelm to praise by implication those Barking nuns such as Cuthburg[20] who had spurned their marriages; at the same time it allowed him to praise 'pure' virginity in traditional terms. And although 'chastity' must obviously occupy an inferior position to 'virginity' itself, Aldhelm was able to pay an indirect compliment to the Barking nuns by suggesting that virginity, because of its exalted station, is susceptible of pride, whereas chastity, because it starts from a lower station, is inclined to continual striving after perfection. Thus at one stroke Aldhelm was able to flatter his audience of once-married nuns and to maintain an orthodox position on the question of marriage-versus-virginity. And, not surprisingly, perhaps, a large proportion of the female martyrs whom Aldhelm adduces in his *De Virginitate* as examples of virtuous behaviour are those who have rejected betrothal or marriage.

These remarks may suffice to indicate some of the novel doctrinal implications of Aldhelm's prose *De Virginitate*. In the structure of the work, likewise, Aldhelm departed from patristic tradition. To some extent, Aldhelm's *De Virginitate* is modelled on Ambrose's treatise *De Virginibus ad Marcellinam* (the one patristic treatise to which it bears any structural resemblance). Ambrose had begun his treatise with a theoretical discussion of virginity, a discussion which he had illustrated by the simile of the chaste bee which gathers honey but does not undergo intercourse. After this discussion, Ambrose exemplified his argument by giving a short catalogue of female virgins, beginning with the Virgin Mary, followed by Thecla, then Antiochena, and so on. It is clear that Aldhelm was influenced by this structure, both in the theoretical discussion (together with its bee-simile[21]) and in the catalogue of female virgins (which in Aldhelm also commences with the Virgin Mary). But Aldhelm did not follow Ambrose slavishly: his doctrinal position is different, he produces his own catalogue of female virgins (and does not simply re-employ Ambrose's examples—Antiochena, for example, is omitted by Aldhelm), and he adds a catalogue of male virgins that had no antecedent in earlier patristic treatises on virginity. One wonders why Aldhelm should have included both male and female virgins: possibly the answer lies in the fact that Barking, the immediate destination of Aldhelm's treatise, was a double monastery.[22]

At all events, the structure of the prose *De Virginitate* consists, first, in an elaborate theoretical introduction to the problem of virginity (cc. III–XIX); a catalogue of male virgins (cc. XX–XXXVIII) in roughly chronological order—Old Testament, New Testament, martyrs and Church Fathers—and then a catalogue of female virgins (cc. XL–LII), similarly ordered. At this point, for no apparent reason, Aldhelm reverts to a few Old Testament patriarchs (Joseph, David, Abel, Melchisedech), all of whom prefigure Christ in one way or another (cc. LIII–LIV). From here, Aldhelm begs leave to return to his original topic, asserts that virginity is an interior not exterior quality, and so launches into a long diatribe against ostentatious dress by members of the Church (c. LVIII); from the description of apparel we easily see that once again Aldhelm has his audience of Barking ladies firmly in view.[23] The work ends with an apology for its brevity and for the fact that it is long overdue (he has been busy with pastoral care), but Aldhelm promises to send the ladies a poem on the same subject in compensation (cc. LIX–LX).

In spite of Aldhelm's apology for the work's brevity (a much abused topos in the hands of medieval authors), it is not brief by any stretch of imagination. Like its individual sentences, the work is sprawling and Gargantuan. I suggested that a definite doctrinal position underlies the argument of the first nineteen chapters; but this position only emerges with difficulty from the profusion of similes which accompanies it. The driving force of the work is Aldhelm's sheer delight in prolixity and in words for their own sake. Only rarely is this prolixity restrained by the exigencies of economical argument or by the demands of tightly devised structure. One looks in vain, therefore, for any structural principle informing the catalogues of virgins. What criteria of selection did Aldhelm follow in drawing up these catalogues? It may not be a truism to say that Aldhelm's selection was limited only by the texts available to him. The list of texts from which he drew his examples was an extensive one, as even a cursory look at Ehwald's source material will indicate (see Appendix III). Yet Aldhelm included Ambrose among his male virgins, for example, presumably because he had access to the *Vita S. Ambrosii* by Paulinus of Milan; but why, on the other hand, did he omit St Felix of Nola when he must presumably have had before him a copy of Paulinus of Nola's poems on that saint?[24] How are we to account for the omission of Anne, or Perpetua, or Catharine from the list of female virgins other than by assuming that Aldhelm did not possess their *vitae*? Except by the simple terms of availability of texts, Aldhelm's choice of examples often seems capricious: he includes Amos of Nitria, for example, who was apparently never venerated in England and who never appears in English calendars.

In the end, it may be futile to seek a clearly designed structural principle in Aldhelm's prose *De Virginitate*. His purpose may simply have been a didactic one: from his own vast reading in hagiography and patristic literature he was attempting to compile an anthology of saintly models for the Barking ladies to peruse at leisure, 'plucking', as he says, 'crimson flowers of purity from the meadow of holy books' (c. XIX). Aldhelm's *De Virginitate* is therefore an 'anthology' or *florilegium* in the proper sense of these words. We will do best to approach it with no demands for coherent structure or concise expression, but with a preparedness to be transported by Aldhelm's *verbosa garrulitas*.

THE PROSE DE VIRGINITATE

To the most reverend virgins of Christ, (who are) to be venerated with
every affection of devoted brotherhood, and to be celebrated not only
for the distinction of (their) corporeal chastity, which is (the
achievement) of many, but also to be glorified on account of (their)
spiritual purity, which is (the achievement) of few: Hildelith, teacher
of the regular discipline and of the monastic way of life [p. 229]; and
likewise Justina and Cuthburg; and Osburg too, related (to me) by
family bonds of kinship; Aldgith and Scholastica, Hidburg and
Berngith, Eulalia and Thecla—(to all these nuns)[1] unitedly or-
namenting the Church through the renown of their sanctity, Aldhelm,
dilatory worshipper of Christ and humble servant of the Church,
(sends his) best wishes for perpetual prosperity.

I. Some time ago, while proceeding to an episcopal convention[2] accompanied by brotherly throngs of associates, I received most
pleasurably what had been written by your Grace to my humble self
and, with my hands extended to the heavens, I took care joyously to
extend immense thanks to Christ on behalf of your welfare. In your
writing[3] not only were the ecclesiastical compacts of (your) sworn
vows—which you had pledged with a solemn promise—abundantly
clear, but also the mellifluous studies of the Holy Scriptures were
manifest in the extremely subtle sequence of your discourse.

II. And when, reading aloud the individual texts of your letters, I
had scanned (them) with the keen gaze of (my) eyes and had thought
them over with a certain natural curiosity about hidden things—as, it
is said, is innate in me—and had very much admired the extremely
rich verbal eloquence and the innocent expression of sophistication [p.
230], then, I say, the governor of lofty Olympus and the ruler of
heaven rejoices with an inexpressible exultation on seeing, thus, the
catholic maidservants of Christ—or rather adoptive daughters of
regenerative grace brought forth from the fecund womb of

59

ecclesiastical conception through the seed of the spiritual Word—growing learned in divine doctrine through (the Church's) maternal care, and like talented athletes under some experienced instructor training in the gymnasium through wrestling routines and gymnastic exercises, who eagerly win the crown of the laborious contest and the prize of the Olympic struggle by the strenuous energies of their own exertions; so that, let's say, one (athlete), smeared with the ointment of (some) slippery liquid, strives dexterously with his partner to work out the strenuous routines of wrestlers, sweating with the sinuous writhings of their flanks in the burning centre of the wrestling-pit; another, taking the missiles of javelins and the shafts of arrows from the hidden recesses of his quiver—not in order to relax the passive gaze of his eyes freely through the skies but in order to demonstrate the accurate focus of his vision—with his flexed bow humming and the bow-string twanging he guides (them) unswervingly to their destined mark; another, trusting to his fleet feet in the stadium of the panting runners—concerning whom the excellent competitor and teacher of the Holy Word said 'all run indeed, but one receiveth the prize' [I Cor. IX. 24]—overcoming the crowds of participants in the race and his companions in this competition, has good luck and happily enjoys the palm of victory; another man together with a crowd of associates, riding a caparisoned steed which, bloodied by spurs and cut by the whip, they dress up with shining sharp-toothed bits—concerning which the elegant poet: 'The field shook and crumbled under the four-hoof beat of the horses' [Vergil, *Aen.* XI. 875]—quickly linking circuit to circuits he measures out the surface of the grounds; another one, surrounded by the naval companies of sailors and encircled by dense throngs of rowers, driving his swift galley or skiff through the glassy waters of the ocean, with the steersman urgently inciting (them) and the master-rower beating time with his truncheon, presses on with foamy and sea-weedy strokes of the oars.

III. And truly all these things, which we have singled out as being performed by athletes among the teachable skills belonging to worldly matters, are not, according to the industry of your discipline, performed with the motions of the outer man, but with the actions of the inner man, given that I do not think it concealed from your wisdom that the microcosm [p. 231]—that is, the 'smaller world'—consists in a two-fold and twin substance of material; but rather, just as the nature of the outer man—having been formed in open view is seen clearly—can be perceived with no difficulty, so the quality of the inner man—who is believed to have been breathed in by the divine Spirit according to the account of *Genesis*—has, I think, been subtly investigated bit by bit and stage by stage by your intelligence. And, truly, that most celebrated proponent of the name of Christ suggested the contest of athletes as an example for the Christian army, saying: 'And they indeed that they may receive a corruptible crown; but we an incorruptible one' [I Cor. IX. 25], and elsewhere, '(I so fight), not as one beating the air' [I Cor. IX. 26]. And however much the examples of athletes, who with (their) bodily agility win popular honours in the theatre and the applause of the circus, might properly pertain to a comparison of those who, traversing the spacious race-courses of the Scriptures, are known to exercise the most subtle industry of their minds and the quality of (their) lively intelligence through assiduous perseverance in reading;

IV. nevertheless the richest experience of life clearly declares that the industry of the highly ingenious bee might be adapted to the aforementioned schemes of examples—(the bees) who, when dewy night is departing and the light of the bright sun has risen, straightway pour out dense armies of rejoicing throngs in swarms through the open fields: at one moment, settling on the honey-bearing petals of marsh-marigolds or the purple flowers of mallows they gather honeyed moisture drop by drop in their mouths and, as if with the treacly must of the sweet wine made for royal feasts, they struggle eagerly to fill the greedy receptacles of their stomachs; at another moment, swarming round golden-yellow willows and the saffron tips of broom they transport /p. 232/ their fertile booty in numerous loadings of their thighs and hips, out of which they build waxen castles; later still, pressing together the smooth flower-clusters of ivy and the tender buds of the blossoming lime-tree, they construct the multi-dimensional edifice of the honey-comb with angular and hidden cells. The excellent poet [i.e. Caelius Sedulius], sustained by his poetic eloquence, is believed to have sung in catalectic verse of the endeavours of their craft, when he said,

Waxen honies turn golden in the jewel-studded baskets,
[*Carm. Pasch.*, praef. 13]

and further on, in a brachicatalectic or colophon,

And the golden vessels shine with their honey-combs.
[*Carm. Pasch.*, praef. 14]

For just as the swarm, having left in companies and throngs the restricted openings of the windows and the narrow entrance-halls of the beehive, pillages the beautiful meadows of the countryside, in the same way your remarkable mental disposition—unless I'm mistaken—roaming widely through the flowering fields of scripture, traverses (them) with thirsty curiosity, now energetically plumbing the divine oracles of the ancient prophets foretelling long in advance the advent of the Saviour with certain affirmations; now, scrutinizing with careful application the hidden mysteries of the ancient laws miraculously drawn up by the man [i.e. Moses] who is said to have cruelly smitten the Memphitic realms [i.e. Egypt] with ten most savage afflictions of plagues, and to have separated on different sides, into the likeness of a wall, the swelling waters of the Red Sea and the surge of its foaming waves, receding at the touch of the sacred rod once transformed from a serpent, and, after divine confabulation, to have put to flight the incredulous people with his horned face; now, exploring wisely the fourfold text of the evangelical story [i.e. the four Gospels], expounded through the mystical commentaries of the catholic fathers and laid open spiritually to the very core and divided up by the rules of the fourfold ecclesiastical tradition according to *historia, allegoria, tropologia* and *anagoge*; now, duly rummaging through the old stories of the historians and the entries of the chroniclers, who by their writing have delivered to lasting memory the chance vicissitudes of times gone by; now, sagaciously inquiring into the rules of the grammarians and the teachings of experts on spelling and the rules of metrics (as they are) measured out into accents (and) times, fitted into poetic feet, broken up into cola and commata—that is, into pentimemeres and eptimemeres—and, indeed, divided individually into a hundred kinds of metre.

V. *[p. 233]* The bee, I say, by virtue of the special attribute of its peculiar chastity, is by the undoubted authority of the scriptures agreed to signify a type of virginity and the likeness of the Church: robbing the flowering fields of pastureland of an ineffable booty she produces her sweet family and children, innocent of the lascivious coupling of marriage, by means of a certain generative condensation of a very sweet juice; and in truth, the Church, striking vitally into the hearts of men with the double-keen sword-edge of the (two) Testaments, fertilizes through the chaste seed of the Word the offspring who are lawful heirs of eternity.

VI. This also is to be remembered, I suggest, concerning the harmonious fellowship of the bees, and to be admired as some theatrical spectacle—I mean the spontaneous inclination to voluntary servitude which they are known to exercise in obedience to their rulers. In respect of this sort of consideration, are not all the disciplines of the monastic way of life and the regular practices of monasteries indicated by an extremely close comparison? For as long as that bee who among the others discharges the office of magistrate, shall decree that they should inhabit their ancient dwellings and care for their little cottages woven with slender cane or knitted together with hollow stems, no bee from the immense multitude roams through the air on wandering routes or with undirected flights; but if, when strong reasons exist and a necessity for travel urges, that bee, to whom in the role of consul the rule of the others is entrusted, shall give preference to the seeking out of foreign realms, nowhere among living things would you see exile(s) driven from their own homeland crammed into such dense columns of armies and such crowded cohorts of legions—so much is this the case, in fact, that out of reverence for their leader they set out for foreign parts (in search) of a residence more willingly than they would remain at home in their cells (where they are) used to domestic comforts and content with subservient tranquillity. What, I ask, in the nature of visible things can be seen, that obeys the command of its begetter and strives to fulfil the order of its king with such great desire *[p. 234]* that, appropriately, because (it is) a symbol of unstained virginity and (because of its) spontaneous acceptance of devout servitude—whereby it offers an example of obedience to mortals living in this vale of tears—above all other creatures it may produce nectared food and store up the nourishment of honeyed sweetness in its golden dwellings of wax, (nourishment) which may not only excel all dishes of delicacies and the seasoned richness of sauces, and surpass all the incense of sweet ambrosia and the odour of fragrant balsam, but also—in order that, leaving out the particular, the course of my discussion may hasten to the general—may exceed all delights of worldly sweetness and the exquisite pleasures of sumptuous gourmandising and may leave far beneath it the gulping down of sweet wine?

VII. Therefore, if the glory of holy virginity is believed to be next kin to angelic beatitude, and the beauteous company of the heavenly citizens wins praise for the merit of chastity, it ought to be extolled with the acclaim which is its due, since among the other ranks of the virtues it is singled out to wield the sceptre of the highest sovereignty and the sway of government; since, indeed, just as the taste of honeyed sweetness quite incomparably excels everything that is experienced as pleasing and delectable when brought to human mouths and the palate of mortals, so the divine majesty—though I speak however with the peace and indulgence of those saints once bound by the ties of matrimony—set the special attribute of virginity before all the ranks of virtues in general which are enumerated in the list of the gifts (of the Holy Spirit). A clear enough proof of this exists, since, when from the highest summit of the heavens the venerable offspring of God descended to rescue the straying sheep and to recover the lost farthing, he entered the womb of an uncontaminated mother, made capable of virginal birth without danger to her perpetual purity or loss of her chastity. For this reason I think also that the holy recliner on the

Lord's breast and the 'fourth river of Paradise' [i.e. John, author of the fourth Gospel], who above all others irrigated the seven churches of Asia with the inexhaustible waters of divine doctrine, deserved the special prerogative of divine love and the intimate lavishing of affection before all the renown of the other apostles, since he offered up to Christ—who is a passionate lover of chastity and a jealous teacher of /p. 235/ holiness—the welcome sacrifice of virginity made with spontaneous devotion. For this reason the true physician, when, considering the wounds of evil and the scars of sin by which souls of the sick were prostrated by a cruel overthrow, he mixed a health-giving potion and vitally administered an antidote of celestial medicine to the fibres mortally infected with a virulent dose of spiritual wickedness, and ascending the summit of the gallows on the sixth day after the sabbath—that is, the 'day of preparation'—he was suffering, mindful of reverence towards his mother he dutifully enjoined the disciple who was awaiting the outcome of things among the dangers (presented by) the perfidious soldiers to look after his mother—as can be not inappropriately expressed in a rhythmical poem[4],

> Christ, having suffered the cross
> and the hiding-places of death,
> himself a virgin commended a virgin [= Mary]
> to a virgin [= John] for safe-keeping.

Afterwards, when decades had elapsed, John, having been banished as an exile to Patmos by Domitian—who at that time, reliant on his imperial power, was inflicting the cruel pains of torture upon the worshippers of the true faith—and having been transported in a vision of ecstasy, was found worthy to hear the 144,000 virgins singing a new song with sweet-sounding harmonies of melody and to behold (them) with his pure eyes. Of them it is said: 'For they are virgins; these follow the Lamb whithersoever he goeth' [Apoc. XIV. 4]. The rest of the faithful are to hear, but these are to sing the holy songs, and to walk with the Lamb through the august glory of the heavenly kingdom.

VIII. On the other hand, (while we are) augmenting the virginal glory of chastity with immense praise, and inciting the minds of those bearing arms for Christ to the example of a strict way of life and to the model of a strenuous resolve, we do not consider that the immaculate cohabitation of matrimony and the legitimate union of lawful wedlock is to be scorned, as /p. 236/ the ravings of heretics blather. Far be it from the catholic faith of the churches, particularly since we know for certain that in ancient times the patriarchs who maintained the bonds of marriage according to the precept of divine decree were pleasing to the heavenly majesty, and, filled with the grace of the Holy Spirit, prophesied the birth of the future Incarnation in presentient voices of prognostication, as is said: 'The sceptre shall not be taken away from Juda, nor a ruler from his thigh, till he come that is to be sent: and he shall be the expectation of nations' [Gen. XLIX. 10], and so on—which can be clearly proved and established by a thousand-fold mass of witnesses. But now, with the dusky shadow of the ancient document [i.e. the Old Testament] receding and the clear beauty of the Gospel flashing forth, we say that there is as great a distance between the flowers of virginity and the virtues of marriage as is between east and west. Whence one of the catholic fathers [i.e. Jerome], explaining that the flowering glory of virginity arises from the root of marriage, through the agency of a metaphor began elegantly as follows: 'I select gold from the earth, the rose from the thorn, the pearl from the shell' [*Ep.* XXII. 20].

IX. For the radiant beauty of pure silver is not shamefully debased, even though the refined metal of shining gold is preferred; nor does the gloss of dazzling white marble suffer any loss of splendour, though the loveliness of the red-glowing jewel is praised as more beautiful; nor do the woollen threads of fibres wound from off a ball of yarn or from bobbins become objects of careless contempt, even though the taffeta garment of royal purple or the silken robe of emperors is more resplendent. Are pomegranates stuffed with pips and red seeds and protected with a single covering of rind, thought to suffer a contemptible calumny of nature, even though we believe that the juicy dates of the palm and the honey-sweet nectar of Nicolian dates are incomparably better by far [p. 237]? In no way is the utility of the rough anvil or the rigid hardness of the striking hammer or the holding power of the rusty tongs or scissors scorned and despised, although the studded girdle and the royal diadem and the diverse glories of ornaments—which are produced and forged by the aforementioned instruments of iron—are preferred; nor does the smooth sphere of the lunar globe suffer any loss of its own beauty, though the bright splendour of the clear sun is thought to illuminate the tripartite orb of the world more clearly. And are the waters of the deep well or the icy liquid of the cistern—which we draw up by means of an *anthlia*, that is to say, a drawing-wheel—to be thought of as of little value, though the alternating jets of the purest fountain may seem to excel (them), and the constant down-pouring of aqueducts with their frequent lofty vaults of arches, raised aloft in an elevated water-pipe, and their overwhelming cataracts, may seem to surpass (them)? For the dusky constitution of the greedy ouzel is not put to confusion, nor the black coloration of the crow despised, although the multi-coloured glory of the peacock, with the smooth perfection of its (feathered) rings, takes precedence—the peacock, the beauty of whose feathers now grows golden with a saffron hue, now blushes red with a purple sheen, now shines with a bluish depth of colour or glows with the tawny glint of gold. The excellence of its beauty, (which may be) compared, not in vain, to the model of virginity, scorns the other baubles of the world and counts at naught the ornamented trappings of this life, and indeed St Augustine, in his *De Civitate Dei* [XXI. 4], testifies that he has found it to be empirically true that the flesh of the peacock is of an incorruptible nature. And is the nature of woodland trees and the sterile greenness of leaves or the sappy stems of terrestrial vegetation scorned, even though purple and crimson flowers—sprung from the very boughs of these trees or born from the plants of the green meadow—are more beautifully flushed and are more sweetly redolent with the sweet fragrance of scent, since it is well known that from the flowers, the rewards of the fruits which are to follow ripen in a wonderful fashion, with an abundant yield and profit many times over, while the flourishing leaves on young branches and the dense tendrils of vines miserably wither once the sap in the inner cortex has stopped flowing, and with the torrid heat of autumn advancing they fall in large numbers like the thickest of slaughter? The sublimity of praiseworthy virginity, like a lofty lighthouse placed on the uprearing promontory of a cliff, does not shine so resplendently that the strict moderation *[p. 238]* of chastity, which is the second grade, is scorned as completely inferior and grows vile; or so that the legitimate fertility of marriage, undertaken for the issue of children, becomes perceptibly foul. Nor by a comparison of this sort do I see that what is good is disparaged but rather—which is better—I think that it is more willingly praised.

X. And yet—unfortunately—it usually occurs the other way around with the hierarchical positions reversed, so that the station of the inferior life, advancing on all fronts little by little, takes the place of the superior grade as it languishes tepidly; and urged on by the goad of most bitter remorse obtains its wish and overtakes the once superior victor; and he who was counted last through the negligence of his past life, henceforth, kindled by the flame of divine love, is in first place, reminding (us) of the maxim in the Gospels, 'Many sins are forgiven her because she hath loved much' [Luc. VII. 47]. And he who had been merely a follower in pious resolve, rejecting the pleasures of the world with contempt like the scourings of filth and repressing the enticements of carnal delight, and having undertaken manfully the novitiate of a chaste way of life and, trembling at the horrifying abyss of hell and burning with desire for eternal life, relying on the freely

66

given grace of Christ, becomes the leader through the diligence of his labour. As far as the others are concerned, what is, I think, to be lamented mournfully with tearful outbursts of sorrow and to be bewailed dolefully in querulous plaints with profound sighing of breasts, are those of either sex who, inflated with the puffed-up arrogance of pride, exult in the integrity of the flesh alone; while the others, sailing (as it were) near the perilous shipwreck of this world with the whirlwind of a dreadful tempest raging, as though between the Sicilian Scylla and the gulf of the whirlpool [i.e. Charybdis], hasten towards the harbour of the monastic life, and with Christ as their pilot arrive safely, even though the timbers of their ship are somewhat shaken. The former lot, seeking the condition of the holy life with the life-rafts of their soul all sound, and the ship of their uncontaminated body unbreached, without any risk of rocks, are so much the less eager to devote themselves to moans of lamentation or to seek to wash their faces with floods of tears, inasmuch as they trust themselves to be deformed by no blemishes and stains, and fouled by no blackness /p. 239/ of secular slag. The others do not cease from watering their sad countenances continuously with the dewy fountains of their eyes and their dripping eyelids: all the more so, since they remember that they have perpetrated illicitly certain forbidden things prohibited by the severity of the law, by reason of their association with the world. But the former ones, because they judge themselves to be chastely celibate and to be thoroughly free from all the dregs of filth, inflated with (over-) confidence in their virginity they arrogantly swell up and in no way do they turn away the most cruel monster Pride, devourer of the other virtues, with the nose-ring of humility [cf. Iob XL. 21].

XI. For in the conflict of the eight principal vices, although Pride is placed last, yet like a fierce queen she is known to usurp for herself the authority of tyrannical power and the sway of government more so than the others, since without any wavering uneasiness of ambiguity it is to be truly believed that Lucifer—surrounded by parasitic accomplices and hemmed in by apostate followers—fell reeling into the profound abyss of pride and the foul pit of swollen arrogance, before the first-created (man), the inhabitant of the newly made Paradise and the inexperienced owner of all the earthly creation which the smooth circling of the heavens encircles like a whirling sling, tasting the forbidden nourishment with stuffed cheeks and smacking lips, fell cruelly into the chasm of gluttony. Now if the angelic loftiness of heavenly citizens, swelling so greatly with the arrogance of pride, was deprived of the blessed companionship of the other angels and its share in contemplating the godhead, how much the more will the frail weakness of mortals be unhappily defrauded of the wedding-feast of the celestial bride-groom, if it has swelled up like an inflated bladder with the merit of its own attainments, and has taken on the notoriety of vainglory because of its virginal chastity—as if it were some special sanctity? Virgins of Christ and raw recruits of the Church must therefore fight with muscular energy against the horrendous monster of Pride and at the same time against those seven wild /p. 240/ beasts of the virulent vices, who with rabid molars and venemous bicuspids strive to mangle violently whoever is unarmed and despoiled of the breastplate of virginity and stripped of the shield of modesty; and they must struggle zealously with the arrows of spiritual armament and the iron-tipped spears of the virtues as if against the most ferocious armies of barbarians, who do not desist from battering repeatedly the shield-wall of the young soldiers of Christ with the catapult of perverse deceit. In no way let us sloppily offer to these savage enemies the backs of our shoulder-blades in place of shield-bosses, after the fashion of timid soldiers effeminately fearing the horror of war and the battle-calls of the trumpeter! Rather, as combatants in the monastic army, boldly offering our foreheads armed with the banner of the Cross among the ranks of our competitors, and carrying tightly the warlike instruments of armament—which the distinguished warrior [St Paul] enumerates, that is to say, the sword of the Holy Word and the impenetrable breast-plate of faith [Eph. VI. 17]—and protected by the secure shield against the thousand harmful tricks of spiritual wickedness, we shall then blessedly rejoice in the heavenly kingdom, revelling in celestial glory (and) ready to receive the due triumph of victory from Christ our paymaster—if we now fight strenuously in the forefront of the battle as rulers of the world or as warriors of the Lord, steadfastly struggling with steadfast foes, against the dominion of Leviathan and the powers of darkness.

XII. First of all, as I said, let us—sustained by divine approbation—strive to conquer the eight leaders of the principal vices, to whom the Cerethi of crimes and the Phelethi of evil deeds [cf. II Reg. VIII. 18] with their horrendous apparatus of war, are subject: (these vices), who never cease from struggling indefatigably against the throngs of Christ's recruits and the warlike squadrons of virgins with savage armies of foes, a multiple bombardment of stratagems and a full armoury of deceptions, even though—when Christ offers a defence and urges on the phalanxes of His soldiers with the prize of a predestined victory—they often shamefully turn their backs in flight. But—alas!— the prosperity of peace, when acquired, is not safe; nor is the happiness of the triumphs achieved secure, or the victory over deceptive fortune unchangeable and lasting. For the enemies—who were thought to have been cut down to the point of extermination

68

[p. 241] in a final massacre and were (thought) to have been successfully overcome by the desired outcome of events—again in their turn challenge the victors to a savage battle, take up bloody arms, renew a horrendous war, and equip themselves for renewed struggles against those who had obtained their (earlier) desire. Wherefore, in the first place, let the cruel serpent of gluttony who lethally vomited the pestilent poison of transgression on the inexperienced inhabitants of the flowering earth [i.e. Adam and Eve] from his venomous jaws, be driven away by the restraint of frugality; and, last of all, on the other hand, let the ferocious adder of pride—which lamentably threw into confusion the blessed company of heaven and the dwellers in the holy city—(be) banished from the hidden recesses of our soul and the secret corners of our hearts (and) be driven far away by the fear of God, just as the army of the Hebrews, advancing with six hundred thousand marching men and hordes of followers, when the greedy army of the Pharoah had been submerged in the waters of the Red Sea and drowned in the deep floods of the tide—through which army gluttony is figurally represented—gave over the seven peoples of the Canaanites—which foreshadowed typologically the seven-fold armies of the vices—to the jaws of gluttonous death by frequent destructive slaughter; and, as long as it did not oppose the sanctions of the Decalogue, happily inhabited the Promised Land which was divided among the twelve tribes by lot of territory; and this race of paternal generation, by its ancestors and forefathers so left it to be possessed by the grandchildren and great-grandchildren of future posterity through the perpetual law of legitimate heredity.

XIII. However, if the alert interest of your wisdom sagaciously desires to know how many companies of legions serve the aforementioned leaders of spiritual wickedness and the foul princes of darkness; how many tyrannous fellow-soldiers bent on harming human nature follow (them); how many attendants of (these) evil-doers, who have conspired to attack our army and to demolish the fortresses of faith, have gathered together in hordes; and how (both) the servants and the hangers-on belonging to the lower ranks of this evil soldiery, with their throngs of camp-followers, not to mention the governors and generals who claim for themselves a shameful command over these same spirits, are called by name by the exact designations of words *[p. 242]*—these (leaders) who incite to battle the profane armies of the Philistines, crowded together in hundreds and thousands against the Israelites on top of Mt Gilboa—that is to say, the horrendous throngs of loathsome vices, which with the leaders set over them, strive to attack in hordes the universal diocese of the Church, and with poisoned arrows of sin and the dire sword of crimes not only wound the sluggish, but also sometimes bring down the veteran soldiers of Christ, with a virulent wound to (their) chastity and deadly toxin, so that not undeservedly might the clairvoyant David—that is, the flower of the branch, coming forth from the root of Jesse—dolefully compose, in a mood of compassion, an elegiac poem and mournful song—which is called a 'dirge' or 'epitaph'—for the peoples of the Church (who are) falling in droves to the onslaught of the vices: if, I say, your shrewdness of careful attention would wish all these things to be more fully considered, not only will the ten *Collationes patrum* composed by Cassian, the abbot of the diocese of Marseilles (who was) particularly endowed with eloquence in writing, clearly set them forth, but also Gregory, pontiff of the apostolic see, from whom we (English) took the rudiments of faith and the sacraments of baptism, elaborated (them) more clearly than light through allegorical exposition in his book of .*XXXI. Moralia in Iob*. But what compelled me to debate and discuss concerning the disgraceful roots of the eight sins, whence the entangling shrubbery of the other crimes grows up like dense saplings of bushes with tenacious foliage, was that certain people, elevated on the lofty pinnacle of virginity and raised up on the peaks of a chaste way of life, considering the second grade of chastity as if it were contemptible and far remote from themselves, believe that they have incomparably surpassed the renown of the others, somehow forgetting and placing behind themselves that (biblical phrase): 'And whosoever shall exalt himself shall be humbled; and he that shall humble himself shall be exalted' [Matth. XXIII. 12]. For if the uncontaminated virginity of Mary bore for us the incarnate Word of God in celestial childbirth /p. 243/, yet when the circle of one forty day (span) had been measured out, the prophetess Anna, the daughter of Phanuel, prophesied the same redeemer through the presentiment of the Holy Spirit, and accordingly both grades, consecrated to both virgins and widows, are honoured in the very beginning of the divine nativity, so that he who is bountifully enriched by the abundance of the hundred-fold reward should in no way presume to disdain boastfully him who is enriched with sixty-fold bundles of sheaves; nor should the mere possession of corporeal virginity produce in the mind the wound of pride, nor the remedy for salvation feed the tinder of perdition. For it is a calamity to be lamented, if the pliable stuff of humility, by which the growths of the other virtues are healthily preserved, (should be used) to weave the net of pride or the snare of self-exaltation for holy virginity; if panaceas or antidotes which usually remove the deadly virus are detriments to health, with the condition unaffected.

XIV. On the other hand, however, there are certain aspirants to the blessed life, who from the very commencement of first infancy never cease from persevering indefatigably in the high pursuit of virginity, and (who) strive blessedly to preserve to the very end the unbreached barriers of their modesty without any disparagement of their purity; and yet they are so goaded by the spur of divine love and inflamed by the blazing torch of heavenly ardour, that every day they eagerly long to depart from the prison of the body, transported from the adversity of this world; and through the chariness of their abstemiousness they bring it about that they hasten as quickly as possible to the celestial homeland of Paradise, while, with secret singing of psalms and salt fountains of tears they fail to dissimulate the burning desire of their minds and groan aloud because of the frequent sighings of remorse drawn from the deepest recesses of their hearts: and, thus sweetly filled with the delight of the contemplative life and fattened with the nectarine food of contemplative sweetness, so that no-one in the pursuit of practical living, which we call the active life, can manage to match their rule of life, even if he dissolves his sins in tears—to such as these, therefore, who are known to accumulate the glory of virginity by holiness of morals and by the reinforcement of virtues of this sort, (to these) all the lofty greatness of (merely) temperate persons, all the sublime loftiness of wedded folk, takes second place.

XV. *[p. 244]* Wherefore let no-one trust that the sole attribute of purity without the assistance of other virtues will suffice in attaining fully to perfection, and as if, were it alone preserved, he might be relaxed and confident without (taking on) the conflict of the remaining vices! No, it's rather the case that, in order that the special worth of high-born virginity should not (become) cheapened and less beautiful, it should be supported by the concurrence of the other precepts of the law and be fitly honoured by the manifold variety of the commandments, so that—according to the words of the Psalmist—like 'a queen on the right hand' of the divine majesty, radiant 'in golden vestment' and resplendent in the 'surrounding variety'[5] of merits [Psalm. XLIV. 10], she may, accompanied by heavenly cohorts, blessedly be found worthy to be perpetually present at and have joy of the indivisible fraternity of angelic companionship! Otherwise the unadorned diligence of virginity, without the assistance of the other virtues, will not be enriched with the opulent abundance of the ecclesiastical harvest by a hundred-fold return on its merits, but withering with fruitless and barren sterility will be punished along with the foolish virgins carrying burned-out lamps since, indeed, (in the case of) the weaving of hangings or carpets, if threads dyed with purple and indeed with diverse varieties of colours do not run here and there among the thick cloth-fibres and according to the

71

embroiderer's art ornament the woven fabric with the varying outlines of pictures, but it is made uniformly with a monochrome dye, it
is immediately obvious that it will not appear pleasing to the glances
of the eye nor beautiful against the most exquisite elegance of ornaments. For the curtains of the ancient temple are not read to have
glowed with one simple and single kind of dye, but are described as
having blazed with gold, blue, purple, twice-dyed scarlet or vermilion
with twisted cotton of diverse tints. But why are we rhetoricising
about the tintings of fabric-dyes? Clearly, the pure sheet of gold itself,
which excels all the other metals of silver and brass and tin, will seem
somehow to lose its gloss without the topaz and the garnet and the
ruby glory of jewels or the precious stone of amber. But consider the
separate varieties of colours and the kinds of metals [p. 245], adopted
(here) in order to augment and amplify the rewards of chastity
through the scheme of allegory; and investigate (them) with the help
of the mystical explanations of the Fathers through the figural
scrutiny of tropology!

XVI. Therefore let the true and not trivial glory of delicate virginity be protected by the true and not false precaution of humility, and
let it be restrained as if (it were) the gentlest playfulness of a noble infancy (restrained) by the stern tutorship of discipline, since the mind
which is wounded by the spear of self-exaltation is exalted in vain
about chastity alone, and the spirit congratulates itself in vain on the
grace of integrity if it is wounded by the arrow of swelling arrogance!
In short, very often, as we have found, the consciousness of chastity is
assailed by the vainglory of pride, and where it imagines that it is
more excellent than others in the Church through the merit of its acquired sanctity, there it will be cheated of the due profit of its reward
and deprived of the prize for its laborious struggle. For the Gospel
parable did not promise that the entire crowd of the ten virgins is to be
welcomed to the marriage of the celestial bridegroom and to be blessed
with equal joy in celestial glory, but only those who, keeping wedding
etiquette with shining lamps of modesty and torches burning with the
oil of chastity, will be found worthy to run happily to the celestial
bridegroom on his return. Hence it seems worthwhile that first the
grasses of wickedness and the thickets of pride are to be entirely
uprooted, and the most fruitful slips of the apple-bearing tree (with its)
flowering branches are to be mulched, so that (when) the underbrush
of vices has been destroyed and the roots of the passions have been
pulled up, we may plant the fruit-bearing saplings of the virtues with
Christ as our gardener. Therefore carnal integrity is in no way
approved of, unless spiritual purity is associated with it as companion.
Whence the 'vessel of election'[6] [i.e. St Paul] says, 'And the unmarried

woman and the virgin thinketh on the things of the Lord; that she may be holy both in body and in spirit' [I Cor. VII. 34]. Clearly, it is shown by the apostle's statements that the stainlessness of bodily purity by itself cannot unlock the gates of the heavenly kingdom, and on its own can in no way serve to reopen the door of Paradise—which the summary verse of *Genesis*[7] declared the Cherubim to have closed originally with a fiery weapon that turned every way—unless a dual sanctity on each side glistens in harmony. Whence the same writer says, 'I chastise my body and bring it into subjection' [I Cor. IX. 27], which is to say, so that the flesh does not contumaciously grow insolent with tyrannical power against the spirit and, swelling /p. 246/ with the impudent arrogance of liberty, scorn to subject its neck to the yoke of legitimate servitude. Therefore the pure steadfastness of uncontaminated virginity is made a servant of God through the tireless constancy of contemplation; and, on the other hand, the freedom of restrained conjugality is made into a servile poverty of complacent spotlessness.

XVII. The excellent preacher distinguishes this bipartite aspect of life in this manner: the married woman and the virgin, he says, are distinct—'And the unmarried woman and the virgin thinketh on the things of the Lord; that she may be holy both in body and in spirit. But she that is married thinketh on the things of the world; how she may please her husband' [I Cor. VII. 34]. In truth a great interval and a large dissimilarity of vast proportion exists between the munificence of divine dilection and the affection of baser love: the one rejoices at being a companion of angelic chastity, the other is pleased to be the kindling of marital wantonness. The latter strives that her neck be decorated with necklaces and her arms with bracelets and that she be adorned with gem-studded rings on her fingers; the former desires to be radiant with the most beautiful adornment of shining modesty and to gleam with golden necklaces of virtues and at the same time to be decked out with the dazzling pearls of her merits. The one is busy being alluringly coiffed with the twisted curls of her ringlets curling round the tongs, and to paint her cheeks and lips after her own fashion with the scarlet rouge of artificial colour; the other, with an uncombed mane of hair and with her tresses carelessly matted bears the crown of glory with the palm-wreath of virginity on her head; the one, parading[8] with the senseless pomp of her ornaments—in the likeness of that woman offering the lethal drink of the brothel in a golden chalice, whom the *Apocalypse*[9] describes as having sat on the beast—when turned out offers a sight which is equally pleasing and harmful to the spectators; the other never ceases from displaying the lessons of chaste behaviour and the example of the citizens of heaven to those desiring to emulate (her)

XVIII. Therefore the future eminence of the angelic life is now in a certain sense seized by violence beforehand by the male and female followers of intact virginity (who are) 'bearing a treasure' pleasing to God 'in an earthen vessel' [II Cor. IV. 7]—although it is spontaneously laid hold of by unforced impulses—since *[p. 247]* 'the kingdom of heaven suffereth violence and the violent bear it away' [Matth. XI. 12]. For it is assuredly clear—because the violence is of the strictest and the way of life most difficult—that the man, whom maternal fecundity brought forth into the world from the natural womb of nativity, if he spurns the laws of nature, is bound to exist as an inseparable fellow of angelic chastity, and, before the dominion of horrendous death is driven into black hell by the supreme glory of the resurrection and 'this corruptible (body) puts on incorruptibility' [I Cor. XV. 53], earthly celibates are compelled in a wonderful manner to become heavenly citizens. Whence our Lord dismisses the factious slander of Pharisaical temptation, confuting (it) with the argument of a true response, saying: 'In the resurrection they shall neither marry nor be married, but shall be as the angels of God in heaven' [Matth. XXII. 30]. O excellent grace of virginity, which like a rose grown from thorny shoots blushes with a crimson flower and never withers with the defect of dread mortality, and although the tired fragility of the moribund flesh droops and ages with stooping and bent senility as the terminus of death approaches, virginity alone in the manner of happy youth continually flourishes and is constantly growing! 'Now, concerning virgins,' says the apostle, 'I have no commandment of the Lord' [I Cor. VII. 25]—so that the gift may be of greater merit, because it is offered with the free will of spontaneous choice, than what is ordered to be fulfilled by the rigid command of a forcible precept. Formerly, when the three-cornered expanse of the world was not yet replete with a race of fruitful offspring, the divine commands ordained as follows: 'Increase and multiply, and fill the earth' [Gen. I. 28]; but now the decrees of the same (heavenly) King are changed because of the nature of the times, and they are thought to promulgate the law differently: 'He that can take, let him take it' [Matth. XIX. 12]. Indeed, the (evangelist here), aware beforehand of human fragility, seems to urge this not by the rigid stimulus of precept but by the gentle counsel of suggestion, so that whatever individuals who are dedicated by the free will of their choice and endowed with the consciousness of their election may be able to test the capacity of their strength, and, exploring the quality of their own virtue, they may strive to endure the long-drawn-out exertion of patience, the blessed possession of which gift is especially obtained from Christ by earnest prayers through the industry of one's own virtue, as Christ

74

himself attests: 'All men take not this word, but they to whom it is given' [Matth. XIX. 11]. Therefore, let human diligence work together with divine indulgence and—what we [p. 248] earnestly beseech with faithful prayer—let us also run together with harmonising desires for action, thereafter expecting faithfully the prize for patience from the true athlete watching the course of (this) struggle, (the prize) which without doubt that person shall then deserve to receive when the time of his contest is completed, who is now seen in no way to flag in maintaining his virginity, so that, when he has overcome his enemy rivals, he may as hymnist joyfully proclaim, on the point of singing a sweet melody and a triumphal chant, with the joy of apostolic jubilation: 'I have fought a good fight; I have finished my course; I have kept the faith. As to the rest, there is laid up for me a crown of justice which the Lord the just judge will render to me in that day' [II Tim. IV. 7-8].

XIX. Moreover the catholic Church accepts a three-fold distinction of the human race, which increases orthodox faith, as it is described by an angelic narrative in a certain volume,[10] how 'virginity', 'chastity' and 'conjugality' differ the one from the other in three ranks; which, as they are each in turn isolated by the triple quality of different life-styles, so they are separated on three levels by the different order of their merits—with the angel distinguishing (them) in turn in this manner: so that virginity is gold, chastity silver, conjugality bronze; that virginity is riches, chastity an average income, conjugality poverty; that virginity is freedom, chastity ransom, conjugality captivity; that virginity is the sun, chastity a lamp, conjugality darkness; that virginity is day, chastity the dawn, conjugality night; that virginity is a queen, chastity a lady, conjugality a servant; that virginity is the homeland, chastity the harbour, conjugality the sea; that virginity is the living man, chastity a man half-alive, conjugality the (lifeless) body; that virginity is the royal purple, chastity the re-dyed fabric, conjugality the (undyed) wool. All these things are not external to the palace; but the dignity of the prefecture sits one way in a carriage, the baseness of the muleteer sits another way, and he who keeps the mules in check by their feet sits yet another way: and yet [p. 249] all these are known to bear arms for the one commander-in-chief; and so on. From the evidence of this distinction, it is permissible to deduce or conjecture what virginity is, which unharmed by any carnal defilement continues pure out of the spontaneous desire for celibacy; (and) chastity on the other hand which, having been assigned to marital contracts, has scorned the commerce of matrimony for the sake of the heavenly kingdom; or conjugality which, for propagating the progeny of posterity and for the sake of procreating children, is bound by the

75

legal ties of marriage. To these three levels of rank, therefore, into which the flourishing multitude of believers in the catholic Church is divided, the gospel parable has promised hundred-fold, sixty-fold and thirty-fold fruit according to the outlay of their merits, even though certain (authorities) are accustomed to allot the sheaves of the hundred-fold harvest, sprouting abundantly in the fallow lands of the gospel and putting forth grain-bearing ears of corn, to the martyrs who pour out their holy blood in the manner of a stream for the glory of the Christian faith. But so that, lacking the firm support of the scriptures, I am not blamed by someone for the verbose garrulity or garrulous verbosity of my dissertation, I shall attempt to weave with Christ's favour a most beautiful crown of virginity, plucking crimson flowers of purity from the meadow of holy books.

XX. ELIJAH, a prophet adorned with the favour of virginity and inspired by the prophetic spirit, opened the locks of heaven and the obstacles of the clouds [i.e. produced rain] with his prayers, and (also) scorched the two captains of fifty men, blazing with the lightning of celestial fire, and consumed them with cruel flame—who are to be burned (in any case) with the heavenly conflagration; he who thereafter, as the poet [i.e. Caelius Sedulius] says in an epic hexameter,

Borne aloft to the golden stars in a fiery chariot
Entered the sidereal path ...   [*Carmen Paschale* I. 179–80]

And further on [p. 250],
He did not arrive at the limit of human life.

[*ibid.*, I. 183]

Elevated to the heavens in a certain region of secluded country, continuing alive in the perpetual vitality of his members, he is known to have remained aloof thus far from the general destiny of death which all people, subject to the laws of nature's will and fettered by the bonds of the first transgression, are compelled to pay as if it were an inevitable tax or a fiscal tribute.

But ELISHA, enriched with a double portion of the spirit of Elijah and endowed with two-fold grace, at whose birth the golden calf is said to have bellowed out a moo with booming voice in Gilgal, signifying the fall of idolatry and the banishment of the veneration of effigies—did he not, because of the distinction of his virginal modesty (and) relying on his master's [i.e. Elijah's] mantle, divide the mighty waters of the Jordan; (did he not) deliver the children (who were) mocking the prophet [i.e. Elisha himself] with yelping derision, to the savage jaws of the bears' ferocity; (and did he not)—though he himself was at peace in death—give back the spirit of life to a corpse crushed in the jaws of chill death?

76

Now, the holy JEREMIAH presents himself clearly to us as an example of the topic of virginity, who before he had been brought forth through maternal parturition, was dedicated to the Lord by blessed predestination and from the very early tenderness of the cradle was consecrated to virginity, concerning whom the divine sentence declares: 'Before thou camest forth out of the womb, I sanctified thee' [Ier. I. 5], that is, by the beautiful prophecy of virginity; Jeremiah, I say: how greatly he shone, glistened and flowered through the bounty of the prophetic dignity—who would be sufficiently sustained by the polished eloquence of words to relate?

XXI. DANIEL—through the prophetic meaning of his name the 'judgment of God', (and) often called 'the man of desires' by the archangel on account of his investigating the hidden recesses of secrets—is recorded to have offered up the most pleasing gift of voluntary virginity, like the fragrance of burning incense to the father of odours, up to the final conclusion of this fleeting life. He, in fact, with /p. 251/ the evangelic trumpet not yet blaring out 'he that can take, let him take it' [Matth. XIX. 12], immune nonetheless from all carnal filth and secure from the deceptions of allurements, is clearly stated to have been completely pure. To him above other mortals, as a reward in exchange for his chastity, hidden things lie open and things closed in the mystical coverings of the sacraments are divinely unlocked. For which of the prophets foretelling things to come, whose minds the free gift of the Holy Spirit abundantly fecundated, inspiring (them) with the virtue of prophetic gifts, is recognised as having woven together a series of oracular sayings concerning the divine incarnation more copiously and more clearly? For in the seventy weeks of years, under which index of computation 490 years are calculated, the saving nativity of our heavenly Lord is prefigured; and he expounds minutely and in detail the statue made from the four kinds of metal—signifying as many ages of kingdoms—(and) shattered by the cornerstone of the two Testaments, cut out from the summit of the mountain without the hand of man, that is to say, without the marital embrace. He also explains through an appropriate prophetic interpretation the tree sprouting with dense branchy twigs and flowering with fruit-bearing boughy wands, the top of whose immense height, stretching upwards, is raised as far as the sky, which under the cone of its topmost point bountifully fed with lush nourishment of food feathered flocks of birds penetrating the obstacles of the clouds with swift flight, and at the same time the multifarious kinds of beast ranging through the world with four-footed motion, until, shaken by celestial power it collapsed cruelly, and, sadly cut down by the agency of heavenly power, it toppled and was deprived of luxuriating verdancy

77

of leaves and the apple-bearing fronds of shoots for the space of seven years. Daniel interpreted these things in prophetic exposition; and he also is said to have expounded wisely the frightening fingers of the celestial hand prophesying in the curved outlines of letters inscribed on the four-fold page of the wall the ruin of tyrannical dominion and the threat to royal monarchy, under the three-fold indication of words, that is, *mane, techel, phares*, which translated means 'he has numbered, has weighed and has divided' [Dan. V. 24–8].

Also [p. 252] at that time three youths [*scil.* Shadrach, Meshach, Abednego] born of the ancestral race of the Hebrews and carried off to the Chaldeans in the transmigration to Babylon, are read to have devoted themselves in no wise to the pleasures of carnal copulation, but are said to have persisted in the strict resolve of voluntary virginity, even though the troublesome chattering of the Jews fabricates frivolous absurdities of falsehood, asserting that in no way were these youths, or their aforementioned fellow, the sharer of their journey into foreign lands, voluntary devotees of chastity, but rather unwilling eunuchs—who are (accordingly) assigned to the second rank of eunuchs by the evangelical affirmation of the truth [Matth. XIX. 12]. These (youths) in fact are recorded as having kept the rule of their paternal tradition and the law of divine sanction to such an extent, that for (the purpose of) obtaining the glory of integrity and continence they even spurned the opulent delights of regal feasts and the sauces of princely food in their tenderest youth; content to sustain their life merely with humble pulse, they curbed the playful high spirits of their youth. As a result of this, they refused to behold on bended knees the enormous statue of the Chaldean tyrant—which exceeded the height of the Colossus of Rhodes, lifted 170 feet high with its (immense) stature of 60 cubits—even though the horrendous blaring of trumpets thundered and the musical harmony of psalteries echoed resoundingly, and at the same time the flame-belching volcano of the furnace, stoked up with the kindling of naphtha and the fuel of firewood, blazed fearfully; and, supported by angelic assistance because of the inflexible constancy of their fixed resolve, they conquered with their unconquerable faith the scorching engines of incineration and the crackling flames of the furnace.

XXII. But why do we, seeking accurately the treasure of virginity like bees mending with cohesive glue (drawn) from diverse flowers of the field the framework of their golden honey-combs, link fetters of delay in (considering) men of ancient times, to whom the licence of the ancient law benignly permitted nuptial bonds of marriage for the sake of a family of offspring and for propagating the progeny of descendants? And [p. 253] why do we expend the leisure of time, since even

78

among the early and recent followers of the catholic faith—after the hidden obscurities of the earlier document [i.e. the Old Testament] had totally disappeared and the clear lights of the subsequent testament, illuminating the darkness of dense night through the grace of the gospel preaching, were distributed more widely in the three-cornered ambit of lands [i.e. the three known continents: Europe, Africa, Asia]—innumerable examples of blessed virginity abound in profusion and are copiously at hand? From these (ancients) we have compiled selectively and briefly these few little (things), which came to our recollection, whereby the longed-for gift of integrity may be openly displayed in public to people dealing in the market (of life), and with them as its originators, the lofty height of purity, like a lighthouse looming over all the virtues or the round globe on top of a square column, rose aloft to such an eminence of perfection and peak of divine contemplation, that it is deservedly thought to reach the sixth degree of evangelical beautitude, concerning which the evangelist—the figurative river of flowering Paradise, whom Ezechiel describes as having a human face—thus appropriately affirms: 'Blessed are the clean of heart; for they shall see God' [Matth. V. 8]. Oh, how the pellucid pupil of virginal purity shines, oh how the brilliant eye of holy chastity beams forth, which neither the carnal darkness of lasciviousness dulls nor the glaucoma of foul obscenity overspreads, by which very often—alas, it is painful to say—the eyelids even of the perfect grow ponderously heavy and those who were thought to be endowed with purity—though often human judgment is deceived—are closed over with hideous shadows just like the eyes of sightless persons! From this fetid bilge-water of impurity, dolefully submerging the ships of souls, those people are truly believed to be immune who are perfectly possessed of the glorious palm of a purity which is not feigned, and who are to proceed in throngs through the gates of the heavenly Jerusalem with the company of chaste soldiers carrying victorious arms, and who shall joyously carry the trophy of virginal triumph and the standard of uninjured chastity before the angelic assembly of the celestial audience and (before) the dreadful tribunal of the Judge weighing out the deeds of (all) individuals with the just balance of discernment.

XXIII. JOHN THE BAPTIST, a holy prophet even before he had issued from the maternal womb, the boundary of the ancient text [i.e. the last of the Old Testament prophets] and the first file of the roughest penalty while an infant grace held sway, a voice smoothing out the rough divergencies of the Word, a herald proclaiming the saving advent of Christ the king, the bridegroom's assistant regulating the first principles of the primitive Church [p. 254]: is he not, because of the integrity of his chastity, described as having baptized—himself pure and a virgin—a pure virgin, the author of all chastity, submerged in the river Jordan with the heavens opening, with the voice thundering through the skies and with the Spirit descending in the likeness of a dove? (It is the same John the Baptist), who, burning with the torrid ardour of chastity, reproving the forbidden nuptials of the king's [i.e. Herod's] marriage and putting a check on the polluted cohabitation of a reeking union, resisted (them) with the severity of harshest invective; and for the sake of this he was ready to endure willingly the putrid squalor of a prison; (and) with the crimson gore of his flesh, poured out in the ruby rivulets of his entrails, he portended in mystical tropology the holy passion of (our) Redeemer.

JOHN, the author of the fourth part of the (Gospel) story and the true tetrarch of the evangelical narrative, whom our Saviour, the unique redemption of the world and the benign model of how to preserve chastity, loved specially among the other (disciples) with holy affection because of the glory of his virginal purity, was famous through the entire world by the wondrous signs of his virtues. For he changed the branches of forest shrubs, brought to him from leafy groves, into the purest metal of yellow gold; relying on heavenly power, he also with the greatest of ease converted the smooth pebbles of the cliffs and the rounded little grains of rock fetched from the sandy gravel of beaches, against the customary law of creation, into rubied heaps of jewels. In addition, he reformed to their pristine state the scattered fragments of jewels which the duped simplicity of (two) brothers, following the advice of an extremely stupid sophist, had smashed into tiny bits as a public spectacle. But by means of intermediating prayer he also raised from deadly sleep the matron *[*p. 255*]*, whom the final destiny had sentenced with a double urn of death,[11] at the entreaties, with earnest supplication, of crowds of peasants whom (the matron) had sustained with the lavish nourishment of donated alms. And when he was cruelly compelled by the insane ferocity of pagans to consume by drinking the deadly draught of a cup in which were contained the virulent juice of deadly herbs together with the grim poisons of adders and asps and a pestilent confection of the venomous four-footed toad and of the poisonous fly harmful to mankind, protected by the ensign of Christ going on before and armed with Christ's standard he did not shrink trembling from the poisonous contagion of the serpents nor did he dread with pallor the terrifying perils of death. He also restored to their original state of vitality two corpses of dead people whom a lethal venom had suddenly laid low with the cruel onslaught of death; and so, flourishing in chastity, he persisted in blessedness up to the snowy whiteness of old age. Certain people contend indeed that he did not depart according to the usual death, but that he lies alive in the tomb, put to sleep in a special trance, because of that which the Saviour had said: 'So I will have him to remain till I come' [Ioan. XXI. 22]—particularly since the dust bubbles up from the vault of his sepulchre and gently eddies on the surface of his crypt as if with the alternating inhalations of someone breathing.

DIDYMUS [i.e. Thomas], at one time the disbelieving doubter of the Lord's resurrection—but once the scars of (Christ's) wounds had been seen, (became) its confident preacher—who illumined the tripartite provinces of eastern India with the clear light of evangelical preaching and totally annulled the execrable rites of (pagan) sanctuaries and the empty offices of their priests, when he spoke for the instruction of chaste partners in marriage in the praises of virginity, said: 'You have integrity, which is the queen of all virtues and the fruit of perpetual virginity. Virginity is the sister of the angels and the possession of all good things; virginity is victory over desires, the trophy of faith, a triumph over enemies and the surety of eternal life'.[12] See how the blast of the apostolic trumpet, blaring as if with the roar of thunder, urges the devout minds of virgins to the veneration of integrity, when it honours (integrity) with the mighty commendation of renown!

XXIV. PAUL [p. 256], once (called) Saul, the vessel of election, a figural Benjamin 'devouring the prey in the morning, in the evening dividing the spoils' [Gen. XLIX. 27], who with a terrifying command compelled the sorceress to place a door of mute taciturnity in front of her insolent lips, when she was prophesying frivolities of falsehood through the spirit of necromancy, and for this reason piling up in abundance the sumptuous wealth of princes, and richly accumulating the delightful treasures of profit: (it was Paul) who—marvellous to say—spent twenty-four hours unharmed on the deep bottom of the sea[13] and received on five occasions forty stripes save one, in the severest torture of cruelty—does he not, because of the privilege of his pure integrity, traverse the third heaven contemplating the secrets of the heavenly citizens with chaste vision, and exploring the mysteries of the celestial army with (his) ineffable account of events, even though the so-called *Revelatio Pauli* says foolishly that he came to the delights of flowering Paradise in a golden ship? But divine law forbids the followers of the catholic faith to believe more, in any respect, than what the judgment of canonical truth promulgates, and the decrees of the orthodox fathers in decretal writings have sanctioned the utter rejection and complete banishment of the other absurdities of the apocrypha as being a cacophonous thunder of words.

LUKE, described by Ezechiel in the figural image of the calf, and the third historiographer of the evangelical mission, who acquired at Antioch the poultices of medicine and first healed sanatively the festering sicknesses of bodies and the diseased fibres of inwards, and thereafter (healed) the spiritual disorders of souls with the searing cautery of doctrine or the blood-letting of the divine Word. He is said to have persevered as the purest devotee of unimpaired chastity up to the seventy-fourth year of his life. Therefore, when he had paid the universal debt /p. 257/ to nature of death by his final dissolution, his bones were, as we read, translated to Constantinople for the safekeeping of the Roman dominion when Constantine was governing the monarchy of the world.

XXV. CLEMENT, the first successor of the celestial key-bearer [i.e. St Peter] and the second steward of the Roman Church—although some people, without any grounds, place Linus and Ancletus before him in the government of the papacy—makes manifest in the very writing of his own letters that he profoundly loved the chastity of the celibate life even before he was purged of original sin (by being) immersed in the redeeming baptistry of the font, saying, 'I Clement, born in the city of Rome, pursued the study of chastity from my earliest infancy'. Therefore if he, not yet regenerated (by baptism), so greatly esteemed and took possession of what was most excellent among all the grades of the virtues and most difficult for the nature of mortals, how much more is it appropriate to believe that, after he had accepted the principles of the faith and had spurned the religion of the gentiles, he conserved (this virtue) more fully and perfectly when he followed Peter through the provinces sowing the seeds of the divine Word and cultivating the shoots of the gospel-vine in the ditches of the believing, and destroying at the root the lethal wild vines of Simoniacal necromancy! (It was Clement) who afterwards wrote up, clearer than daylight, the *Itinerarium Petri* [i.e. the pseudo-Clementine *Recognitiones*] arranged in ten volumes, which Rufinus translated into Latin from the Greek text.

SILVESTER, who took up the office of the pontifical see at Rome, was renowned for the famous signs of his miracles throughout all the provinces of Europe and the parishes of blossoming Italy, which is bounded by the icy passes of the Alps /p. 258/ with their sheer cliffs of rock—since indeed, relying on uncontaminated chastity of body and endowed with the abstemiousness of continual abstinence, he is said to have gone down inside, through the hundred steps of its den, to the lethal dragon of Rome lurking in the secret cavern of the crypt, which, fouling the air with its poisonous maw and the pestilent exhalation of its breath, was fiercely molesting the miserable populace. Silvester punished for ever this very monster of amazing size—to

82

which the beguiled heathenism of the pagans offered up the pollutions of idolatrous sacrifice in order to appease the insanity of its fury—with the chastisement of perpetual revenge, constricting (the dragon) with an inextricable collar. And so he reformed Rome, the worshipper of deceitful idolatry, from the fatal practice of offering victims by his evangelical declarations and by miracles of equal luminosity. I also think that that (incident) should not be omitted, in which an outstanding proof of preserved chastity is made evident, namely that the long illness of the emperor Constantine and the elephantine disorder of his body was cured more quickly than the telling of it, as soon as the sacrament of baptism had been accepted, to his salvation, from the aforementioned Silvester; and the fever of the interior man as much as the condition of the exterior was healed by a double remedy through the celestial poultice, without any interference of quackery.

Besides, I would think it absurd if that most celebrated form of miracle, bruited through all the corners of the world, were to lose its lustre, stopped up by the silence of speechlessness, and, not touched on by the letter-forms of my script, should remain secret—(that phenomenon) in which the victory of Christ triumphant and the chastity of Silvester militant are spread abroad by the renown of a dual praise. For, when Constantine was governing the world (and) people were flocking in throngs to a synodal council, Silvester, trusting in the divine shield, confutes twelve instructors of the Jews and rabbis of the Pharisees who were savagely hurling the dire shafts of disputation against this soldier of Christ. And the same bishop wisely explained with marvellous acuteness a dream of Constantine which portended the indications of hidden things; namely that when the emperor, (being) in the city which was called Byzantium, had given his limbs over to sleep and was paying the debt of nature, there appeared to him in a nocturnal vision a certain old woman, very decrepit—in fact near to death—whom he is ordered at Silvester's command to resuscitate by praying. (When) Constantine prayed, that old woman arose and became an extremely beautiful young lady, blushing with the glowing flower of exquisite youth. When she had pleased the royal inspection /p.259/ in chaste contemplation (of her), he covered her with his cloak and placed a diadem adorned with burnished gold and shining gems on her head. But Helena his mother said to him: 'She shall be yours and shall not die except at the end of the world'. Thereupon, when he awakened, the emperor was bitterly constrained by his ignorance of future events until, after the simple space of a week—his body (having become) lean with the abstemiousness of temperance—he is again given over to sleep. Silvester, the man of venerable life, is present before him on the seventh day of his fast, saying to him once again in his vision: 'The decrepit old woman is this city in which you are staying, called Byzantium, whose walls are now wasted away because of their age, and nearly all its fortifications have collapsed. Mount, therefore, that horse of yours, on which you sat when you were baptized, in white linen, in the city of Rome, and (on which) you toured the shrines of the apostles and martyrs; and sitting on him take up your ensign which is decorated with the sign of Christ in gold and jewels. Holding this ensign in your right hand, release the reins of your horse so that he may go wherever the angel of God shall lead him; and you drag the point of your ensign fixed in the earth in such a way that it makes a path by its passage; along this path you shall have walls constructed and (so) shall resuscitate this veteran and nearly dead city into (the likeness of) a young lady; and you shall name her with your own name so that you make her the queen of all cities. The name of the Lord Jesus Christ shall be glorious in it, and there shall be in it temples of God built in honour of all the saints; and your sons after you and the sons of your sons shall reign in it'. Now, waking, Constantine went directly to the church and telling to the bishop of the city, a holy man called Sisinnius, the dream which he had just had, and offering gifts to God and taking the sacrament of Holy Communion, he mounted his horse and set out where the angel of the Lord led him; and the foundations grew along the paths of his ensign *[p. 260]*. And it is called the 'city of Constantine', which in the Greek language is rendered 'Constantinopolis', up to the present day. Thereupon Silvester, having completed his (term of) office as pontiff and having accomplished the span of his life, ascends Jacob's ladder with the palm of virginity (and) is introduced into the companies of angels, and enjoys in blessedness the holy fellowship of heavenly citizens.

XXVI. I shall not indeed allow AMBROSE, redolent with the ambrosia of heavenly nectar, to lie hidden behind a veil of silence—(Ambrose), whose mellifluous sweetness of doctrine and the privilege of pure virginity were prefigured by beautiful omens since, when as a baby he was lying quietly on his back in his cradle, a swarm of bees unexpectedly filled the mouth and lips of the resting child without any danger, and eagerly jostled for room to come and go through the child's tender lips; and, at length, with Ambrose's father awaiting the outcome of the event and commanding that (the bees) not be driven off by the servant-girl, who was the child's nurse, (the bees), flying away through the atmosphere to heavenly regions of the sky, fled in swarms from the sight of mortals. In what way and how greatly this same patriarch shone through the glory of his virtues and the signs of his miracles, I think no-one (will have) discovered, except the person who has studied the accomplishments of his life as they are set forth by the venerable Paulinus [i.e. in Paulinus's *Vita S. Ambrosii*].

Nor should it be an embarrassment for Christ's celibates (who are) constraining the unruly impulsiveness of their nature with the strict laws of chastity and curbing the bodily gestures of titillation with iron bridles, as if they were untamed cart-horses, to call to mind the bishop of Tours [i.e. MARTIN], whom, before the womb of regenerating grace had born him and (before) he came to know the elementary doctrines of holy baptism, in the grade of a catechumen and with the status of those suitable (to be baptized), (even then) offering alms to the poor /p. 261/ and distributing charity to the needy, a celestial oracle rewarded when (once) he had given his limbs over to nocturnal rest; and who, because of the crown of integrity he had acquired and the blessed distinction of virginity—which he was able to preserve with tireless efforts right to the end, like a royal diadem or the jewelled necklaces of amulets—is said to have shone forth in the marvellous miracles of his virtues. For he raised from death's door back to the light of life the corpse of a catechumen whom the grim ferocity of Fortune, as they say, and the violent cruelty of the Fates (who) spare no one, or rather the pitilessness of chill death, had suddenly overcome, while he was (still) bereft of the sacrament of regenerating grace. Two others, tormented by the cruel limit of death and deprived of the hoped-for bounties of life, Martin brought back from the mysterious abyss of death and the torments of fierce hell to the upper regions [i.e. earth], (thereby) obtaining his wish. As for the lofty trunk of a branching pine-tree which had been designated for the forbidden ceremonies of the heathens, (and) although the numerous axes of the inhabitants were eagerly cutting through the tree with a sideways tilt, he watched it tottering without fear, and scorned it, even though it was about to topple with a deafening crash. Through the superior grace of his merits he made the deceitful tricks /p. 262/ of that rascal Anatolius fall completely apart and vanish into thin air like a ridiculous phantom—deceits which the fraudulent company of his spiteful rivals, armed with a thousand devices for doing evil, was audaciously pushing forward under the demonstrable sham of a cloak of deceit. The sanctuaries of the ancient pagans, which had been constructed from stones polished by the mason and covered with red roof-tiles, he shattered, overturned and destroyed by casting them to the ground, distrusting the assistance of mortals and relying on the help of the angels, who are said to have come armed with spears and shields to bring aid to the servant of God.

XXVII. GREGORY, the governor of the church of Nazianzus, was incomparably educated in letters at Athens, where at the same time the renowned glory of grammarians and the recondite sophistry of academic disputation flourished, (and was) a fellow student of Basil in philosophic doctrine, as the eleventh book of (Eusebius's) *Historia Ecclesiastica* attests: since from the tenderness of early infancy he was a despiser of bodily allurement and a passionate lover of chastity, he was benignly consoled, when (once) he was lulled to sleep, with a vision of beauteous appearance. Because of the virginal resolve of his purity and his strenuous pursuit of philosophy, Chastity and Wisdom are described as having appeared to him in his sleep in two figures of the *[p. 263]* female sex; they spoke in this way, urging the saint on to the crown of integrity: 'One of us is called Wisdom, the other Chastity; and we are sent from the Lord to dwell with you, since you have prepared a pleasing and fully pure dwelling for us in your heart'. From these statements it is fitting to observe, and from the interpretation of this dream it is fitting to conclude, that this saint, endowed with the munificence of merits of this sort, had safeguarded the crown of undefiled purity with tireless energy in every way (possible) up to the limit of his last end, especially since concerning him it is stated in admonition: 'Nothing more commendable or holy than his life, nothing more distinguished or illustrious than his eloquence, nothing more pure or righteous than his faith, nothing more full or perfect than his learning is to be found (anywhere)'—which Rufinus, endowed with an amazing verbal elegance, has more amply elaborated in the prologue of his *Liber Apologeticus.*

BASIL (was) the most renowned Cappadocian bishop, trained at Athens in the rhetorical disciplines of sophistic like his previously mentioned colleague, who expounded with certainty (and) more clearly than light the regular practices of the monastic life [i.e. St Basil's *Rule*], by replying to the varying inquiries of correspondents with the answering exposition of his letters. Relying on the marvellous refinement of his eloquence he also produced his *Erga ta ex emeron* or *Hexaemeron*, that is, 'The Works of the Six Days (of Creation)', which (may be) read in Latin translation [i.e. that of Rufinus]. That this Basil, I say, flourished corporeally incorrupt, by virtue of his integrity, I shall understand as an interpretation of his own maxim, as follows: 'I do not know a woman *[p. 264]*, and yet I am not a virgin'. For in fact it is said to be an ancient practice of skilled orators who, standing high up in their pulpits harangue throngs of people, that, in the audience of the diverse assembly with its difference of sexes, they sometimes use a different *persona* just as their own; and, disclosing the secrets of the minds of these persons and unlocking what was hidden in the depths of their hearts to their astonished audience and their unwitting listeners, they reveal (these things) with the key of their eloquent speech. The

86

previously mentioned bishop is therefore thought to be speaking in this manner of oratory, thinking that the stainlessness of bodily chastity—which is only external—was in no way suitable for acquiring the distinction of a vigorous integrity, unless chastity of the spirit, by whose command the untamed impulses of bodily wantonness are restrained—just as a servant-girl, lest she become stubbornly insolent, is subjected to the control of a mistress—inwardly cleaves to it harmoniously with comradely solidarity.

There was a certain man graced with episcopal authority who was deservedly called FELIX [i.e. 'blessed'], who, when for the constancy of his faith he was tortured by torturers and was agonizingly martyred by the horrendous torments of his executioners, is said to have exclaimed: 'I give thanks to you, oh Christ: I have kept my virginity in this world for 56 years'.

XXVIII. ANTHONY, the driver of the celestial plough and the sower of the evangelical seed, by (means of) whom the fertile crop of cenobites and the fecund harrow of (monastic) life first put forth fruit with grain-bearing ears throughout Egypt; whence, afterwards, the Egyptian land, which the Nile fecundates with recurring floods, brought forth thousands of sheaves of souls, springing up in the fruitful fallow-land of the Church, whom the angelic reapers, when the semblance of the universe shall vanish in a moment and an instant, and the vast elements of created nature, transformed into a better (arrangement), shall reappear, having separated out the bundles of tares [p. 265] shall carry in heaps for the inexhaustible granary of the kingdom of heaven: and was he not, because of the surpassing purity of his soul, endowed with the ineffable grace of his virtues, proclaimed by his reputation to the furthest corners of the earth? As for the power of Anthony's miracles, Athanasius, the bishop of Alexandria, treated this more fully in a single volume, (and) Evagrius translated it into Latin.

PAUL (THE HERMIT), likewise glorious and most renowned of fathers, who, betrayed in violation of the laws of nature by a deceitful brother-in-law (who had been) deceived by the greed of blind avarice, and prostituted from the first immaturity of adolescence, entering the deserts of the Egyptian wilderness—where the attractions of carnal filth grow faint and the pleasures of worldly delight become worthless—fearlessly scorned the horrendous trumpetings of elephants and the savage roars of lions, protected by the rampart of burning faith. Sustaining his starveling little body merely with a woven patchwork of palm-leaves and with the sweet nourishment of dates, he paid his debt to nature. Was he not found worthy, because of the stainlessness of his flowering chastity, preserved to the very end with an indissoluble restraint for twice six *lustra*—that is, for an interval of sixty years—to receive a half-mouthful of bread which a feathered bird brought in its open beak—and he giving thanks for the gift—with tireless service and recurrent flights, never running out right up to the feeble old age of his life?

XXIX. HILARION *[p. 266]*, the most famous inhabitant of the Palestinian desert, born of heathen parents given to the worship of idols, a crimson rose flowering—as it is said—from thorns burgeoning everywhere, was famous at the time when the aforementioned Antony was celebrated by reputation throughout Egypt. St Jerome, the distinguished student of the celestial library and the most excellent of all exegetes, praises his life with such a babble of good reports, that he says that even Homer—if he were to emerge from the underworld—would envy or be overcome by such a subject. Hilarion, for the sake of preserving the integrity of his chastity, rejecting the cohabitation with (other) mortals, ready from the first times of his infancy to range over the empty expanse of the foul desert as an early inhabitant (of it), practised a contemplative life, contrary to the usual nature of things, almost earlier than an active one. Chastising severely the sportive high spirits of his starved youth with the abstemiousness of frugality, he said: 'I shall arrange it, my dear ass [i.e. addressing his body], so that you do not kick back, for I shall not feed you with grain but with straw: I shall wear (you) down through hunger'. Wherefore, he resplendently equalled the ancient patriarchs with innumerable prodigious miracles: for example, with the weaponry of prayer he killed a dragon, horrendous with its scaly body, near Epidaurus, a town in Dalmatia, a dragon that they called a 'boa' for the reason that it was of such enormity that, slaying cattle [i.e. *boues*] with the poisonous teeth of its jaws, it is accustomed to swallow them whole with the greedy appetite of its stomach—and it not only gulps down cattle and sheep, but also farmers and ploughmen and swineherds, drawn to it by the force of its breath. O gods, avert such a serpent from our lands![14] (Hilarion killed it) in this way: compelling the aforesaid serpent of wondrous size with a commandment of terrifying authority to ascend a pyre built high with a heap of logs and fired by flaming brands, as the people watched *[p. 267]* he burned up the scaly framework of its rib-cage and the rigid curvature of its spine on the burning coals, and cruelly incinerating (it) with roasting balls of firebrands he snatched the people from the lethal breath of the monster. In addition to this, when (once) the floods of the seething ocean and the blue-green depths of the foaming deluge were exceeding their proper bounds and, as if the judgment of divine power were threatening the irruption of the Flood, or else all things were being compelled to return to primordial chaos, the citizens of Epidaurus, driven by unfamiliar terror, stationed the same servant of God against the roaring waves and the salty mass of the sea. When Hilarion had furrowed three signs of the cross in the gravelly sands of the shore—a marvel to relate, how (then) the swelling sea grew to a height and with what immense loftiness it stood like a wall of ice before him! Oh how great is the force of virginity, which curbed the insanity of a raging monster with a humble prayer, and held back the swelling fury of the sea with the power bestowed upon him (from above)—so equalling the deed of the prophet Daniel with regard to the dragon and those of (Moses) the law-giver in regard to the sea!

But JOHN, a hermit of the Nilotic [i.e. Egyptian] desert, who, while Theodosius governed the monarchy of the world, toiling for forty years in the pursuit of the active way of life—which Martha, the sister of Lazarus, prefigures in offering to Christ the vowed obedience of humanity—went further in the marvellous fervour of his devotion, and thereafter, burying himself away in a remote hut for the space of fifty years, he led the contemplative life of seclusion. It is clear that he preserved the unimpaired gift of pure virginity up to the non-agenarian age of decrepit senility from this: that he is said to have replied with resolute purpose to the chiliarch, that is, to the soldiers' tribune, who was earnestly beseeching him [p. 268] with importunate prayers for consultations concerning the troublesomeness of his wife—so she should be allowed to go and visit John—that it had never been a habit of his to see women, and, above all, that he had shut himself up in the monastery on that cliff for that very reason. Therefore, because of the cloak of his acquired integrity, whereby he was assimilated to the form of angelic purity as if by the family solidarity of a household, he experienced the prophetic spirit of inspiration, the future declarations of presentient divination which were hidden from other mortals.

XXX. Nor do I think that BENEDICT of blessed memory should be by-passed, who from the very cradle of infancy was so cherished by the blessed prediction of the name [i.e. *benedictus* = 'blessed'] that he simply could not live in the resolve of divine religion otherwise than the dignity of his own name and the privilege of celestial bounty would permit. For since he showed his worth as a boy, honoured with the generous munificence of heavenly bounty, and became widely renowned throughout the august kingdom of Italy through the favourable achievements of his merits, not in vain did he share the blessed privilege of the appellation [i.e. 'blessed'] with our Intercessor and Redeemer, of whom the evangelizing babes, hymning with a melodious harmony of voice, had sung euphoniously: 'Blessed is he that cometh in the name of the Lord' [Matth. XXI. 9]. My mediocre talent too, supported by the authentic authority of ancient writers [p. 269], celebrates with the melody of joyous jubilation this exemplary fact, ringing out with harmonious voice in the holy celebration of the Psalms with its two divisions, and reverberating 'Osanna' among the twin melodies. Therefore, prophetic omens followed this aforesaid soldier of Christ, protected by the vigilance of the Holy Trinity, because of his uncorrupt and constantly sparkling garlands of unfading chastity; and heavenly miracles accompanied him from above: since indeed, after the sanctuaries of idols had been destroyed and the ceremonies of fanatical paganism had been routed—(paganism) which thinks according to the gang of astrologers, that life, empty of true meaning, is governed by the decree and formation of Fortune—(Benedict) is said to have constructed twelve monasteries, in which the rich treasures of a holy life and the abundant profits of souls plentifully acquired through orthodox doctrine were produced for Christ, which the clever cultivator of the Lord's vineyard, cutting down as it were the maturing grapes of the vine and the ruby-red clusters of the branches with the evangelical sickle, brought in baskets crammed full and loaded panniers to the wine-press to be trodden and to be pressed out according to the rule by the treaders of the Church, so that he might bring in with blessings the vinolent must of clarified wine for laying-down in the celestial cellars and for distributing to the angelic wine-merchants, so that the banquets of the heavenly citizens may rejoice, revelling in gifts of this sort brought from commerce in the terrestrial market.

XXXI. Great, therefore, is the privilege of purity: and if anyone who is compelled by force to relinquish it shall for that reason, contemptuous of human society, voluntarily separate himself from this life shared by all, he shall rejoice triumphantly in the celestial society among the 144,000 singing the virginal song [cf. Apoc. XIV. 1]. As Eusebius, the historian of the Greeks, records some virgins devoted to God to have done, who, in order to preserve the purity of their integrity, immersed themselves headlong in the swift channel of the cataract—whence one of the Church Fathers [i.e. St Jerome] says, 'It is not allowable to die by one's own hand except in cases where chastity is endangered' [*in Ionam* I. 12]. Oh, matter of wonder!—and an almost unfathomable pronouncement! When anyone forced unwillingly to be subject to other outrageous sins—which grievously disturb the state of the world—and, his freedom of will having been ignored, is compelled to commit a criminal offence, if, under the pretext of avoiding sin and shunning transgression, he shall by any manner of death inflict violence on his life [p. 270], he is considered, among (other) suicides, an

90

outcast from the society of the Church! From this one may infer how precious to the heavenly citizens is the nobility of chastity, which cannot by any means be destroyed or obliterated by that which is able to make mock of the merits of the perfect and to make void every kind of virtue.

Hence MALCHUS, when he was being forced into a carnal union [i.e. marriage] by the violence of paternal severity and at the same time by maternal pressure—they being concerned about the offspring that were to result—he decided to scorn (the marriage) on the pretext of chastity and for the sake of the heavenly kingdom. But when, from the fervour he entertained for the monastic way of life, he began little by little to decrease in ardour, and was slowly cooling off from the torrid intensity of cenobitic life, and, at the prompting of the deceitful Enemy, he was ready to leave, out of concern for his family ties, he was captured by Saracen pirates and Ishmaelite robbers (who were) ravaging violently whatsoever was in their way, so that he was commanded to serve (as) a submissive slave, by a very appropriate turn of events, seeing that he who was seeking a forbidden journey homewards, was in bondage as a base slave, (and) he who in no way feared that loss of the woman perishing at Sodom, suffered painfully the handicap of a protracted slavery and the loathsome servitude of a master. And, while, glancing backwards, he was guiding the handle of the plough without care, the harrow pointlessly shattered among the sods of furrowed earth; and, when, in the same place, he was forced at the point of a sword into abandoning the glories of the chastity he longed for—which he had preserved in his native land—he preferred to die transfixed cruelly by the sword rather than to defend his life by profaning the laws of chastity, fearing in no way the danger to his soul if the status of his virginity were preserved intact.

XXXII. Furthermore, I shall not allow NARCISSUS of blessed memory—at once enriched with the prerogative of virginal purity and adorned with the authority of the episcopal insignia—to lurk in the recesses of silence [p. 271]; (Narcissus), whose life was distinguished with signs and resplendent portents of miracles to such an extent that, relying on the armament of his prayers, contrary to the nature of things he converted the quality of the liquid element—mutable to God alone—into another form, seeing that it happened by chance at the Paschal vigil when, after the returning cycle of a year the Lord's resurrection is celebrated with the festivity of the usual celebration, that the appropriate liquid of fatty oil was lacking in the torches and lamps of the church. Then the man dedicated to God, exorcising the liquid waters of the fonts and enriching them with the fullness of his holy benediction, by a stupendous show of divine power made them grow fatty—and to such an extent, that the water poured into the holders of the lamps quickly was turned into the viscosity of oil and the papyrus wick placed in the centre shone more brightly than normal, like tinder-wood drenched in suet or tallow. But the ancient assailant of mankind, as a result of the extraordinary nature of (Narcissus's) renown by which the praises of the faithful proliferate, is fired by the devious fury of envy to shatter the popular reputation of the man of God and bring it down through false evidence of suspicions. For (certain) deceitful fabricators of lies, sitting in the seat of the scornful, concoct a completely infamous crime and an unheard-of offence against Narcissus, perjuring themselves deceitfully in a council under the testimony of three witnesses, just as the Psalmist writes: 'Unjust witnesses have risen up against me, and iniquity hath lied to itself' [Psalm. XXVI. 12]. Of these (three witnesses) the one swore that he was speaking truthfully, else may he be burned up by crackling fire; the second likewise, else may he be destroyed by the virulent ravages of jaundice; the third likewise, else may he be deprived of the sight of his two eyes. Whence Narcissus, trusting in God, does not in any way seek a defence hearing, as both guilty and innocent customarily do; but abandoning the height of his episcopal see on the finding of this opportunity, he sought the remote waste /p. 272/ of the desert; and, fleeing the frivolous machinations of his detractors and the factions they had created, he hid himself away. Afterwards the avenging judgment of divine power struck down pitilessly the deceitful personages of the witnesses—who rivalled the elders testifying against Susanna!—by those very disasters to which, in perjuring themselves, they had destined (themselves). The first of them is said to have burned, together with his entire household of domestic servants and his relatives nearest of kin, in avenging balls of fire in the thatch of his own house; the second, swelling up with jaundice from the top of his tripartite brain right down to his feet—as he, mindless, shameless and insolent, had once wished—breathed his last fetid breath; the third, observing the unhappy fate of his (two) companions, revealed openly with belated penitence to all listeners the whole sin of the plotted crime; and, giving way to tears, the lamentable (wretch) wept mournfully with such great sobs of lamentation and such bitter cries of remorse that at length he was totally deprived of the twin lights of his eyes. Hence the cautionary statement: 'Revenge is mine, I will repay, saith the Lord' [Rom. XII. 19].

Why should I mention ATHANASIUS of blessed remembrance, the renowned glory of whose merits and the flourishing report of whose virginity, although particularly illustrious in Alexandria and Egypt, yet resounded far and wide through all corners of the world where the catholic faith is putting forth fruit-bearing shoots? His tutor and instructor from the very tenderness of the cradle is said to have been the blessed Alexander, bishop of Alexandria, who taught him in a kindly manner the written characters which scribes use, as well as the periods of the grammarians, distinguished separately by cola and commata. This is the same Alexander who, after the bowels of Arius the heretic had flowed foully into the hidden hole of the latrine, is honoured with the triumphal trophy of the Church. But is it surprising that Athanasius was to show his worth in the highest summit of (ecclesiastical) stations *[p. 273]* through the divine grace of his gifts, when even the most tender age of the infant in no way lacked a prophetic augury of his genius, but rather his childish behaviour in games portended the episcopal authority of the future bishop? For (once after) he had performed the sacrament of the Mass, Alexander caught sight of beardless crowds of children on a gravelly sea-side beach confer the priestly office on (the young) Athanasius, and saw certain catechumens and novices being regenerated by him in the mystic office of baptism—which, performed (then) as the pantomime of a game, was (later) seriously conferred by the decrees of episcopal synods. Therefore Athanasius took on the episcopacy of the church after the death of Alexander; and what great machinations by heretics he experienced, how many fraudulent plots by schismatics—which they cooked up in cunning factions against the guiltless man—he endured, the tenth book of (Eusebius's) *Ecclesiastical History* translated by Rufinus explains. (These schismatics went) to such length in fact that they showed an arm which had been torn from a corpse and put into a tomb to Constantius Augustus—who was the emperor of the East—(and) which they perfidiously alleged to have been taken by Athanasius's deceptive necromancy from the body of Arsenius. Whereupon the emperor, persuaded by the seductive falsehoods of the heretics and deceived by their disgraceful factions, inadvisedly ordered the bishop to be condemned in council. But Arsenius, who had formerly held the office of lector in the pulpit, betrayed the entire farce of plotted crime and declared that the holy bishop was free from such shameful crimes. Oh, what great pallor of impudent face accused certain of the trembling (conspirators) on account of the detection of their crime! And, on the other hand, what glowing redness of the cheeks coloured the faces of others as if with rouge, when they saw in the council alive and well the man whom they had said was maimed, with the joints of his arms amputated! But, put to silence by a holy victory of this sort, they devise the building up of another kind of proof, so that a deceitful prostitute would impudently contrive to accuse the thoroughly chaste man of debauchery in a brothel—from which, his body uncorrupted from puberty onwards, he was completely free. When *[p. 274]* the prostitute had vomited up from the recesses of her false breast the entire lewdness of false verbosity, like the stinking vomit of biliousness, (Athanasius) is immediately defended by the priest Timothy—whom the insolent woman was clasping in the foul embrace of her arms—by a veracious verbal defence, as if by a fixed phalanx of shields. But Athanasius, giving in to the insanity of his rivals—who in their zeal against the man of God were twisted with the loathsome envy of spite—(and) setting out to wander far away exiles himself, so far that hiding in the dry hollow of a cistern for the space of six years, he in no way received a clear ray of the sun; but his mind dedicated to God—harder than whetstone, stronger than iron, more rigid than adamantine steel—suffered impassively with the constancy of an unbending spirit all the calamitous persecutions which the clandestine conspiracy of envious people were malevolently bringing against him.

XXXIII. What shall I say about the blessed BABILAS, who kept the watches over the Lord's flock, and the sheep-folds of the Church, against the cruel madness of tyrants, as if against the bestial ferocity of wolves, not in the manner of a hireling, but with a shepherd's care? When he was adorned with the insignia of the highest pontificate, he did not allow Numerianus Augustus, defiled with the blood of those he had killed, to profane the sanctuary of the basilica by entering with his polluted feet, but rather prevented the entry of the death-dealing king from the holy threshold of the church by the severity of his vehement castigation. Nor did he show terror at all by trembling or growing pale, fearing the expropriation of his possessions or the loss of his life. Then he was led to the palace buildings and (hence) to the forecourt of the imperial hippodrome, so that he might argue with the baleful king, disputing alternately in reciprocal exchanges. But the ferocity of threats did not deflect, nor the softness of blandishments weaken, the mind dedicated to God so that it would swerve from the uprightness of catholic faith to the distorted rites of idol-worship. Soon, at the command of Augustus, they bound a yoke on his neck and shackles on his feet, to the calumny of the pontiff and the infamy of the clergy; what is more, they flayed the most holy limbs of their living victim with refined instruments of torture. Also, they brought into the king's presence at the same time three young brothers, whom Babilas had taken into the guidance of his tutelage to be duly instructed *[p. 275]*. When the emperor could not deceive them with verbal arguments—since they were armed with an amazing constancy of faith—he ordered them to be flogged with bloody strokes of the lash. But seeing the boys' constancy unvanquished, the raging ruler asks the venerable bishop whether these boys were truly his sons. He is said to have replied: 'They are truly my sons according to God; but in the presence of my God, since I was born, I have known no woman'. Then the saintly Babilas, receiving the sentence of decapitation together with his three pupils, was beheaded and (so) sanctified by the red rivulets of his veins.

XXXIV. But I think it worthwhile that we do not in any way exclude from (our) historical account of virgins—as if unworthy of the company of the others—COSMAS and DAMIANUS, the most famous warriors of spiritual warfare and arch-physicians of celestial medicine. We confidently trust that these two, predestined to citizenship in the heavenly Jerusalem and inscribed in the register of celestial writing, will rejoice with their aforementioned colleagues. For in the times of Diocletian and Maximian, at the two hundred-and-sixty-seventh Olympiad, when as a result of cruel edicts the followers of the catholic faith, whom they called 'Christians' and 'cross-worshippers', were compelled to burn incense at the petty little statues of the pagans, and those not wishing to apostatize, that is, to revert to (wallowing in) the mire of apostasy, were compelled to undergo capital punishment—at this time a devout mother gave birth to twins, the aforementioned novices of Christ (Cosmas and Damianus). (These twins), gradually instructed in medicinal treatments from the beginnings of their adolescence /p. 276/, were able to cure by means of celestial poultices both the diseases of dropsical persons and (other) internal discomforts and spiritual disorders as well: imparting sight, that is, to the blind and emollients to the one-eyed, opening the door of silence in the dumb, renewing the harmonies of the outside world in the ears of the deaf, granting correctness of speech to stutterers and stammerers, restoring the lame and the maimed to their former healthiness, reviving through the grace of their merits those possessed by devils and the short-sighted, and even recalling to earthly life those overthrown by the accidents of fortune. Nevertheless, enriched by the munificence of powers of this kind, they conferred the wished-for health on the infirm, not for the traffic of avarice but out of a freely-given generosity, (thus) conforming to the message of the Gospel: 'Freely have you received; freely give' [Matth. X. 8]. Meanwhile, at the time of the aforementioned persecutors (Diocletian and Maximian), when holy martyrs were being sacrificed 'like sheep for the slaughter' [Psalm. XLIII. 22] by the bloody swords of butchers, and these athletes of the Church in no sense terrified were struggling, as if they were in a wrestling-arena, who would be able to describe the many great instruments of punishment with which the aforesaid confessors were tortured at the jurisdiction of the tribune Lysias? Since

95

indeed, with their arms bound and the shanks of their legs tied together, they were cast into the depths of the sea; but, sustained by angelic intervention, the wild ferocity of the waves, not daring to touch them, returned them unharmed to the shore. Again the savage governor, confounded and put to silence by so brilliant a triumph by the holy soldiers, orders them to be cruelly thrust into a furnace which was stoked up by much tinder of brushwood and crackling with diverse flaming logs. But in no way did the conflagration of the raging furnace burn (the twins), who were as salamanders which, by nature, burning lumps of coal are unable to scorch or consume. Next, the patronage of angels protected them (while they were) tormented by the anguish of the rack and suspended from the fork of the gallows, and in addition buried under the dreadful blows of arrows. In the end they were sentenced to be beheaded: with their palm of virginity they earned a martyr's triumph.

XXXV. Nor let it be disagreeable to remember the renowned soldier of Christ CHRYSANTHUS, whom his father, leaving Alexandria, handed over to the philosophers and rhetors at Rome and had him instructed in all liberal studies of the arts. He was, so they say, of so burning an intellect and so retentive of memory *[p. 277]* that, whatsoever he investigated through reading and studying diligently very quickly stuck—as if fastened by glue—in his young intelligence, and would cleave, firmly rooted, within the receptacle of his subtle mind. When, therefore, the studies of the grammarians and the teaching of the philosphers—which are divided into seven kinds, that is, arithmetic, geometry, music, astronomy, astrology, mechanics and medicine—having been completed, he came to the most holy scripture of the Gospels, without delay and quicker than the telling of it he rejected all the arguments of the Stoics and the Aristotelian categories—which are distinguished by ten kinds of predication—as soon as he shrewdly perceived how much the doctrine of celestial philosophy excelled the teachings of the world and the fictions of mortals. And when, having been conceived in the womb of regenerating grace and having been brought forth by the fertile delivery of baptism, he was nourished in the reverend cradle of the Church, straightway the young neophyte, after receiving the rudiments of faith, becomes an outstanding teacher and, fearing in no way the dangers of perfidious (enemies), he preaches Christ the son of God openly to all people. When his father learns of this through the reports of relatives and friends, he imprisons his own son—against (all) laws of nature—restricted to the confines of a cellar, to be wasted away by the deprivation of hunger, fearing otherwise both proscription of his property and the loss of his patrimony, and the danger of capital punishment besides, so that the abundant wealth of his riches would be completely confiscated by the imperial treasury, together with the loss of his life. Accordingly, when he discovered that Christians would willingly undergo the severity of punishment *[p. 278]*, he now strives to bend his son to his wishes not with the pain of tortures but with the allurement of pleasures. Taking him from his squalid prison, he dressed him in silken garments and sent him into the dining-room where very beautiful girls adorned in sumptuous dresses had prepared the luxurious delights of wine and the sumptuous entertainment of a feast, combining unrestrained shrieks of joy with the light-hearted embraces of sexual play, so that they might soften the iron resolve of the youth with such blandishments. But the man dedicated to God is not overcome by the sweet richness of the feast, nor is he deflected from the rigour of his intention by the alluring beauty of the young women. Rather, he avoids the girls' soft lips as if they were the baleful venom of vipers, caring little for the line of (Claudian's) *Epithalamium* where it is said,

The honeyed lips cling together in rosy kisses . . .

[*Epith. Laurentii*, 80]

Thereafter, some of the relatives urge the father that his son be bound with the pleasant chains of marriage and be fastened down by the seductive allurement of matrimony; so that Daria, a very beautiful vestal virgin of elegant appearance, radiant with jewels and gold, should approach Chrysanthus boldly, in order that both the polished eloquence of her speech as well as the ornamented gew-gaws on her bosom should incline the soldier of Christ to the tie of marriage. But (Chrysanthus) gave in in a different way than they anticipated. For there arose between Daria and Chrysanthus a very lengthy verbal debate and a reciprocal exchange of ideas—since Daria was said to have been so well trained in dialectical arts and so well versed in the sophistical procedures of the syllogism that even the most eloquent orators feared to test the sagacious intellect of the young girl in an argument. Why say more? At length the man of venerable life achieved the palm of victory in their reciprocal debates, not by an argument of deception, but through a demonstration of reason; and taking this very Daria, who now believed in the sacraments of the catholic faith, they live together under the simulated intercourse of marriage, until at length Daria was purified through the water of the redeeming font. Abandoning at once the disciplines of dialectic, with which she had been occupied in her school-studies, she is instructed in canonical writings and exegetical commentaries. Nor could one enumerate in a list or compute in any way by any system of reckoning

97

what a great multitude of either sex would flock in crowds from the fanatical superstition of pagan shrines to the catholic faith as a result of the instruction (of Daria and Chrysanthus). As a result of this, the blessed Chrysanthus is given over at the command of the tribune Claudius to seventy soldiers to be punished by varying excruciation, unless he would consent to burn incense in the pagan manner in the temple of Amphitrionades, that is, Hercules *[p. 279]*. He obstinately refused, and then the soldiers bound him fiercely with wet, raw thongs of leather, so that when the thongs dried out gradually in the torrid heat of the sun, he would not be able to bear the force of the binding; but in the nick of time the cruel bindings of the thongs came undone through divine command. In the same way they cram the shins and calves of the man of God into the confinement of the crippling stocks: immediately the hardness of the rigid stocks is reduced to nothing, ground down by some invisible power. But the soldiers, thinking this to have been done by sorcery, soak him in the most stinking clouds of urine, by which they think that all the deceptions of Chaldaeans and hierophants as well as the machinations of sorcerers and wizards (would) disappear; but the anointment of reeking urine is changed into fragrant ambrosia and into the rosy aroma of nectar. Then they order a young heifer to be flayed so that the naked limbs of the martyr might be bound with the rawhide of the recently-flayed skin, such that under the burning heat of the sun he would be fiercely tortured in the freshness of the rawhide; but sustained by the favour of Christ, he escaped free of danger and unharmed. Straightway they bind his neck, his arms and legs with the iron links of chains and throw him into the dark recess of a prison; but the tight chains are swiftly broken like husks of flax, and the murky darkness abates as if by the translucent light of a lantern. In the end, when he was about to be beaten by the bloodthirsty cruelty of executioners with rods and knotted scourges, these very sceptre-like rods, which beforehand were stiff with knotty hardness, were made softer than a feather and smoother than paper. When he saw these great marvels, Claudius the tribune was stupefied and, being touched to the quick, he, together with the seventy soldiers and all his family and his following of slaves as well as other guests and companions, put his faith in Christ the son of God, saviour of the world; and straightway all these people, reborn through the waters of baptism, achieve the glowing crowns of paradise by the blessed spilling of their blood; and their holy bodies, buried together, lie in a subterranean crypt, ready to arise to glory at the final judgment.

With these people all passing on to heaven, Chrysanthus and Daria who survived them were separately constrained by alternate punishments. He was bound in iron and put in the murky recesses of a rock-prison, where the underground drains of the sewers carry in the stench of excrement; but the stench and darkness are put to flight by serene light and nectared aromas. She was thrust into a brothel of harlots and the fellowship of whores [p. 280], where a lion from the cages of the amphitheatre is sent by God's command for the protection of the holy virgin so that, if any wanton whoremonger or licentious fornicator might wish in his aimless strolls to enter the brothel, he would be mauled with savage jaws. But sometimes out of the heaped abundance of miracles a scarcity of words (to describe them) is created; for, overwhelmed by the huge pile of these miracles, I shall by-pass many more with an abridgement of brevity. After these (aforementioned trials), by the decree of Numerianus Augustus they died as martyrs, put to rest together in the one crypt in the company of saints, ready to receive together the rewards for their merits, just as they had shared together their torments.

XXXVI. Moreover, I shall not allow the virginal glory of the martyr JULIAN to lie hidden in the secret recesses of silence. Julian was born in the time of Diocletian and Maximian of a noble stock. When his parents, while he was still blooming in the first stages of childhood, had arranged for him to be master of the dialectic art as well as to be a participant in the arts of rhetoric, they gave him over to tutors and teachers to have him instructed in the various disciplines of philosophy; and already in the tender beginning of boyhood, his parents observed the grown man (that he was to be), having discovered him (to be) a lover of the catholic faith, hanging round the sacred portals of the church and also visiting often the prisons of the confessors, (and) they feared greatly that, if their only child were to be deprived of offspring because of his choice of religion or the practice of a holy way of life, they would—as the patriarch said, pouring out a tearful lament, 'bring down his grey hairs with sorrow unto hell' [Gen. XLIV. 29]—be completely deprived of heirs for their hoped-for succession and of children to come to their children. Therefore [p. 281], they attempted to influence the youth with earnest prayers and unheard-of incitements of flattery, so that they might incline the young man's disposition—which was not so much iron, as harder than adamant—to wedding-festivities and the companionship of marriage. For this argument of urgent persuasion, they even use the pronouncements of the apostle in which he says: 'I will, therefore, that the younger should marry, bear children, be parents of families,[15] give no occasion to the adversary to speak evil' [I Tim. V. 14]. To whom he is reported to have replied, 'It is not the appropriate time according to my will nor to my age that I should do these things which you urge';

99

likewise, when they persevered obstinately in their entreaties, he said: 'I have not the capacity to promise, nor have I the power to refuse; what you urge, I commit to the power of my God', and so on. However, he asked from his parents a respite of one week so that he might discover the will of the heavenly majesty by evident proofs. When this interval was up, and he was laid in sleep and sunk in slumber, he saw Christ say to him in a vision: 'Arise! Do not fear the persuasions of words nor shudder at your parents' wish! For you shall take a wife who shall not separate you from me by fleshly pollution, but through you shall remain a virgin', and thereafter, 'Many young men and women through your teaching shall be recruited into the life of the heavenly army', and so forth. Accordingly, a blessed virgin named prophetically Basilissa, that is 'queen', is accepted in marriage, beautiful in the features of her face, yet more beautiful in the chastity of her heart; lovely, I say, in each and every one of her physical features but more beautiful inwardly through the adornment of her spiritual robes.

Oh, what a crowd of believers of either sex, treading down the fetid sewers of sin and abominating the stinking mire of vice, rejoicingly attained to the trophy of martyrdom, having been converted to the catholic faith by the instruction of Julian and Basilissa, since indeed they constructed through Christ's assistance many monastic work-houses /p. 282/ in the celebrated town of Antioch, which is the capital of Egypt.[16] In these establishments approximately ten thousand soldiers of Christ practised a regular monastic life, living under the rule of Julian alone and in no way deviating to right or left on crooked by-ways from the (straight) path of holy religion. And Basilissa, (equally) dedicated to God, reaping one thousand sheaves of the holy harvest with the scythe of gospel preaching, took them to be threshed on the threshing-floor of the executioner and to be stored in celestial granaries. Ultimately, when the savage insanity of persecutors went on the rampage, attacking violently the holy soldiers of the Church by means of deadly edicts and ferocious instruments of torture, and was striving to destroy completely the fortress of catholic faith, rocked by the missile of worldly reason and weakened by the battering rams of dreadful conspiracy, who could eloquently express within the restricted style of (literary) composition how much Julian suffered being martyred together with his other comrades and fellows in the same resolve? With Martianus presiding on the raised platform of the tribunal or haranguing in the orator's pulpit, Julian—flayed with knotted cudgels and bloody scourges without any consideration of mercy—could not be deflected from the worship of Christ. What is more, he restored to health the eye of one of his torturers, who was cruelly inflicting on him the lashes of the whip—and even though he was drenched in stinking urine as (being) a sorcerer! Furthermore, he threw to the ground, shattered and overturned more than five hundred impious statues of idols, to which temple-priests were offering incense, offering up libations like dervishes.

Likewise *[p. 283]* Julian, together with a young son of the governor—a youth on the threshold of puberty who was a neophyte and recently converted to the faith—was thrown into the remote depths of prison, where the fetid corpses of the damned, due to the long interval of time, were bubbling over with horrid swarms of worms, and where (Julian) suffers the nausea of filth; but with a reversal of events divine compassion, which always remembers its champions, mercifully bestowed on those suffering the filth and darkness of the dungeon the sweet smell of ambrosia and the fragrance of nectar in place of the reeking dung-heap, and clear light as well. When the soldiers who were deployed in guarding these confessors saw these great miracles, they scorned their worship of fanatical superstition and are added to the ranks of the faithful. Meanwhile, Julian, at the insistence of the governor, by pouring out prayers to heaven, resuscitated the corpse of a dead man which was wrapped up in the lengthy windings of bandages but not yet buried in the enclosure of the tomb. This man, rising from the depths of hell, revealed to the astonished onlookers all the misery of departure and all the tranquillity of returning hither.

Therefore, under the pressure of the emperor's decree, the holy martyrs are placed, in full view of the circus, within thirty vats which were filled up with masses of black pitch and the kindling of bitumen and the stench of sulphur; and on the outside they are set alight by torches of crackling fire beneath and by flaming firebrands of brushwood to such an extent, that the summits of the flaming pyre exceeded the threatening height of an obelisk, and the rounded top of its ball (which was) thirty cubits to the cone.[17] But nevertheless the burning conflagration was suppressed through heavenly power and the triumphant men walked out into the open like burnished gold (from the fiery forge) in full view of the circus-crowd. Thereupon the renewed ferocity of the abominable torturer, which is always fed by the pains of the guiltless and nourished by the spilling of blood, increased the glorious merits of martyrdom for (these) champions and contestants of Christ *[p. 284]*; they wrapped the thumbs of their hands and the joints of their fingers with strings soaked in oil and at the same time they harshly tied up the toes of their feet. But, when the threads of the strings were ignited, divine protection safeguarded these champions of God struggling in the arena of the world like wrestlers, (keeping them) immune from the smoking balls of fire. So the bloodthirsty executioner, confounded by this victory of the soldiers of Christ, orders the saints to be led into the amphitheatre bound up with iron neck-chains, so that they might be devoured by the teeth of bears and gnawed by jaws of lions once the gates of the dens were opened and the bars of the cages were removed. Thus the stupid mind of the governor, hateful to God, is fed by vain hopes, while the raging fury of beasts and the gluttonous voracity of wild animals was constrained by heavenly command, (and), not daring to devour the prey offered to it, closed up the gaping entrance of its gullet; just as the poet [i.e. Caelius Sedulius] said of the prophet,

And they taught fierce lions to protect their prey.

[*Carm. Pasch.* I. 203]

In the end, Julian, together with his other fellow-combatants, was ruthlessly struck down by a drawn sword and died blessedly, pouring out a ruby river of blood. When ten lepers came to the venerable tombs (of Julian and his companions), lepers whom a rough callousness of skin, defiling (them) with an elephantine disfigurement, had blotched not in a few places, but on every limb, having been in that very place reborn in baptism by the grace of a second nativity, they who when they were diseased were wrapped in linen and muslin are restored to health through the merits of the saints and depart, having obtained their wishes.

XXXVII. AMOS, the first renowned citizen of Nitria, who, although he was compelled unwillingly by his parents [p. 285] to the intercourse of marriage—and yet he, unwilling, would in no way be deprived of the palm of chastity—resisted more and more the proffered lot of this detested marriage, as if it were the contagion of squalid filth or the poisonous bite of an asp. This Amos, therefore, was born of a respectable family which was renowned in Egypt for the outstanding affluence of its riches and the sumptuous wealth of its estate. Accordingly his parents, when they saw their most affectionate offspring growing up and maturing in youthful years, thinking as it were of posterity to follow, they urge Amos to the nuptial bonds of marriage, even though he was resisting strenuously. When he could no longer disappoint their obstinate importunity by refusing, he unwillingly chooses a young virgin who is betrothed with a ring under a simulated connivance of matrimony; (and) in the secret seclusion of their wedding-chamber he persuades her with private verbal exhortations to (strive after) the rewards of chastity. Complying with his prayers and admonitions she aspires to the highest summit of virginity. The two of them are said to have lived together—with God alone as witness—in chastity for a lengthy period of time; and they continually prospered, with an increase in virtue, in their strict observance of the holy way of life. Under their instruction a numerous crowd of either sex streamed to the faith of Christ and to contempt of this world; and when Amos had prevailed in practical affairs through the favourable outcome of his merits, he set out for the wilderness of the dreadful desert, where he practised the contemplative life of an anchorite.

He is endowed with an infinite number of prophetic signs by the true rewarder of virtues. For a certain young man, turned to insanity by the rabid bites of a dog, was brought to him [p. 268] bound tightly in chains; he is immediately restored to his pristine health, but with the condition first imposed, that what had been stolen and plundered be returned to a certain poor little lady. And these (people), recognizing that the deceit perpetrated in stealth was now revealed through the prophetic power (of Amos), restored of their own volition those things which they had removed by fraud. And this (following) story ought to be retold briefly and cursorily: that two certain men had promised that they would bring a large jar to the man of God. The one of them, when he had broken his promise, lost his hump-backed camel which died thereafter; the other man, fulfilling his promise, has the benefit of a healthy donkey. How great is the virtue of chastity shall be more clear from the following (anecdote)—that the man of God, when he was endeavouring to cross the waters of the river Nile, was ashamed to shed his sheepskin cloak and his other clothing lest the shameful nakedness of his body and its improper indecency were to offend chaste eyes; he is said to have been transported suddenly to the far bank of the river by divine power. And, lest this seem incredible, recall how Habacuc, the bearer of food to the reapers, swiftly brought a meal from Judea to the (land of) the Chaldeans [i.e. Babylon] in one split second, supported by angelic aid, and over so great a distance of land amply fed the starving prophet of God [i.e. Daniel] and abundantly nourished him (while he) was in the den of roaring lions. St Anthony the hermit saw the soul of this Amos being borne aloft by a band of heavenly soldiers into the starry orbs of heaven when it was released from the bonds of the fleshly prison.

XXXVIII. In the time of the most wicked (emperor) Julian, who, departing from the ecclesiastical rank of office and deviating from the straight path of religion with wandering digressions [p. 287], had begun most lamentably to apostatize in favour of the pagans' cult, there was a certain man of venerable life from the Thebaid [i.e. Thebes, Egypt] by the name of APOLLONIUS, who, in the fifteenth year of his life, entering the retreat of the vast desert and avoiding the company of mortals, is said to have sheltered himself not far from that ancient sanctuary into which our Redeemer—whom the nefarious son of Antipater was persecuting—entered and overthrew all the statues of idols, toppling (them) to the ground, in accordance with the prophetic pronouncement of Isaiah: 'Behold, the Lord will ascend upon a swift cloud and will enter into Egypt. And the idols of Egypt shall be moved at his presence (and shall fall to the ground)'[18] [Is. XIX. 1]. 'The cloud', he says, 'is swift': it prefigures, that is, the most chaste bosom of the Virgin Mary which is devoid of the filth of human corruption and of masculine embrace. At length the aforementioned servant of God, (Apollonius), tolerating the horror of the desert not with flagging but with indefatigable energy for the space of eight *lustra*, that is to say, forty years, was the abbot and rector of approximately five hundred monks. It is written that Apollonius—shining forth in many evidences of marvels and miracles as a result of the bright glory of his virginity—had called on the Lord on bended knee a hundred times in the space of the daylight hours, and as many times at night. Although his tunic was produced from the thread or rather the husk of flax without any ostentatious variety of threads, (his) robe of muslin (was made) from a smooth ball of thread, and was woven from the spindle, made into cloth with the shuttles humming and the reed beating; these vestments, although he was so long in retreat in desert places through so many revolutions of time, never came to pieces at all through old age. His sustenance—or rather his abstinence!—is said to have been so sparing /p. 288/ that he would rather be fed on green bunches of herbs and freshly picked garden vegetables, as if he were getting a well-seasoned repast from the kitchen, whereas he would refuse cooked or roasted food prepared in the oven for (his) nourishment. Apollonius was thrust at one time into the obscurity of a dungeon when Julian, who had taken on dictatorship and apostasy together, compelled not only those who held some ecclesiastical position, but even those engaged in the monastic vocation, to enter military service. But in the stillness of the dead of night an angel blazing with the most brilliant ray of light (and) opening the doors of the prison while the guards trembled, snatched the man of God from the obscure filth of the underground cell.

On a particular day, when Apollonius was taking a journey, with the chains of his prayers he made some crowds of pagans revelling everywhere around an effigy remain immobile, fixed as if rooted to the ground, in the open air and in the burning heat of the sun; nor were they able to proceed further in any direction. But when they discovered what had been done by the man of God, they promised straightway by intermediaries[19] sent (to him) /p. 289/ that, if the means of moving were given to them, they would all reject the idolatry of their heathen ceremonies and would put their faith in the orthodox belief, and would smash the worthless statue of their idol into smithereens, or would burn it to cinders and ashes; and the ending of the affair showed that so it was done.

At another time, likewise, a very bloody battle was being waged between two populous settlements, one of believers, one of non-believers. It just so happened that the aforementioned man of God had come upon the crowds armed with a phalanx of shields and with their swords already drawn on each side in readiness for slaughter. When Apollonius sought earnestly to mitigate the disorderly belligerence of each group with words of peace, and attempted to soothe the bloody-mindedness which had arisen in each of the raging bands, a certain pugnacious troublemaker, instigator of the encounter and leader of the worsening quarrel, is said to have resisted with an insane and furious outcry, saying that he scorned any peaceful settlement and would fight to the death. Then the saintly man said, 'May the outcome you have wished for follow on your words! The others have harmoniously repaired the lesion of the violated alliance; you alone shall pay the vengeful punishment of a bloody death! What is more, no tomb shall ever receive your wicked corpse—as it does other mortals—but, torn apart by the beaks of birds and gnawed by the jaws of wild beasts, you shall be deprived of the burial which is common to all'. Thus the bloody event came to pass, just as the prophetic announcement had forewarned.

At another time, the holy festival of Easter was being celebrated within the retreat (of Apollonius), and many were eagerly gathering at the cave of the man of God like a swarm (of bees) at the beehive, in order to participate in the celebration. When it was over they were feasted with the banquet of his accustomed frugality, that is, with dry and tiny crusts of bread and with bunches of vegetables sprinkled with salt; then, pouring out prayers to the heavens, they faithfully implore the protection of God. And, no sooner had the word been spoken than Christ, with his usual compassion in abundance for his hungry servants, sent to the cave-entrance porters whom none of them had seen before, bearing such an abundance of delicacies, that they were plentifully nourished with this divinely-sent gift of food up to the day of Pentecost, which is calculated by the lapse of seven weeks, just as the year of Jubilee is reckoned (to fall) after an interval of seven years [p. 290]. That this, moreover, was a donation of heavenly munificence rather than a gift of human generosity, is deduced from the following by the most evident proofs: that (heavenly munificence) divinely provided the fruitful bounty of the donation brought by unknown servants at an unseasonable time, that is, in the spring rather than in the autumn—(the donation consisting in) 'Punic' apples, which are called pomegranates, together with the dates of the palm which they call 'Nicolian', honeycombs, grapes and figs, that is, bunches of Carian [i.e. dried] figs—since we well know that the rows of vines and the shoots of the vineyards become leafy and blossom in the spring, but in the autumn they soften and grow ripe, with swelling clusters and yellowing grapes.

It happened one time, while the calamitous atrocity of a famine was ravaging the people of Egypt indiscriminately, that many flocked to (Apollonius) in hordes for the sake of a handout. And he showed to the starving throngs of people three tiny baskets filled with crusts and buns—which were to provide the sustenance of food for the monks for a space of one day only [p. 291]; and he gave them the power of increase through a fertile benediction. These crusts and buns, reviving the indigent populace with their abundance of bread, kept the people from hunger and danger of imminent starvation; he is said to have done this same thing with wheaten flour (and) corn-meal together with the thick richness of oil. In the earlier miracle Apollonius imitated the baskets and hampers of the Gospel [cf. Matth. XIV. 20]; in the second he equalled the flask of oil and the handful of flour which were filled with the amplitude of fecund benediction by the prophet Elijah [IV Reg. XVII. 14–6].

XXXIX. Having, therefore, completed in a cursory fashion the examples of the masculine sex—who supported the edifice of chaste behaviour with anything but a crumbling foundation of integrity—and moving on gradually with verbal footsteps to the equally distinguished personalities of the second sex, who continually endured in the perseverance of holy virginity with an inflexible strength of mind: let us strive to pluck successfully the most beautiful flowers of purity from these (women), so that we may be able to embroider with a braid that cannot be unplaited the crown of eternal beatitude—provided He benignly grants the benefit of His protection, who being born a virgin from the womb of a virgin expiated the sins of the first man, and who, having overthrown the princes of darkness, made happy the condition of the entire world; and just as we first of all collected examples of the principal sex from the course of either testament [p. 292], for whom the virginal resolve above all the other gifts of virtue revealed the mansions of celestial paradise and the halls of the kingdom of heaven—in the same way, as we shall demonstrate with evidence below, let us strive to set out skilfully the abundant examples of chastity in the race of women.

XL. Well now, as we mentioned above, the blessed MARY, the perpetual virgin, 'a garden enclosed, a fountain sealed up' [Cant. IV. 12], 'the rod out of the root of Jesse bearing a flower' [Is. XI. 1], the dawn of the sun, the daughter-in-law of her Father, the mother and sister of the Son and at the same time his bride and blessed handmaid, the mother-in-law of holy souls, the queen of the heavenly citizens, 'a dove ... among threescore queens and fourscore concubines' [Cant. VI. 7–8]: because of the privilege of her perpetual purity, was blessedly found worthy to beget, with joyful heart, the ransom of the world, the monarch of the earth, with the archangel announcing (this to her) and the Holy Ghost enveloping (her).

Truly, it suddenly came into my mind as I am writing carefully about the perpetual virginity of Mary—who was a virgin full of grace before receiving the sacred seed, and who remained a virgin of even greater grace after the honour of her divine child-bearing—how CAECILIA, a most holy virgin, refused the companionship of a conferred marriage and the betrothal ceremonies of her suitor on the grounds of her chastity, and scorned, despised and rejected them with laudable spiritual fervour, just as the foul excrement of the latrine. And although the music of the organ with its one hundred and fifteen musical notes was sounding,[20] she listened with deaf ears, under the pretext of her chastity, as if to the deadly harmonies of the Sirens when they entice each and every inexperienced person towards the dangers of life. As a result of this, she converted her own suitor and her future brother-in-law—if the condition of virginity were to allow (it)—from the superstitious worship of pagan shrines; and when they were reborn through the baptismal font she made them visibly enjoy an angelic presence: for an angel sent from the stars brought to them some garlands woven with white and crimson flowers, saying. 'Guard these crowns with an immaculate heart and a pure body, since I have brought them to you from the paradise of God (himself)'.[21]

XLI. But also /p. 293/ the universal renown of the virgin AGATHA was growing far and wide and had spread through the entire province of Sicily at that time when the emperor Diocletian, exercising the authority of imperial power, was inflicting grim decrees of punishment on the followers of the orthodox faith. The cruel rending of her limbs could not subdue, the vicious persecution of the lictors could not impede, the sharp splinters of potsherds could not weaken, the searing heat of coals could not in any way overcome (Agatha's) innocent purity; rather, like an adamantine rock, she became harder than iron in the face of the tortures imposed by the executioners. The attestation of this fact, and the proofs of a not fictitious truth, are jointly confirmed by a native of Sicily and a citizen of the town of Catania: when the fires of Mt Etna boiled over with lava throwing off sparks far and wide and the streams of its torrents ablaze with sulphureous balls of fire roared as they flowed headlong (down the mountainside), these men opposed the holy coffin in which lay the virginal little body (of Agatha) to the engulfing streams of fire, as if it were a towered bastion or a walled fortress; and in the twinkling of an eye, with the virgin's assistance, they straightway calmed the terrifying inferno of flames which was going to burn everything in its way and devour the liquefied masses of rock.

XLII. To me it also seems worthwhile that the fame of St Agatha should be followed by the glories of the most chaste virgin LUCIA, which two our teacher and instructor St Gregory the Great is known to have coupled together in the daily litany, when the solemnities of the Mass are celebrated, placing (them) in the catalogue of martyrs in this order: Felicity, Anastasia, Agatha and Lucia, so that these (two), who were born in Sicily to a kindred race, and rejoice together in heavenly glory, should not be separated in the sequence of narratives. For, just as the town of Catania is happily distinguished from the other cities of Sicily by the martyrdom of Agatha, so Syracuse, another Sicilian town, is elevated with fortunate events through the claims of the renowned novice of Christ, Lucia. When (Lucia) and her mother were once speaking together [p. 294], and her mother had been worn down by a prolonged illness and then cured by a flow of blood through the merits of Agatha, Lucia bombarded her with entreaties of this sort: 'I beseech you, by the one who has cured you [i.e. Agatha], that you do not name for me a husband, and that you do not seek for the fruit of mortality from my posterity; but that you give to me all those things, which you were going to give to me when I went to the author of my corruption, a mortal husband, when I go to the author of my purity, our Lord Jesus Christ'. Thereupon—after her mother had agreed to this—there is an immediate division of property: the recesses of the treasure-chests are opened up, purses of coins are filled, wedding fripperies are disbursed, and a heavenly banquet is prepared; and while a fleshly inheritance is being uprooted, a spiritual contract is being settled. But because of this settlement the bridegroom is kindled with the flames of anger; Paschasius,[22] the consul with tribunal power, was troubled with bitter anguish because he was not able to deflect Christ's recruit at all from her rigid resolution of virginity, neither by castigating her with the harshness of reprimands nor by giving her over to the deceptive seductions of panders—even though they attempted to drag (or thrust)[23] her, bound in ropes, to a detestable brothel and a loathsome bawdy-house of whores. But the protection of Christ kept her unharmed from every machination of magicians and uncontaminated by the superstition of soothsayers. In the end the furious consul handed her over to be burned with flaming brands, so that they heaped up lumps of black pitch and resin as kindling together with searing oil on the fires of the pyre: but quicker than the telling these (fires) were put out by rainshowers (sent) by divine power, (and) died away. Therefore the blessed Lucia, having preserved the seal of her chastity and having finished the course of her life, was found worthy of the glorious triumph of a martyr, since she preferred to spill out her crimson blood, having been pierced by the sword, rather than to lose her precious virginity. Nor did the blood-thirsty executioner [i.e. Paschasius] derive any pleasure from observing the dying virgin; instead, he was bound in chain-shackles and put to scorn by the entire population of Sicily, as a barbaric robber or cruel buccaneer; and when he was led to the city of Romulus [i.e. Rome] weighed down by these chain yokes, he was sentenced by the Roman senate to capital punishment, and so provided a wretched spectacle.

XLIII. As for [p. 295] the great and mighty (sufferings) which JUSTINA, a handmaid of justice and a heroine not to be disdained by the orthodox, endured on behalf of her virginity at Antioch, at the time when Diocletian cursedly was in control of the sceptre of imperial power, what author, who could call on only mediocre talent, will boast that he can narrate them, if he has not diligently learned all the occurrences of signs and miracles which are inscribed in written characters (in books)? Her suitor could not force her from the citadel of her purity, nor could the magic incantations of sorcerers overcome her in any way; but rather the entire scenario of illusions' which the false scoundrels had projected by their cunning fantasy had disappeared like a wisp of smoke, melted like liquefying wax, and was dissolved like a dwindling shadow in the twinkling of an eye. When Cyprian, I say, who at that time was the most renowned of soothsayers,[24] and is said to have been the most outstanding of sorcerers after Zoroaster and Simon Magus, was unable to bend her towards the bond of marriage and matrimonial fellowship by using the arguments of Leviathan [i.e. Satan] and the deceptive snares of the devil, he recognized on the spot—through the chaste virginity of Justina, by which she had cast out and nullified all the instruments of his opposing forces—the unconquerable victory of Christ and his ineluctable prize, though he was a pagan, so thoroughly that he was straightway catechized through ecclesiastical purification, was reborn through the womb of regenerating grace in baptism, where six, or two sets of three,[25] ranks are established, and was admitted to the catholic faithful—to such a degree that, having completely rejected the works of sorcerers and entirely cast them away, he on the other hand came to know the divine sacraments sent from heaven and became a fearless preacher—who had been a stubborn opponent of the faith—and so proceeding slowly through the seven offices of the Church, he arrived blessedly at the highest summit of the episcopacy.

Justina [p. 296], however, not only remained to the end in blessed possession of the glory of her purity, but even when she was afflicted with diverse instruments of torture she did not give in, (being) harder than adamant for the sake of laying hold of the prize of suffering, since she had in no way placed the foundations of her unvanquished mind on the powdery grains of sand, shifting this way and that, but had established the lofty structure of her dwelling on the most solid rock, just like the wise man whom the Gospel parable describes. While she was being cruelly lashed with rough scourges of leather, and was being beaten with plentiful blows of the fist, she was ordered at length to climb into an iron cauldron which was sizzling with tallow and pitch, in order that she, the gentlest of virgins, be cremated in such a torture-chamber. But Christ with his accustomed clemency—through which he knows how to show compassion of his own accord, taking thought for the humble and those who are contrite of heart—checked the force of the flaming furnace and protected with his power the virginal limbs from the threatening death of the cauldron, to the illustrious glory of his own name. In the end, when Claudius Caesar was torturing these voluntary martyrs of God with the foulnesses of the dungeon, and was forcing them with cruel edicts to the rites of pagan shrines, (Justina) received the sentence of decapitation, together with Cyprian—not then involved in necromancy, but rather endowed with his bishopric—and was reddened with the holy purple of her blood.

XLIV. What shall I say of the blessed EUGENIA, crowned with the garland of perennial chastity and armed with the banner of flourishing virginity? When, being instructed in the liberal arts, she had learned perfectly all the syllogisms of the philosophers and the doctrines of Epicurus and the arguments of Aristotle, together with the five-year silence of the Stoics, according to the teachings of these wise men, (even though) urged by her father Phillip, and sought in marriage by a suitor born of a noble family, for the sake of the greater glory of her virginity she spurned (the idea) like foul excrement; like tossed-out garbage she scorned it; as from the swarthy blackness of dusky soot she recoiled from it, and ran to the maternal bosom of the holy Church [p. 297], accompanied only by two eunuchs, having rejected the conveyance of a sedan-chair, and having abandoned her retinue of other attendants, to receive the sacrament of baptism and take service in the monastic army—not like a woman, but, against the laws of nature, with her curling locks shaved off, in the short crop of the masculine sex—and she was joined with the assembly of saints and was recruited to the troops of Christ's army with the seal of her purity unbroken, and with no blemish on her chastity. Since all the affectionate relatives of her family and the friendly concern of her domestic household thought that she had been carried off by some unfortunate accident—like Prosperina abducted by Pluto, as the fictions of poets maintain—and was lamenting her mournfully with tearful groans, they sought straightway some stupid advice from the soothsayers and sorcerers, who babble out the ravings of falsehood (and) who vainly flatter themselves on possessing a knowledge of hidden things beyond that of other mortals. But while the soothsayers were fashioning trifles to remove (the family's) anxiety, trifles which truly lacked any prophetic truth, the habitual clemency of our Saviour did not allow to remain hidden any longer the 'city seated on a mountain' or the 'candle under a bushel' [Matth. V. 14–15]: since the renown of Eugenia's hidden chastity was revealed through the perverse reproaches of infamous slander, even though the author of the virginity herself had resolved to hide away her virginal gift in secret corners, and had taken care that it was known only to the observation of the divine majesty to whom the hidden mysteries of all secrets are revealed. For when Melanthia—inspired by the black omen of her name [μελανθής = 'black']—whom the amusements of wanton obscenity and the impulses of the flesh impelled with their tantalising goads, and who, forgetful of her own matronly modesty, deceitfully tried to force upon the same Eugenia the false debauchery of the bawdy-house and the wickedness of the polluted brothel, Eugenia hurled back *[p. 298]* the missiles of deceitful accusation (taken) from the quiver of falsehood against those who had launched them, blunting (them) with the manifesto of her self-defence, as if with an iron-clad shield—as the book of Eugenia's life [i.e. pseudo-Rufinus, *Vita Eugeniae*] fully explains; similarly, in ancient times, when those fabricators of lies—rather than elders of the people—whom the spur of adulterous desire had bloodied with the sin of sexuality, conspired falsely to incriminate Susanna with the discrepant impudence of their words, they were buried with dense and terrible showers of stones, and so presented a cruel spectacle of death: so, the sentence of the Psalmist may, on the historical level of interpretation, be seen to square and to agree with the happy outcome of the lives of both (Eugenia and Susanna)—even though it be believed on the anagogical level to be a prophecy concerning the Redeemer: 'For unjust witnesses have risen up against me, and iniquity hath lied to itself' [Psalm. XXVI. 12]; and as if because of this abuse of calumny, which the innocent tolerate from deceivers, the Psalmist continues with this apt change of sentiment: 'I believe to see the good things of the Lord in the land of the living' [Psalm. XXVI. 13].

XLV. And it seems important that the glorious example of the dis-

tinguished AGNES should not be concealed from the celibate im-
itators of her purity and from the despisers of carnal filth—rather, that
it should become known to the adherents of the same virginal under-
taking and to the companions of chaste fellowship. Agnes, in order to
preserve her purity, scorned like the yellow-brown scum of a reeking
sewer all the array of ornaments which were offered by her suitor, a
prefect's son, so that he might obtain the marriage he wanted; and she
is said to have replied in the following way: 'Depart from me, oh in-
centive to sin, nourishment of evil, food of death; for I am already
engaged by another lover who has betrothed himself to me with a ring
of his good faith, surrounded me with glowing and glistening gems,
and dressed me with a robe woven from gold; whose father knew no
woman, whose mother is a virgin, whom the angels attend and whose
beauty the sun and moon admire'. And although because of this she
was thrust—despoiled of her own clothes, to the infamous disgrace of
her family—into the loathsome harlotry of a brothel, where the
detestable wantonness of prostitutes runs wild and the shameless impudence of whores is disgustingly flaunted [p. 299], nevertheless,
walled about by the shining splendour of a mighty light, she gazed on
angelic faces and was covered with her Lord's robes. Oh, how great is
the savagery of raging sexual desire, and, on the other hand, how great
is the mercifulness of placated chastity! For when the aforementioned
lover of lewdness [i.e. her erstwhile suitor], on fire with carnal passion,
entered the brothel accompanied by his partners in crime, so that he
could impose with his impudent lips the foul sports of his lechery on
the sacred virgin, suddenly, struck down by the sword of celestial
anger, he died, and paid on the spot the penalty of an untimely death,
just like Uzzah, who had not feared to touch with his profane hands
the ark of the testament, where the pontifical rod which had flowered,
and golden urns filled with celestial bounty [i.e. manna], and also the
tablets inscribed with the letters of the decalogue, were hidden [II
Reg. VI. 6]. But again, to the greater glory of God, so that the mockers
of the catholic faith, who had plotted a scheme which they could not
execute, might fall silent with the stammering lips of their mouths, and
the swinish snortings of the pagans, raging with foaming teeth against
the stainless chastity of the Church, should cease their violent grunt-
ing, Agnes brought the same young man back from the abyss of hell
with renewed health to the threshold of life. And straightway,
drenched with the rosy blush of crimson blood, she offered the immaculate sacrifice of virginity to Christ in martyrdom. Her tomb
(was) placed in a cemetery, where it restored to pristine health, as if by
celestial medicine, the serious illness of the virgin Constantina, whose
mention we shall pen below.

XLVI. I have also thought it inappropriate to by-pass the glorious personalities of the celebrated young ladies THECLA and EULALIA, (who) fit well into the development of the theme of virginity *[p. 300]*. Of these (two), Thecla, a devout virgin of Christ, when she was a betrothed bride in the first bloom of adolescence and was a young girl of pure and modest behaviour not yet reborn in the baptismal font, having heard the teaching of the excellent apostle (Paul) discussing the gift of virginity, she was not to be inclined to the companionship of marriage and the wedding feast, (even though) she was urged by her mother's coaxing and her suitor's entreaties. Brought in front of the cages of the theatrical arena by the bloody bands of executioners striving zealously to deprive her of the prize of her virginity, with Christ granting his protection she nonetheless kept the token of her chastity unbroken and the precious mantle of her virginity undestroyed among the fierce roaring of lions and the ferocious jaws of hungry bears. She even blessedly escaped, safe and sound, from the crackling furnaces of huge pyres and from the half-burned timbers of the funeral pile (which were) quenched by the fountain of celestial clemency.

Eulalia, however, endowed with a double victory and adorned with a two-fold trophy—in that she was to finish her course and preserve her faith—is inscribed in the heavenly register. For after the glory of her far-famed virginity, through which she shrank from the filth of the carnal sewer and rejected the companionship of the marriage bond, she blessedly arrived at the glorious palm of a martyr.

XLVII. Next, SCHOLASTICA and CHRISTINA and at the same time DOROTHEA, who was born in Caesarea in Cappadocia, although separated by different periods of time, were yet crowned by Christ with the same diadem of purity.

Of these (three), Scholastica, under the title of a confessor, even though no opportunity for a bloody martyrdom presented itself, lived in a manner worthy of praise among the company of the faithful; and she shone at so high a peak of purity that, when her only brother, whom she had importunately entreated with earnest prayers (to stay) for the space of a night, was obstinately refusing to agree, by means of profuse fountains of tears she immediately changed the serenity of the sky into a stormy tempest; and, arousing thunder to terrify the trembling earth with horrific rumbling, and at the same time eliciting fiery flashes of lightning, she displayed a marvellous spectacle to the world.

The second, Christina, is said to have been kindled with the flames of divine love *[p. 301]* to such an extent even before she received the rudiments of baptism, that she is said to have been a despiser of fanatical superstition and a worshipper of heavenly decrees right from the eleventh year of her life. Although her father, who had the position of *magister militum* at the palace, also instructed his daughter in the liberal disciplines of learning, he erected for her a tower that stretched aloft with a menacing height and was constructed with a strong framework of cement, in which she was confined, without her consent, by her father—who was dedicated to the worship of pagan shrines—in the company of twelve young girls, so that she should honour the gods with incense according to the rites of the pagan service-books and offer sacrifices (to them). But when he learned that he had been—deservedly!—rejected by his only daughter, and when he discovered that (his) gilded statues of the pagan gods, that is, of Jupiter and Apollo and also Venus, the lover of debauchery, had been smashed to tiny pieces, this blood-thirsty butcher and savage infanticide rather than affectionate father cruelly devised on the spot various sorts of torture to harness his daughter. Nevertheless, the (young) mind devoted to God did not shrink from the stinking filth of the dungeon; nor did it fear the rock tied to her neck and immersed in the waves of the sea; nor did it weaken when sticks were cruelly flogging her tender limbs; nor did the disfigurement of her pretty head, even though her golden hair was shaved off and she was dragged shorn in public, influence the state of her mind; nor did the girl show amazement at the torrid flames of the furnace, which equalled the ovens of the Chaldaean tyrant, or tremble with fright at the poisonous bites of asps, which sorcerers aroused with chants of incantation: rather, with Christ offering his protection, she happily overcame all these things, keeping safe the treasure of her virginity. In the end, wounded by two arrows and pouring out her crimson blood, she suffered martyrdom for Christ.

When Sapricius, a bloody butcher of the faithful, failed to compel the third virgin, Dorothea, not only to marriage but also to the wicked worship of idols or the foolish ceremonies of the heathen, immediately the raging maniac inflicted the savagery of the scaffold, laid on the livid bruises of fists, applied the burning flames of torches. He also gave (Dorothea) over to be corrupted by two women who had recently shipwrecked in their faith and who had apostasized from the fellowship of Christ *[p. 302]*; but instead Dorothea so wholesomely healed the shameful wounds of these apostate women with the medicine of penitence, that at once, in a reversal of the proper order, they preceded their teacher to her own palm of martyrdom. But when she left the cruel palace, and Theophilus demanded with a jeer of laughter that she be sure to send him small gifts of fruit from the paradise of her heavenly groom, to whom she said she was going, what was requested with a snarl of malice was fulfilled in reality. For, well before she suffered (martyrdom) and was given over to be carved up with bloody swords, she is said to have sent three apples with as many crimson roses to this Theophilus. As a result of this action, Theophilus, seizing the occasion for his own salvation, was crowned with the scarlet garlands of martyrdom.

XLVIII. As for CONSTANTINA, a heroine of most intact virtue, the daughter of Constantine, who at that time is known to have governed the monarchy of the tripartite world with beneficial results, did she not incite with her conversation, persuade with her speech and arouse by her example nearly all the daughters of Roman praetors, nearly all the high-born offspring of the feminine sex, and the most beautiful flower of its youth, through the manifest renown of her own famous virginity, to the worship of the Christian religion and to the crown of chastity—to such an extent that they confessed that each one, rejecting their marriage bed and the self-indulgent intercourse of wedlock, yearned more eagerly for the embraces of a heavenly bridegroom, and were hastening, with shining lamps and frequently uttered sighs, among the wise virgins—all of which is abundantly recorded concerning her behaviour in those works drawn from her teaching? Of this fact, Attica and Artemia, flourishing with the purity of unimpaired virginity, provide a quite evident proof. Their father Gallicanus who, while Constantine—the son of Constantius born in Britain of the concubine Helena—controlled the sceptre of government, was more renowned than anyone else in the Roman empire, and whom alone he [i.e. Constantine] considered to be the most worthy of all those of the status of tribune and all the leading magistrates, and to whom, because of the fortunate outcome of his wars and the prosperous results of his victories he would have betrothed Constantina /p. 303/, the daughter of his royal family, with a nuptial dowry, and (would have) arranged the espousals for the fellowship of the marriage-bond, if the proper order of things had allowed—having torn up by the roots his pagan beliefs, (Gallicanus) was converted to the catholic faith. It was said that Gallicanus alone at that time could sustain the attack of the Scythians who, invading from the north with an infinite apparatus of war, were devastating aggressively the province of Thrace.

XLIX. Accordingly, the report of the virtues of EUSTOCHIUM and DEMETRIAS, which, growing apace, is spread everywhere throughout Europe, should not be excluded from the previously mentioned throngs of virgins by the sheets of our writing and by the parchment-leaves of our letters. The first of these, (Eustochium), the beloved daughter of Paula and the sister of the blessed Blesella, was renowned to such an extent throughout the western Empire for the brilliant quality of her book-learning, that in libraries of patristic writings, where the commentaries of the wise Jerome are read, her reputation too is made known by the frequent repetition of reading, since the eighteen volumes (of Jerome) on the prophecies of Isaiah are dedicated to this same virgin in a lengthy series of words. But it is most exacting to enumerate one by one all the remaining commentaries on the canonical scriptures which the aforementioned interpreter of the divine law, driven on by the intelligence of the mother (Paula) and the diligence of the daughter (Eustochium), laboriously produced—I think that these (commentaries) are in no way unknown to the wisdom of your intelligence, racing *[*p. 304*]* curiously through the wide-open fields of books. Jerome also produced for Eustochium in a most polished way a small exhortatory work on preserving virginity [i.e. *Epistola* XXII].

Wandering reports of fame extolled the second (virgin), (Demetrias)[26], born from the stock of a noble family, to such an extent that, imbued with instruction in letters from across the sea, she ascended the highest beacon of virtue on the virginal stairs of her merits; since indeed, at her mother's request, a volume written in a developed and elegant style was sent over the sea to the aforesaid servant of Christ, in which the principles of her life were thus described. 'Therefore I must write to Demetrias, a virgin of Christ, a noble virgin, a wealthy virgin and, what is greater than these things, a virgin spurning her nobility and wealth in the ardour of her faith', and further on: '(Demetrias), born in this high station, nourished with the greatest riches and the greatest luxuries, and ensnared with so many and so various attractions of this life as if (entangled) in exceedingly tenacious chains, suddenly broke free and transformed all her bodily goods by the power of her soul'; and a little later he says: 'For she recalls what riches and glory of this world she has rejected, and what allurements of this present life she has scorned, what pleasures she has renounced' [*Ep. ad Demetriadem*, c. 1]. Again, just before the end of the book, when he finely was expounding the subject of the Last Judgment, and the severity of the Judge who shall weigh up the deeds of every person in his just scale of judgment, he began in this way: 'It happened recently, and you yourself witnessed it, when at the sound of the shrill trumpet and the tumult of the Goths, Rome, the mistress of the world, trembled, overwhelmed with melancholy fear', and later on he says, 'If to this degree we fear mortal enemies and human handiwork, what shall we do when the uproar and the terrible trumpet shall begin to thunder from the heavens, and at the voice of the archangel, clearer than any trumpet, the entire universe shall rumble? Then shall you fly to meet your bride-groom, accompanied by holy virgins and choirs of the just' [*Ep. ad Demetriadem*, c. 30], and so on.

L. In the same way *[p. 305]*, let us write out, even in the simple characters of our manuscript, the glorious passions of the three sisters CHIONIA and IRENE and AGAPE, who, by the renown of their suffering and the glory of their holy virginity, triumphed with a similar joy. When their celebrated renown was spreading far and wide, Diocletian, who at that time was wielding to dire effect the imperial sceptre, ordered these aforementioned servants of Christ to be summoned. He promised to them courtly distinctions and rich inheritances if they would apostatize from the worship of Christian religion and, deviating from the true path of faith, would shipwreck in the whirlpool of wicked paganism and would settle for marriages of this world instead. When they refused—with a unanimous decision—the pompous glory and the enticing allurements of this present life, at the urgent command of the evil criminal [i.e. Diocletian] grim torturers immediately thrust these attendants of the holy Church into the recesses of a dungeon; the blessed Anastasia, so that they would not perish through the spareness of their meagre frugality, readily took up her dwelling at the threshold of the dungeon so as to provide them with comestibles for subsistence and alms of food. After this, the aforementioned sisters were given over to Dulcitius, the satrap of Diocletian, to be tortured—unless they would burn incense to the gods. This wanton guard, contemplating (the sisters') comely beauty of face—not produced by make-up, nor achieved by ringlets curling from the crimping-iron, but inborn through natural grace—was immediately caught by the lasciviousness of his eyes and tumbled into debauchery, just as wax melts before a fire. He was, in fact, so consumed as it were by blind passion and pricked on by secret goads, that in the dead of night-time he did not fear to burst violently into the cell in which the aforesaid virgins were singing the harmony of psalmody, and where all the paraphernalia of the kitchen and numerous cooking utensils were kept. Straightway *[p. 306]*, carried away by the fury of his insanity, he began like a madman or a lunatic to embrace blackened pots and cauldrons darker than soot, and to kiss the sooty frying-pans, and when he had raved among them for a long time at the instigation of the deceitful enemy, and had been made a laughing-stock by this ridiculous pleasure, he (at last) departed; and with his wishes not so much fulfilled as expired, he came out as much blackened in the apperance of his body as stained in the sickness of his mind; and darkened as if by Ethiopian sootiness he was not recognized by his own attendants and domestic servants. And truly so dark an appearance of face was hidden from him alone, the circles of his eyes being clear, while it was apparent to his other colleagues and attendants, and when, in his blackened state, he attempted with an earnest effort to break into the entrance-hall of the palace, so that he could voice to the emperor a complaint, in tearful lamentation, about the trickery perpetrated by the (three) girls, some people beat him with tough canes, others pounded him with hands and fists, and several people blew in his face as if he were the black ghost of a villain, so that they drove him far away. Accordingly, he was led to his house in the hands of his attendants and was sadly received with the wailing of the lamenting household. Asserting in vain that he had been tricked by the followers of Christ through (some) magic spell of enchantment, like a snake that's been trodden on hissing with forked tongue, he ascended again the lofty tribunal seat so that, aroused by the filthiness of his disgusting lechery and inflamed by the fires of titillating enjoyment, he could feast his lustful eyes on the holy virgins stripped of their own robes; but the garments of their apparel, tugged at, one by one, by impious hands, could not be removed from the holy limbs at all. At length when the governor Dulcitius had run out of attempts at trickery, and whatsoever he had planned to try out on the virgins had come to naught, Sisinnius his colleague, at Diocletian's command, took over the aforementioned hand-maidens of God to be tortured by the most violent savagery of punishments—unless they would appease the raging divinities and would propitiate anew the favour of the gods by going through the foul ceremonies of pagan rituals, either by celebrating the Lupercalia and the Competalia, or by performing the Portunalia, or by burning incense at the Suovetaurilia or by sacrificing at the Saturnalia or the Nyctelia *[p. 307]*. When they obstinately refused to comply with his detestable command, two of them were thrust into the scorching flames of a crackling pyre; the other was killed with arrows from quivers: and so they went together to Christ to take possession of the rewards of Paradise with their palm of virginity and their crown of martyrdom, and to hymn the virginal melody in the company of the one hundred and forty-four thousand virgins.

LI. Moreover, in the time of the emperors Valerian and Gallienus, when the fervour of raging persecution and the ardour of cruelty was glowing (even) more harshly, and soldiers of the celestial army—who for the sake of confessing (their) faith in no way recoiled from the arena of combat in the manner of timorous contestants—were being killed by the bloody blades of butchers, two sisters named RUFINA and SECUNDA, born from an eminent family, turned away for a short time from the fury of the persecutors and hastened in (their) sedan-litters to their small estate in the region of Tuscany. There, their fiancés, who had recently relapsed into the filth of apostasy, like dogs to their own vomit, betrayed (them), and with a military commander and a mounted escort they were led back to Rome, to be subjected to the stinking cell of a filthy dungeon and to endure the sports of snarling mockery. After this, when Rufina was being flogged in the presence of the raging governor, beaten up with very harsh blows of the whip and bloodied by the livid weals of the lash, Secunda unflinchingly said: 'Lay on fire, stones, swords, whips, cudgels and rods: however many penalties you inflict, that many glories shall I number; however many savageries you impose, that many palms of martyrdom shall I count'. At once, yet again, the holy virgins were shut up in the hidden depths of the prison, which was appalling with its reeking stench of fetid excrement; but the dark blackness was put to flight by celestial radiance, and the stinking manure took on the odour of incense or the fragrance of pure balsam. And again, they were ordered mercilessly to be thrown into the scalding steam of a bath, which was heated (to boiling-point) by a heap of burning coals placed underneath; but they are said to have emerged from this bath unharmed, with the beauty of their bodies unscathed. But the blood-thirsty severity of the torturers, dashed and overthrown so many times on successive occasions, did not know how to grow gentle nor how to be merciful, since, indeed, it ordered the hand-maidens of God to be tied to an immense mass of rock and to be immersed, without any regard for pity, in the channel of the Tiber *[p. 308]*; but the torrents of water, granting to God the glory which was denied (to Him) by the infidels, restored the holy virgins unharmed on the shore of the river-bank. Whence the governor, astounded at such mighty marvels, is reported to have said: 'Either these (two virgins) conquer us by magic powers, or else the sanctity of virginity reigns in them'. In the end they were sentenced to capital punishment; and borne aloft by angelic hosts, they ascended (to) the stars of heaven with the banner of their virginity.

LII. Nor do I think that the renown of the holy virgins ANATOLIA and VICTORIA should be by-passed: their fame and the uniqueness of their miracles spread far and wide through all the corners of the world so long as their names are read out from the written characters (of service-books) from the pulpit of the Church, when catholic (Christians), in the revolving circle of the year, celebrate their birthdays. Therefore, in the reign of Decius, when the unrestrained ferocity of torturers cruelly raged against the warriors of Christ, no insanity of the persecutors, no severity of punishment, was able to drive the aforementioned virgins from the citadel of purity. Rather, they gave away with prodigal generosity all their inheritance and the wealth of their ornaments—both the hair-pins for their coiffure and the anklets for their legs as well as their perfume-bottles of balsam and the pendants hanging from the neck with gem-studded bangles [cf. Is. III. 20]—for the sustenance of the sick and the poor. When this was discovered, the hearts of their suitors were set ablaze with raging torches of madness—since all the income from their wealth and the copious reward for their suit went to the benefit of poor beggars! Then Eugenius and Aurelius, who were considered to be their future spouses, by means of a fraudulent plan and dissembling procedure wangled out of the emperor a note (to the effect that) their fiancées would be taken away from the city of Rome to their own estates, because they wanted to avoid branding them with the name of the Christian religion by accusing them with a public charge, in case the virgins' possessions and their landed property would be confiscated by fiscal law.

Accordingly the blessed Victoria—through her prophetic name truly a 'victory' of Christ—was taken into the territory of Tribula[27] so that, there, she would be tormented by excessive hunger and by a shortage of food and would waste away. At that time it so happened that all the inhabitants whose citizenship was of the town of Tribula were scattered all over in wandering crowds, having abandoned their town, because they were not able to tolerate the venom and breath of a scaly dragon [p. 309]. The holy Victoria voluntarily promised them that, if they would relinquish their petty little effigies of the pagan gods, renounce the Lupercalian rites, and be converted to God, she would drive far away the virulent exhalations of the frothing serpent and would restore the town to its (former) safety. For, as a result of the venomous blasts of this dreadful viper, the miserable people were being massacred in masses with immense slaughter, (and) parents watching in unnatural order the premature deaths of their offspring, were bitterly tortured by tearful complaints of their childlessness. Then the mayor of the city promises that everyone of either sex without exception (will) open his believing heart to the girl's sayings, if she would drive far away the savage cruelty of the dragon, which was inflicting a deadly toll on his miserable citizens. Then the holy virgin, sustained by the assistance of an angel, was led to the dragon's cave, with crowds of the populous city accompanying her in streams for the sake of the spectacle; as the chickens beat their wings and cockcrow sounded, (the girl)—who was in no way trembling with fearful behaviour nor wavering with timid pallor—addressed the lurking monster: 'In the name of Jesus Christ Our Lord', she said, 'go away from here, you foulest of dragons, and do honour to God! Go where no men live!' The dragon obeyed her orders, and, fleeing at an exceedingly rapid pace, he departed. But (Victoria), entering the lair of the beast, asked the people now safe from danger that they build for her an oratory in the very same cave and that they should give her

120

(some) young girls to look after her life. They obeyed this command, and seventy young virgins were subjected to divine servitude, and, hymning in harmonious melody and sweetly intoning the music of the psalms, they adhered to the admonitions and example of Victoria. Afterwards, Procus her suitor, after a space of three years, requested of the Capitoline priest with an earnest prayer, that he send a statue of Diana and compel Victoria to burn incense (on it) in apostatic ritual. When she abominated this wicked deed and condemned the bearer of the statue, she was killed by a stroke of the sword. Nor did her bloody butcher achieve any 'victory' from Victoria, but rather, maimed with a withered hand, festering with an elephantine roughness of skin and crawling with worms, he breathed out his last stinking breath.

Anatolia, however, forced into exile and becoming famous for her miraculous signs, equalled her aforementioned associate in virtue; for, having cursed the son of a consul who was bound tightly by the rigid links of demoniacal chains [p. 310], she cured him (again) in the twinkling of an eye by expelling the demon who inhabited him. As her renown became more illustrious, she restored to their former health those possessed (with devils), epileptics and other diseased persons. As for the snake-charmer who was arousing poisonous adders to attack the holy virgin by musical incantations—just as the poet [i.e. Vergil] says,

By incantation the chilly snake is called up in the fields·
[*Ecl.* VIII. 71]

—and was enveloped in their deadly coils, she swiftly snatched him loose. Then, while the blessed Anatolia was standing in prayer with her hands stretched towards heaven, and pouring out orisons to the sky, an unsheathed sword was driven through both her sides as far as the hilt, and, pouring out her blood, she obtained the ruby garland of martyrdom with the triumph of her virginity.

LIII. But what wonder is it, when the new grace is now gleaming forth [i.e. the New Testament], after the Virgin bore a virgin in holy childbirth, on whose shoulders the government is said to be [cf. Is. IX. 6], if the Church should abound in virgins as the sky shines with stars, when the books of the Old Law also honour the chaste JOSEPH with immense paeans of praise? For as long as he was a companion of pure virginity and a despiser of the enticing bawdy-house, divine protection guarded him unharmed from the menacing danger of multifarious calamities, which were threatened not only by the conspiracy of his envious brothers, who did not shrink at all from fratricide, but also were contrived by the depraved advances of his master's treacherous wife, who had forgotten the modesty (befitting) a matron.

Divine protection (also) inspired Joseph with a certain prophetic vaticination, initiating him into the secrets of future marvels and instructing him miraculously with a foreknowledge of signs and portents which were hidden from other mortals—so that not undeservedly did he appear, when sound asleep, to be adored and honoured by the translucent lights of the sun and moon, and by the remaining stars of the heaven, and at the same time by fruitful bundles of corn-sheaves, since, (when he was) flowering in the exquisite beauty of youth and the loveliness of his handsome face, sustained by his yet more beautiful virginity, he disparaged the deceitful snare of feminine boldness (and) shunned the trap of its cunning [p. 311] deception; and at the same time he spurned, overcame and scorned the fraudulent allurements of feminine provocativeness and the seductive inducements of its prattle (which)—as if with the sticky nectar of wine or the saccharine delight of honeyed mead—pours out the black virulence of its poison and viciously hurls to hell those who are unprepared and who are caught without the breast-plate of faith or any other military armament: from these Joseph fled with the palm of his virginity. Although he suffered the confined spaces of a sordid dungeon and the filthy squalor of a dark prison-cell because of the extraordinary purity of his chastity, nevertheless God, the defender of hidden chastity—to Whom all secrets are known and from Whom no mysteries are hidden—because of the unstained continence of (Joseph's) youth, gave to him the government of the Egyptian people and entrusted him to rule the dominion of its flourishing empire.

As for DAVID also, the most illustrious of kings, endowed with a stainless virginity in the boyhood of his youth before he was tied by the bond of matrimony and the shackle of marriage, did he not soothe the frenzied (Saul) with his clear musical strings and cure the (same) madman by bestowing the gift of health, driving far off the dread fury of black spirits? And also, while still a youth of tender age, he is said to have torn apart the jaws of roaring lions with his strong arms, and to have smashed to pieces the maws of horrible bears; and, advancing alone armed with his sling, to have killed with smooth stones the enormous giant of the Philistines, who was dressed in a plumed helmet and a breast-plate, armed with greaves and a spear, and protected by the bronze covering of a shield. Therefore, although his life was laudable up to the time of (his) death, inasmuch as he alone was able to wipe out the sins of his grandsons and great-grandsons by the privilege of his own merit—just as it is often decreed in (the books of) Kings to those kings who transgress the edict of the ancient law: 'I shall not quench the spark of David'[28]—nonetheless, after he had abandoned the state of virginity, the guiltless Uriah was killed, and David was joined with an illegitimate bond of marriage to Bathsheba [p. 312]; and in order to expiate this rashness, their first offspring was struck down by the sword of heavenly anger.

SAMSON the Nazarene, who from the very tender age of the cradle was sacred to the Lord because of his seven hairs—before he was caught in the fraudulent embraces of Dalila and, weakly deceived by the debauchery of this treacherous concubinage, was entangled in the seductive chains of her allurements—while the mane of his tresses had not yet been shorn by the knife, with what great miraculous signs never experienced in any age up to that time is he said to have shone forth!

Although, I say, each of these patriarchs was most pleasing to the heavenly majesty for as long as he consumed the air of the atmosphere and the breath of life, nonetheless, after their joining in carnal union, the glory of their virtues slackened and became less.

LIV. Therefore, as we mentioned earlier, just as the future virginity of the incarnate Word was prefigured in the mystical foreshadowings of a mystery through Jeremiah and Daniel and other associates in the same resolve and companions of flourishing chastity, so through the guiltless ABEL gentle innocence and suffering, and through MELCHISEDECH the episcopal authority of heavenly power and the sacerdotal office of the divine priesthood, are prefigured.

The first of these, (Abel), if going back further I may begin from the beginning, because of the worthy palm of his innocence and the glory of his original submissiveness, was the first of mortals to be found worthy to offer burnt-offerings, which were approved and welcome in the divine sight, when the sacrifice of his brother's offering had been spurned; because of which his blood was savagely spilt by his treacherous and wicked brother who thus broke the inextricable bond of kinship in defiance of divine law and human custom, and (so), with the crimson covering of his precious blood, he prefigured until the end of time the future passion of our benevolent Redeemer.

Melchisedech, however, flourished at the beginning of the world's age [p. 313] and was the first to attain to the dignity of the highest priesthood and be endowed with the distinguished rank of episcopal authority. At that same time, when a dispute had arisen between kings, Melchisedech went out to meet the patriarch [i.e. Abraham] with his three hundred and eighteen servants bringing back his famous booty, and—after an enormous slaughter of people—bringing home the numerous spoils of the Sodomites, together with his cousin [i.e. Lot][29], and did he not, by reason of the sanctity of his life, in offering up his symbolic libations of bread and wine, prefigure typologically the person of our Redeemer, such that rightly do the

123

oracles of David prophesy concerning the priesthood of Christ, through which he offered up a twofold sacrifice: 'Thou art a priest for ever, according to the order of Melchisedech' [as Hebr. V. 6]? The stock of his paternal kin and the line of his maternal family are obscure, the nature of his real birth being unknown to man, as the apostle [i.e. St Paul] attests, 'without father, without mother, without genealogy' [ad Hebr. VII. 3]—even though the popular tradition of the Hebrews thinks that his father was Shem, the first-born son of Noah, the ancestor of Abraham, Nachor and Aaron. But there is a considerable difference between the dubious traditions of the Pharisees and the elaborate exposition of Holy Scripture; for the catholic Church in no way accepts the trifles of apocryphal (books) and the uncertain tales of (other) absurdities. But let me return to the point!

LV. Let the perfection of blessed virginity be adorned, I say, not with the comely beauty of the exterior person, but by the pious chastity of the interior. For if the exterior, adorned with the precious finery of clothing, flaunts itself in a worldly manner, in vain does the interior rejoice uselessly over its own beauty, since the 'vessel of election' [i.e. St Paul: Act. IX. 15] rejects this in a general statement as if it were an individual one, saying, 'But God forbid that I should glory, save in the cross of our Lord Jesus Christ' [ad Galat. VI. 14]. Why should the ostentatious vanity of the world be admitted into the catholic basilica of Christ? For what reason do the virgins of Christ, living in the servitude of the convent, bother about adorning themselves with a luxurious gaudiness of dress? Did not Achar /p. 314/, son of Carmi, who with secret treachery had 'taken of the anathema' [Ios. VII. 11] of the city fortified with a seven-fold circling of walls [i.e. Jericho], against the commandment of his leader, a cloak of scarlet and a wedge of gold, keeping them for himself, provide a horrendous spectacle of death for the crowds of Hebrews when he was buried by showers of stones together with all the kinsmen of his family and all the domestic members of his household? The precepts of the early fathers decreed that the town of Jericho with its seven-fold circling of walls represented through allegory a symbol of the world with its seven thousand ages. Therefore, the forbidden finery of a world which is to be destroyed, coloured with precious dyes of purple tincture, cannot be duly and appropriately suited to disciples of the convent, to handmaidens of Christ, to virgins of the Church, in contravention of apostolic statutes and legal ordinances, since indeed, the shepherd of the Lord's flock and the gate-keeper of the celestial hall (St Peter)—concerning whom the poet [i.e. Aldhelm himself] said,

Aethereal key-bearer, you who open the gateway to the heavens—
[*Carm. Eccl.* IV. i. 2]

proclaimed with princely weight and authentic episcopal authority as
follows: 'Whose [i.e. wives'] adorning, let it not be (the outward
plaiting of the hair, or) the wearing of gold, or the putting on of apparel; but the hidden man of the heart' [I Petr. III. 3–4]. Whence
Gregory, the watchful shepherd and our teacher—'our', I say,
(because it was he) who took away from our forebears the error of
abominable paganism and granted them the rule of regenerative
grace—when he was explaining the evangelical dictum 'Behold, they
that are clothed in soft garments are in the houses of kings' [Matth.
XI. 8], added: 'Let no one think, therefore, that sin is absent from the
concern for fine clothing, since, if this were not a fault, Peter the
apostle in his letter would not have constrained women from the long-
ing for precious garments, saying, "not in precious garments"; since, if
this were not a fault, the Lord would not have praised John for the
roughness of his dress. Consider what a fault *[p.315]* it would be for
men to want what the shepherd of the Church took care to avert even
women from!' [*Hom. in evang.* I. vi. 3]. For, so it seems to me, the evident disgrace of inexcusable arrogance and the sign of ostentatiousness
is made clear from the fact that no one wishes to be dressed in precious
and colourful clothing when she can be seen by no one.

LVII. Whence the blessed Cyprian[30], speaking of virgins, says:
'Why does (the woman) set out adorned, why made up, as if she either
has or seeks a husband?' [*de habitu virg.*, 5]. And he added further on:
'It is not acceptable for a virgin to be adorned to the beauty of her
appearance, nor for her to take pride in the flesh and its attrac-
tiveness'—since the apostle says, 'God forbid that I should glory, save
in the cross of our Lord Jesus Christ'[ad Galat. VI. 14]—'Let them have
no concern greater than the struggle against the flesh and the determined strife of conquering and subduing the body' [*de habitu virg.*, 5].
'For the regalia of jewellery and clothing and the allurements of
physical appearance are not appropriate to any but prostitutes and
wanton women, and adornment is hardly higher prized than by those
to whom modesty is worthless' [*de habitu virg.*, 12]. (It says) in the
Apocalypse: 'And the woman [i.e. the whore of Babylon] was clothed
round about with purple and scarlet' [Apoc. XVII. 4]. 'Let chaste and
modest women flee from the dress of adultresses, from the appearance
of strumpets, from the furbelows of prostitutes and the trumperies of
whores!' [*de habitu virg.*, 12]. Elsewhere Cyprian says: 'Besides, if you
dress yourself sumptuously and go out in public so as to attract notice,
if you rivet the eyes of young men to you and draw the sighs of
adolescents after you, and nourish the desire of carnal lust, and arouse
the fires of sexual anticipation so that, even if you yourself don't
perish, you nonetheless destroy others and present yourself to your

onlookers as if you were poison or the sword, you cannot be excused as if you were of a chaste and modest mind. Your shameless dress and your immodest jewellery condemn you, nor can she who lives in such a way as to be the subject of passion be counted among the virgins of Christ' [de habitu virg., 9]. Thus far Cyprian.

And [p. 316] couldn't God, the founder and creator of all things, dye the shaggy wool of lambs and the wiry fleece of wethers with the red blood of the shell-fish or with the purple juice of blueberries, or indeed colour them naturally with purple tinctures of dye, if He had foreseen with his wise prescience that this would be convenient to our use and beneficial to our livelihood?—so that what is fictively envisaged by the poet [i.e. Vergil] would truly have been fulfilled:

> Wool shall learn not to disguise itself with various colours;
> But the ram himself in the meadows will alter[31] his fleece,
> Now softly with ruby-purple dye, now with saffron yellow;
> A vermilion colour of its own accord will clothe the grazing lambs.
> [Ecl. IV. 42–5]

And why would He—of whom it is written: 'He that liveth for ever created all things together' [Eccli. XVIII. 1]—when He created the world, not have been able to create at the beginning that which the enterprise of mortals strives to augment and amplify by means of the foolish and superfluous experiments of its inventions? Whence the same excellent Cyprian, bishop of the Africans, says: 'For God did not create scarlet and purple sheep, nor teach dyeing and colouring of wool with the juice of plants or with shell-fish' [de habitu virg., 14]. For the rule of catholic faith denies that the omnipotent (creator) left anything necessary to human nature in any respect incomplete or unfinished in the creation of the visible world. But is it surprising if the precepts of the apostles and the decrees of those learned in the Law should abominate these aforesaid trifles of absurdity, when even pagans and heathens are said to have taunted (other) pagans and heathens, as if with the ridiculous reproach of a derisive jeer, laughing and mocking as follows with the shameful labelling of by-words:

> Your clothes are embroidered with saffron and shining with purple,
> Your tunics have sleeves and your turbans necklaces!
> [Vergil, Aen. IX. 612, 614]

LVII. JUDITH, the daughter of Merari, scorned the flattering allurements of suitors after the death of Manasses, taking up the weeds of widowhood and rejecting a wedding dress—and (this at a time) when clarion-calls of the apostolic trumpet had not yet put out the call: 'But I say to the unmarried and to the widows; it is good for them if they so continue' [I Cor. VII. 8]. Flowering [p. 317] like a bright lily in her devout chastity and hiding from the public gaze she lived a pure life in an upstairs solar. (And) when in company of her hand-maiden she undertook to overthrow the dreadful leader of the Assyrians, who had terrified the quaking world with his innumerable thousands of soldiers glorying in the cavalry and infantry, she did not believe he could be deceived in any other way, nor think that he could be killed otherwise, than by ensnaring him by means of the innate beauty of her face and also by her bodily adornment. Of her, it is written in the Septuagint: 'And she clothed herself with the garments of her gladness, and put sandals on her feet, and took her bracelets, and lilies, and earlets, and rings, and adorned herself with all her ornaments' [Iud. X. 3], and tricked herself out to prey on men.[32] You see, it is not by my assertion but by the statement of Scripture that the adornment of women is called the depredation of men! But, because she is known to have done this during the close siege of Bethulia, grieving for her kinsfolk with the affection of compassion and not through any disaffection from chastity, for that reason, having kept the honour of her modesty intact, she brought back a renowned trophy to her fearful fellow-citizens and a distinguished triumph for (these) timid townsfolk—in the form of the tyrant's head and its canopy [cf. Iud. XIII. 19].

Similarly, that stubborn and insolent woman in Proverbs who foreshadows the figure of the Synagogue, who promised that her own husband would (only) return when the moon was full (and who), in the trappings of a harlot and with alluring luxury, is described as having enticed a foolish young man and, when she had deceived him with the fraudulent delights of her promises, destroyed him pitiably, so that (it was) truly like an ox led to the slaughter, enchained by the wantonness of his own blind desire (that) he entered the vile brothel of this whore without fear, 'not knowing that he is drawn like a fool to bonds till the arrow pierce his liver: as if a bird should make haste to the snare' [Prov. VII. 23].

LVIII. It is a disgrace to mention the shameless impudence of vanity and the sleek insolence of stupidity which [vanity and insolence] are to be discerned in those of both sexes, not only those living cloistered under the discipline of the monastery but even the ecclesiastics whose clerical sphere of duty is under the control of a bishop, contrary to the decrees of canon law and of the norm of the regular life: which (*scil.* vanity and insolence) are adopted for one purpose only, that the bodily figure may be adorned with forbidden ornaments and charming decorations, and that the physical appearance may be glamorized [p. 318] in every part and every limb. This sort of glamorization for either sex consists in fine linen shirts, in scarlet or blue tunics, in necklines and sleeves embroidered with silk; their shoes are trimmed with red-dyed leather; the hair of their forelocks and the curls at their temples are crimped with a curling-iron; dark-grey veils for the head give way to bright and coloured head-dresses, which are sewn with interlacings of ribbons and hang down as far as the ankles. Fingernails are sharpened after the manner of falcons or hawks, or more properly, to the likeness of the night-owl, whom the innate need for food naturally incites to pursue and attack with cruelty small mice and birds with the curved trident of their feet, and the ravenous grappling-hook of their talons.

But, so that I am not accused by the perverse odium of envy or am disparaged by the derision of wicked insults, as a result of the celebrated insolence of these wanton people and the well-known impertinence of the undisciplined, who prefer to be negligently glossed over than to be mildly reproved, a tirade of this sort should not be further prolonged; rather, it should be more speedily terminated with an appropriate conclusion so that, while I am seeking the poultice of medication for the festering wounds of the impudent, I don't experience the stiff scourge of insults nor the virulent whips of harsh invective, fiercely inflicted by my rivals! And nevertheless I am not greatly concerned, however jaundiced, in their fashion, they grow at the proponent of the truth and however vehemently they howl against the persecutor of their swollen vanity, since the wounds inflicted by love are better than the kisses of hatred. For the blue bruisings of a faithful friend are to be borne more lightly than the deceptive adulation of an enemy; whence an epigram is formed:

The tongue of a flatterer heaps up the evil of a sinner,
And binds the man seduced by praise in guilt.
[Prosper of Aquitaine, *Epigr.* LXXXVIII. 1–2]

And further on, he says,

Rather let the voice of a reproving friend be free
So that it won't allow blind venom to creep in his entrails.
[*ibid.*, 5–6]

Accordingly, I think that in general the indulgence of mercy should be obtained from everyone without difficulty, since the harshness of my words in reproof has not distressed anyone in particular. For the common generality of the many ought not rightly to be censured where the particular characteristics of individuals [p. 319] cannot be blamed; for indeed, genus and species, that is to say, the general and the particular, differ a good deal from each other. But as I was about to speak of the glory of intact virginity, I began to harangue un-

128

necessarily about the covering of garments—almost superfluously, since I have decided to discourse only on the renown of chastity, insofar as the freely given grace of God assists, abandoning for a little while the occupation with other things.

For every privilege of pure virginity is preserved only in the fortress of the free mind rather than being contained in the restricted confines of the flesh; and it is beneficially safeguarded by the inflexible judgment of the free will, rather than being diminished out of existence by the enforced servitude of the body. Whence Augustine of Africa, the bishop of Hippo Regis, declares in an elegant sentence of prose, saying, 'Thus the sanctity of the body is not lost provided that the sanctity of the soul remains, even if the body is overcome, just as the sanctity of the body *is* lost if the purity of the soul is violated, even if the body is intact' [*De Civit. Dei* I. 18]. Prosper of Aquitaine sweetened this (statement) into lines and half-lines of verse in his honeyed epigrams, saying:

The unimpaired mind loses nothing in a violated body,
The wounds of the flesh do not stain it, if it's unwilling;
Nor does the unengaged will take on the guilt of the deed:
It's a greater sin to will a crime than to suffer it;
Thus all (sins) revert to the depths of the heart
So that often the soul is guilty without the flesh,
Since it alone conceives and inwardly performs with invisible movements
That which is withheld from the untouched body.

[*Epigr.* LI]

Finally, the aforesaid bishop of the Africans states, 'Virginity of the flesh is an intact body; virginity of the mind is an uncorrupted faith' [*Enarr in Ps. CXLVII*, 19]. Likewise Prosper:

Virginity of the flesh exists when the body is intact,
Virginity of the soul is inviolate faith.
Without this, no concern for corporeal purity is of avail;
But devoutness of mind increases either boon.

[*Epigr.* LXXVI]

LIX. Therefore, with the little book of most sublime virginity set forth—although not remarkably polished—my pen now seeks an end and the course of my writings must be terminated, since the illustrious orator *[p. 320]* writes, 'A time to keep silence, and a time to speak' [Eccl. III. 71]. For I thought that no other little present would be more pleasing and more acceptable to virgins of Christ, than that the rewards of chastity be revealed to the chaste and the benefits of purity be published to the pure. I confess to your kindness, that I have not been able to write this little work, even though it's very small, and send it to you as quickly as you wished, since I have been weighed down with the burden of pastoral care and overwhelmed with the weight of worldly business, (and) because the demanding responsibilities of ecclesiastical administration did not allow any space of undisturbed peace and a leisured interval for writing, and the noisy bustle of practical matters interrupted it. For the leisure of secluded quietude and the remoteness of private solitude abundantly equip authors with copious material for writing; just as, on the contrary, the verbose loquacity of chatterers and the troublesome business of worldly affairs, which the apostle of the Church ordered to be dealt with by those of little account, rob one of it by force. For I have not presumed to use that method of dictating to clerks taking shorthand notes and copying scribes, after the manner of Origen, the renowned teacher of the Greeks, who at the beginning of the third *lustrum* [i.e. his eleventh year] had perfectly completed nearly all the disciplines of learning, that is, arithmetic, geometry, music, astronomy, astrology and mechanics, (while still) on the threshold of puberty.

For these reasons, therefore, the reply due to your letters was delayed as if by a certain obstacle of procrastination, (letters) which accused the interest on my promises of being unpaid as yet, particularly, as I said, (because) the distractions of various business affairs were weighing down the neck of a tired mind with the heavy burden of their load. Through this lingering delay it has happened that the promised recopying of the manuscript has been protracted over so long an interval of time. And so the leaky bark of my weak intelligence, shaken by the whirlwind of a dire tempest, even though the arms of the oarsmen were labouring, attains belatedly the hoped-for port of silence. But nevertheless the enterprise of rusticity, sustained by the heavenly protection of Christ, trusts confidently that the canvas of my sailyards, swelling with favourable gusts of wind, has sailed safely across, with the rigging intact, through the Scylla of solecism and the Charybdis of colloquialism [p. 321], and similarly has not blenched at foundering on the rocks of labdacism [i.e. the intrusion of l-sounds into correct speech] or the dangerous whirlpools of motacism [i.e. intrusive m-sounds], which grimly drive those who are caught without the helmsmanship of grammarians to the shipwreck of error.

LX. Henceforth, just as I have attempted to honour the glory of incorrupt virginity with applause in my rhetorical narratives, in the same way—if this fleshly prison of the soul does not first pass away, prey to the increasing violence of the Fates, as they say, and the stiff repose of the Parcae and the iron sleep of death do not retard the fluttering of my eyelids—I shall try with artistry to adorn the renown of this same chastity, with Christ's co-operation, in the heroic measures

130

of hexameter verse, and, as if the rhetorical foundation-stones were now laid and the walls of prose were built, so I shall—trusting in heavenly support—build a sturdy roof with trochaic slates and dactylic tiles of metre. However, remember that I have pledged the promised little gift of the following composition in no other way—lest the sluggish intelligence of my humble self which, just like a fire covered over with glowing embers of ash, will dwindle in cooling tepor if it is not relit with the tinder of inquiry and writing—but that you deign to stimulate (me) with just as many repeated letters written as you were good enough to resolutely elicit the preceding text of this little book with, which is not arranged in the polished eloquence of sophistication. For I shall not strive to weary myself with these laborious tasks, sweating in vain under the burden of the subsequent composition, unless I find out that the style of the preceding work was pleasing to your intelligence, particularly since the elegance of metrical beauty and the eloquence of rhetorical disquisition differ as much from each other as sweet new wine is different from heady mead.

Meanwhile, I have set out thus far the beauty of comely virginity and the lovely countenance of chastity, and have painted them with the various hues of their virtue, as if with the colours of flowers, just as artists of portraits [p. 322] of the nobility and painters of royal personages are accustomed to adorn their images with gilded flakes of metal and to decorate the most beautiful features of their bodies with forged ornamentation, when nevertheless these same artists are usually ugly and contemptible by the clumsy nature of their bodies, and it is the royal icon painted with its ornamented wreath which is the subject of praise, not the despicable person of the painter which is revered. I think that the bishop of the apostolic see [i.e. Gregory the Great] was speaking of this when he said, 'I, a loathsome painter, have painted a beautiful man; and I who am still tossed on the waves of sin direct others to the shore of perfection' [Reg. past., 4]

Well then, soldiers of Christ: let the welcome reward for my present little work be the frequently conferred exchange of your prayers, and let the mainstay of my sweat and labour be the support (given by) your intercession, so that I, who seem to vacillate shakily and uncertainly in the condition of my own merits and the weakness of my faith, may deserve to be sustained blessedly and fixedly, borne up on the stable column of your patronage; and may the potent assistance of your merits kindly sustain, with its benign mercy, me, whom a sad burden of sin weighs down with a heavy load of faults and misdeeds, so that when in the holy gathering the venerable throng of the monastic army shall unanimously offer on bended knees the rich sacrifice of prayers to the creator of all things, He may deign to have remembrance of my contemptible person in accordance with what your devout prayers shall have promised; so that, too, my prayer may be directed towards you as you pray, just as, according to the maxim of the Psalmist [Psalm. CXL. 2], incense is burned in the sight of the divine majesty, which is represented by the lifting up of outstretched hands and is compared to the evening sacrifice! Whence the holy offspring of the Lord's aunt [i.e. St James], the first bishop of Helia [i.e. Jerusalem], when the splendour of the Gospel was dawning and the radiance of eternal light was growing red, said, 'Pray one for another, that you may be saved'; and he immediately added: 'For the continual prayer of a just man availeth much' [Iac. V. 16]. Since, indeed, frequent prayer is thought to be exactly like a lofty citadel and an unassailable fortress against the poisoned darts of envious persons, let the gracious [p. 323] Trinity—the one substance of the deity and the three-fold subsistence of its persons, controlling the monarchy of the entire universe from the lofty summit of heaven—deign to watch continually over your blessedness as you pray for me!

Farewell, you flowers of the Church, monastic sisters, scholarly pupils, pearls of Christ, jewels of Paradise, and participants in the celestial homeland! AMEN.

THE LETTERS OF ALDHELM

TRANSLATED BY MICHAEL HERREN

Introduction to the LETTERS of ALDHELM

Twelve of the thirteen letters printed by Ehwald (three of which are addressed *to* Aldhelm) are undoubtedly genuine. Only Letter XIII, addressed to Wynberht, has been seriously questioned (cf. Ehwald, p. 502). According to William of Malmesbury (p. 196), we have only a portion of Aldhelm's numerous letters, and those that we have have been 'truncated by the carelessness of our predecessors'. Letters I to XII, then, are the best evidence we possess for Aldhelm's life and deserve close attention.

Letters II, III, IX, X, XI, XII and XIII are preserved by William alone and are only excerpts. Letters IV, VI, VII and VIII are preserved only in Codex Vindobonensis 751, and seem to be complete. Only Letter I, which also seems to be complete, is preserved by both William and the Vienna manuscript. The famous Letter to Heahfrith (No. V) has a completely separate manuscript tradition, which will be discussed below, p. 143.

The formulas used by Aldhelm in his subscriptions to refer to himself are not reliable indicators of ecclesiastical office, or the lack of it, as Ehwald implies in places. Only in Letter XIII, whose genuineness is suspect, do we find the formula *servus servorum Dei*, the mark of episcopal office.[1] The phrase *extremus servorum Dei* of Letter XI may or may not be intended as its equivalent. Specific use of the title *abbas* is found only in Letters IV and VIII—letters wherein Aldhelm is employing priestly authority in ecclesiastical matters. Aldhelm is addressed by the title *abbas* in Letter VII and by *archimandrita* (= *abbas*) in Letter IX. Elsewhere, we find *bernaculus* (= *vernaculus*) *supplex* in Letters I, II and III, of which only Letter I can be assigned with any certainty to the period preceding the abbacy. *Exiguus in domino* is used in Letter V, when Aldhelm was almost certainly abbot.

Ehwald was probably right in stating that the recipient of this letter was Leutherius (Leuthere), bishop of the West Saxons from 670–6, not Hæddi, who inherited the see on Leuthere's death. William of Malmesbury (p. 195) assumes Hæddi to be the *destiné*, but he omits the entire inscription preserved by Codex Vindobonensis 751. Unfortunately, that inscription deletes the name of the recipient. The letter is addressed to a bishop (*fateor, o beatissime antistes*), but all the evidence points to a date before 676, that is, before Hæddi assumed the episcopacy at Winchester. Aldhelm appears to be writing from Kent, where he was engaged in studies (described in the letter) under Hadrian. Most critics assign Aldhelm's stay at Canterbury to 670–2, which is probably correct, for reasons which will be advanced in the discussions of Letters II and IV. The arguments in favour of Leuthere as recipient are as follows:

(1) The inscription of MS Vindobonensis 751 refers to the recipient as *post deum peculiari patrono*. Leuthere, if we can trust William of Malmesbury (p. 231), was responsible for establishing Aldhelm as abbot of Malmesbury. William (p. 189) also quotes a grant by Leuthere to Aldhelm (see Appendix II, p. 173), assigning Malmesbury to Aldhelm and his successors in perpetuity. Even though the charter in question is patently a forgery, it may well preserve some authentic tradition concerning patronage bestowed by Leuthere upon Aldhelm. Since the letter shows Aldhelm to be situated at Canterbury (670–2), the date of its composition falls within Leuthere's episcopacy (670–6).

(2) Aldhelm mentions his desire to spend Christmas with the brethren (presumably at Malmesbury), 'and afterwards, if life is our companion, to enjoy the affable presence of your Goodness'. At the end of the letter the writer begs his recipient: 'Greet in Christ the entire throng of my companions'. Such a request would normally be made of a bishop only if his see included the territory in which the monastery was situated. The abbey at Malmesbury was in the see of the West Saxons, with its seat at Winchester. (For this reason the proposal of Wilfrid as recipient can be safely ruled out: Wilfrid was bishop of York during this period).

The letter is of considerable interest because it provides an eyewitness account of the curriculum of the school of Theodore and Hadrian at Canterbury. The nearly contemporary account of Bede (*HE* IV. 2) tells us:

And because both of them [*scil.* Theodore and Hadrian] were extremely learned in sacred and secular literature, they attracted a crowd of students into whose minds they daily poured the streams of wholesome learning. They gave their hearers instruction not only in the books of the holy Scripture but also in the art of metre, astronomy, and ecclesiastical computation. As evidence of this, some of their students still survive who know Latin and Greek just as well as their native tongue.

Aldhelm goes into some detail regarding his study of the metrical art. He also discusses computation and astronomy, which appears in his description to be identical, or nearly so, with astrology. Moreover, to these he adds the study of Roman law, but gives no details. Interestingly, Aldhelm is silent on the subject of Greek; see the discussion above, p. 8.

Letter II: To Hadrian

The excerpt of the letter to Hadrian is preserved only by William of Malmesbury (p. 189). The phrase *rudis infantiae praeceptori* of the inscription was a source of confusion to William and to subsequent students of Aldhelm (see Ehwald, p. xi). William has Aldhelm studying with Hadrian in early childhood, with Máeldub in adolescence, then again with Hadrian. Indeed, the letter encourages such a reconstruction, as it speaks of a three-year interruption of the relationship between Hadrian and Aldhelm (*ante triennium discedens a Cantia sequestrabar*) and of two periods of instruction (implied in *iterum*), one of which involved 'elementary education' (*post prima elementa*). Hadrian did not arrive in England until late in 669 or 670, having been detained in France on account of the suspicions of Ebroin (*HE* IV. 1). Aldhelm may have been over thirty years old in 670 (above, p. 6). The phrase *rudis infantia* must therefore be taken metaphorically, as most students of Aldhelm are now aware.[2] Aldhelm, in various writings, tends to down-grade his earlier education, possibly at the hands of Irish teachers. Note here the effective slur in his remarks to Leuthere: 'What should be said about the method of calculation, since intense disputation of computation has bent the neck of (my) mind so much that I regarded all my past labour of study (as being) of little value, when I thought all along that I knew the secret compartments of that study, and —to cite the phrase of blessed Jerome, since the opportunity has presented itself—"Shall I begin again to be a student, who thought myself learned?" '

It is likely that Aldhelm studied with Hadrian between 670 and 672, as he may already have been abbot in Malmesbury by 673. (For this departure from the traditional dating of the abbacy, see the arguments presented in the discussion of Letter IV). If we therefore accept Aldhelm's statement that nearly three years have elapsed since he was last with Hadrian, the date of the letter is *c.*675. Ehwald thought that this letter was probably written before Aldhelm became abbot. There is nothing in the body of the letter to support that supposition. Nor should one be misled by the formula *bernaculus supplex* in the inscription as an indication of lowly status, as we have suggested earlier (p. 136).

Letter III: To Wihtfrith

This letter is also preserved only by William, who makes reference (p. 188) to another letter by Aldhelm to someone of the same name. All that can be known of this Wihtfrith is that he was a student of Aldhelm, on the evidence of the writer's phrase *tuum discipulatum*. Whether he was a religious or a layman is not entirely clear. Æthilwald, also a student of Aldhelm and author of certain of the *Carmina Rhythmica* (printed by Ehwald, pp. 519–37), in a letter to Aldhelm (No. VII), refers to Wihtfrith as *meo tuoque clienti Wihtfrido*. *Cliens* in Insular Latin often means nothing more than 'one who is a member of the same monastic community'.[3] It is therefore reasonable to suppose that both Æthilwald and Wihtfrith were students of Aldhelm at Malmesbury.

The date of the letter to Wihtfrith cannot be established with any accuracy, but it almost certainly falls within Aldhelm's abbacy; otherwise, Æthilwald could scarcely refer to Wihtfrith as *cliens* to himself and Aldhelm. We can derive no help for dating the letter from the recipient's proposed journey to Ireland. The emigration of the English to Ireland both for religious and educational purposes had begun in the middle of the seventh century, if we can trust Bede (*HE* III. 27), and continued into the eighth century, for Bede tells us that there was still a community of English monks at Mayo in his own time (*HE* IV. 4).[4] In other words, we can say no more than that the letter was composed between 673 and 706.

Unlike the letter to Heahfrith (No. V), wherein Aldhelm asserts England's educational claims over those of the Irish and questions the wisdom of sojourning in that country for the purpose of self-improvement, the letter to Wihtfrith warns of specific moral hazards indigenous to that country, specifically, an overweaning interest in classical pagan mythology and the allurements of bawdy houses. (The one quite naturally leads to the other, one might infer). One would very much like to know the basis of Aldhelm's information regarding the former peril. There is little evidence, from Latin literature composed in Ireland, that the Irish took much interest in the Latin classics or in classical mythology in the latter part of the seventh century. Irish interests lay chiefly in theological and exegetical studies. The study of the liberal arts in Ireland, as far as one can gather, was based on the use of grammars and compilations, such as the *Etymologiae* of Isidore.[5] It is true that there are several Vergilian echoes in the *Hisperica Famina* and in Adomnán's *Vita S. Columbae*, and at least one in the writings of Virgilius Maro Grammaticus,[6] but it cannot be ascertained whether these were derived first-hand or from intermediaries. In any case, Aldhelm knew and quoted more lines from ancient writers than can be found in the entire corpus of seventh-century Hiberno-Latin writings that we possess. On that basis, it would seem difficult to justify Aldhelm's cavils.

Aldhelm specifically states that the tales of antiquity were passed on in Ireland 'through studying and reading'. Is it possible, however, that the stories of classical mythology were passed on *orally*? James Carney has argued that written adaptations of classical tales into Irish may have begun as early as the ninth century.[7] Such a hypothesis would allow for a period of oral development. Most interesting are the 'free versions' of Greek and Roman heroic tales in Irish; W. B. Stanford has recently made a collection of classical influences and 'free versions'.[8] Whatever the answer, Aldhelm's remarks are discomfiting to the sceptics (now in the majority) of the existence of classical learning in seventh-century Ireland.

Letter IV: To Geraint

This letter has special importance not only for our interest in Aldhelm's character and ecclesiastical work, but also for the reconstruction of the dates of events in his life. The letter is preserved only in MS Vindobonensis 751. William was aware of the letter's existence, but complained that it was lost: *cuius doctrinam nescio quod infortunium usibus nostris invidit, gaudio subtraxit* (p. 196); he later blamed the Britons for its destruction (p. 215). Bede (*HE* V. 18) seemed to possess scant knowledge of the work. He tells us:

> For example, Aldhelm, when he was still priest and abbot of the monastery known as Malmesbury, by order of a synod of his own people wrote a remarkable book (*librum*) against the British error of celebrating Easter at the wrong time, and of doing many other things to the detriment of the pure practices and the peace of the Church; by means of this book he led many of the Britons who were subject to the West Saxons to adopt the catholic celebration of the Easter of our Lord.

Bede is misleading in three important respects: (1) Aldhelm wrote a letter, not a book. (2) The letter is addressed specifically to Geruntius, or Geraint, king of Domnonia (i.e. Devon and Cornwall). Bede makes no mention of that fact. (3) Bede tells us that Aldhelm composed the work *iubente synodo suae gentis*. If *suae gentis* is meant to refer specifically to the West Saxons, then it must have been that Bede at no time had the actual work before him. Aldhelm could not have been more explicit. He says: 'Recently when I was present at an episcopal council, where, out of *almost the entirety of Britain*, an innumerable company of the bishops of God came together', etc. The council Aldhelm refers to clearly was national, not local.

Aldhelm states clearly in the inscription to the letter that he holds the office of abbot: *sine meritorum praerogativa abbatis officio functus*. Was there a major synod involving the bishops from all of England that occurred within the period of Aldhelm's abbacy? Hahn proposed that the synod in question was that convoked at Hatfield in 679,[9] but that proposal does not withstand scrutiny, since the Council of Hatfield dealt exclusively with the heresy of Eutyches (Monophysitism) which Theodore wished to prevent (*HE* IV. 17), whereas the council alluded to by Aldhelm dealt with the problems of Church unity and the Easter reckoning. Within the limits usually assigned to Aldhelm's abbacy (675 × 705), it would appear from available evidence that no such council took place.[10] However, the Council of Hertford, which was convened by Theodore in September, 672, dealt precisely with the issues raised by Aldhelm in his letter to Geraint. To cite the relevant portion of the text of the synod (as reported by Bede):

'Beloved brethren, I beseech you, for the fear and love of our Redeemer, that we should all deliberate in common for the benefit of the faith; so that whatever has been decreed and defined by holy fathers of proved worth may be preserved incorrupt by us all'. This and much more I Theodore added on the need to preserve charity and unity in the Church. When I had completed my preliminary discourse, I asked each of them in turn if they were willing to keep the canonical decrees which had been laid down by the fathers in ancient times ... Chapter I: that we all keep Easter Day at the same time, namely on the Sunday after the fourteenth day of the moon of the first month [*HE* IV. 5].

The prologue of Aldhelm's letter is close to the wording of the text of the synod: '... an innumerable company of the bishops of God came together, having assembled for this purpose expressly, that out of concern for the churches and the salvation of souls, the decrees of the canons and the statues of the (Church) Fathers might be discussed by all and maintained in common'. The themes of charity and unity in the Church and the authority of the Fathers run throughout the letter, e.g. '... their fatherly request and wholesome suggestion, that is, respecting the unity of the Catholic Church and the harmony of the Christian religion' (p. 155); and, '... what a departure from the evangelical tradition it is that bishops of Dyfed, on the other side of the strait of the River Severn, glorying in the private purity of their own way of life, detest our communion to such a great extent that they disdain equally to celebrate the divine offices in church with us and to take courses of food at table for the sake of charity' (p. 158). A large portion of the work is devoted to the need for a common Easter, which subject constituted Chapter I of the text of the synod.

There are, admittedly, problems with assigning the letter to so early a date. If the council in question took place in September of 672, then events in Aldhelm's life become quite crammed. Moreover, as we do not hear of Geraint until 710, when, according to the *Anglo-Saxon Chronicle* for that year, he was defeated by Ine of Wessex, we must assume a thirty-eight year *regnum* for him. Finally, it could be argued that any one of the yearly synods convoked after the synod of Hertford (according to a stipulation of Chapter VII of that synod) could have promulgated texts on the unity of the Church and on the Easter observance. Yet these objections can be at least partially rebutted. In the first instance, we need not assume that Aldhelm was already abbot when he attended the synod (although it is not impossible that he was). Aldhelm may have exercised reasonable delay between receiving the command of the bishops to address the Church of Devon and his execution of the command (implied in the word *nuper*), and could have been elected to the abbacy during that interval. To those who would object that Aldhelm would not have been invited to the council unless he was an abbot or bishop, it can be replied that in all probability by 672 Aldhelm's literary skills were well developed and would be in high demand. As to Geraint, we cannot be at all sure of the identification of the recipient of Aldhelm's letter with the king of the same name defeated by Ine.[11] It is interesting that the *Anglo-Saxon Chronicle* calls him only a king of the Britons, whereas Aldhelm specifies that his intended reader is king of Devon and Cornwall. Even if the personages are identical, there is nothing to prevent us from believing that the king defeated (and killed?) in 710 was not already ruling in 672. We learn from Bede that Ine enjoyed a thirty-seven year rule (*HE* V. 7). As to the third objection, it may be replied that it is indeed odd that Bede, who was painstakingly occupied with the differences between the Roman and Celtic parties, would have neglected to report important developments in that area that may have taken place at the yearly episcopal meetings at *Clofesho*. As Bede had no copy of Aldhelm's letter before him and was ignorant of the date of the work, he imputed its authority to a local council. If all this is right, then William's remark (p. 196) that the letter addressed to the Britons constituted Aldhelm's *primum . . . ingenii periculum* is not wide of the truth.

Finally, a word on style as it might affect dating. The Latinity of this letter is not as bombastic and convoluted as that of some of the other letters, notably the letter to Heahfrith. One should not interpret this fact as a sign of 'earliness' or 'lateness' in Aldhelm's composition. Rather, Aldhelm seems to have adopted a more direct prose style for official purposes, i.e. in letters asserting ecclesiastical authority such as the letter to Sigegyth (No. VIII), whereas he employed the 'hermeneutic' style for letters dealing with literary and educational topics, especially those addressed to students and to members of the learned community.

The letter to Geraint shows Aldhelm as a committed partisan of the Roman cause in the continuing struggle between the Roman and Celtic parties. His impassioned defence of Wilfrid (Letter XII) may be at least partially explained by politics, as Wilfrid was the 'victor' of the Synod of Whitby. Aldhelm's journey to Rome was made possibly after the example of Benedict Biscop and Wilfrid, and may have been intended as a statement of his ideals.

Letter V: To Heahfrith

This letter is not part of the collection of letters contained in the Codex Vindobonensis, nor is it quoted by William. Rather, it has a completely separate tradition. Ehwald (pp. 486–7) lists seven manuscripts which contain a text of the letter; it is usually found just preceding or just following the prose version of the *De Virginitate*. The two works were apparently read together in Anglo-Saxon schools as high examples of the 'hermeneutic' style (see above, p. 3).

Ehwald assigns the letter to the period 675 × 690, the limits usually assigned to the beginning of Aldhelm's abbacy and the death of Theodore, who is mentioned as still living in the letter.[12] It seems difficult at first, from internal evidence, to establish the date more precisely. However, there are a few indications that the letter was composed nearer the earlier date. First of all, Aldhelm makes no mention of his own achievements, as he does in the *Epistola ad Acircium* (c. 685 × 695), where he boldly likens himself to Vergil as a transmitter of a higher culture to his people (p. 46). In the present letter, Aldhelm refers with adulation to Theodore and Hadrian as the great lights of the age: 'the luculent likeness, as it were, of the flaming sun and the moon, that is, Theodore . . . mature in the flower of the arts of learning, and his colleague of the same sodality, Hadrian, equally endowed with ineffably pure urbanity' (p. 163). Moreover, Theodore is portrayed as still very active in teaching. Indeed, he is famous for debating the Easter question with his Irish students: '. . . although Theodore . . . be hemmed in by a mass of Irish students . . . when his bow is tensed and arrows are drawn by his powerful hands and arms from the quiver, that is, from the obscure and acute syllogisms of chronography', etc. (p. 163). This strikes one as a reminiscence of the archbishop shortly after his arrival in England. Bede says:

> *Soon* after he arrived, he visited every part of the island where the English peoples lived and was gladly welcomed and listened to by all. He was accompanied everywhere and assisted by Hadrian, as he gave instruction on the ordering of a holy life and the canonical custom of celebrating Easter [*HE* IV. 2].

However, it is hard to envisage Theodore's teaching activity continuing very far into his episcopacy, especially when one considers his advanced age and the grave ecclesiastical problems he faced upon his arrival in England. If we may trust the contemporary evidence of 'Eddius' Stephanus (*Vita S. Wilfridi, c.* XLIII), Theodore in approximately 685 was 'well advanced in years and nearly always in bad health'. A last observation in support of an early date: if Aldhelm rose to support Wilfrid as early as 677—as some evidence suggests (Letter XII and introduction)—he would hardly have been so lavish in his praise of Theodore as he is here.

These bits of evidence, then, would indicate a date of composition not far removed from that of the letter to Hadrian (No. II, *c.* 675). There remains one problem that has stymied efforts of scholars interested in the chronology of Aldhelm's works. At the end of Letter V we find a five-line pastiche, of which the first line has been adapted from a certain Glengus (= a bogus authority cited by Virgilius Maro Grammaticus, the Irish pseudo-grammarian[13]), the last four—in rearranged order— from a section of the *Carmen de Virginitate*. Ehwald (p. 487) assigns the poem to *c.* 686 and therefore the letter to 686 × 690 (cf., however, discussion above, p. 14). But even if he is right about the dating of the *Carmen de Virginitate*, one cannot conclude that the letter is quoting directly from the completed poem. Aldhelm had the habit of recycling his lines, and it is difficult—if not impossible—to determine the order of his compositions by reference to repeated verses. However, the pastiche did have a purpose. Aldhelm wished to exhibit his own skill as a metrician in contrast to the maladroit attempts of the Irish[14] in order to cap the point of his letter: the superiority of English education in his day over Irish.

The problem of the identity of the recipient of the letter has been a subject of speculation and considerable debate from the time of Ussher almost to the present. Perhaps the best survey of the question is to be found in an article by A. S. Cook.[15] Cook rejects, on phonetic grounds, all attempts to identify *Ehfridus* with any of the following: Eadfrith, bishop of Lindisfarne (698–721); Ecgberht, a Northumbrian priest who lived in Ireland (*HE* III. 27, IV. 3, V. 9 and 22); Aldfrith, king of Northumbria; or Ealfrith (= Alfrith), envoy from Wilfrid to Aldfrith. Cook himself proposes Atfrith or Echfrith (= Heahfrith), fifth abbot of Glastonbury (whose abbacy apparently fell during the decade after Aldhelm's death, and who would therefore have been rather younger than Aldhelm). However, Cook's dubious explanation of the -t- in Atfrith as merely graphic undercuts his argument. It seems doubtful that a final solution to the problem will be achieved.

The letter provides us with a little information about Heahfrith. He has just returned from almost six years of study in Ireland ('a course of almost thrice-two years sucking the teat of wisdom'). That he is described as having sojourned in 'the northwest part of the island of Ireland' and as 'visiting the venerable brotherhood of your paternal country' (i.e. the English) argues for the probability that he was situated with the English monks at Mayo for at least part of his stay (cf. *HE* IV. 4).[16] Nonetheless, he was scarcely isolated from Irish influence, as Aldhelm appears to protest. Peregrination of monks and students throughout Ireland in the seventh century is amply attested.[17] Heahfrith at the time of his return has reached young adulthood (implied in Aldhelm's use of *pubertas*). That he intends to embark on his chosen vocation of teaching would indicate that he was in orders.

Aldhelm (p. 162) addresses him as 'your kindly Discipleship'. Heahfrith, therefore, either had been, or was about to be, a student of Aldhelm. The second possibility, in my view, is the likelier. Aldhelm refers to him as having completed his elementary education in Ireland and as one who must still pursue and achieve a position as a teacher (p. 161). This indicates that Heahfrith intends to do his advanced work under Aldhelm. It is clear from several passages that Aldhelm regards him as a student of exceptional promise.

Letter V to Heahfrith is a central document for the study of the cultural relations between England and Ireland in the last quarter of the seventh century. Aldhelm is the leader of a national awakening of the English in the domain of letters. Irish teachers and monks had dominated English education from the early part of the seventh century. Irish contacts with the continent, especially with Spain,[18] greatly stimulated Latin studies, particularly in the fields of grammar, biblical exegesis, and theology. (If we can trust Aldhelm, the Irish also studied geometry and physics!) One could fairly say that the Irish were at least a generation advanced over the English in most educational areas. However, with the visits of Benedict Biscop to Rome (beginning c. 652–3), things began to change. The defeat of the Irish party at Whitby in 664 was crucial to this development in that the control of important monastic centres began to pass into the hands of the English. A great advance came about c. 670 with the establishment (or revival) of the school at Canterbury by Theodore and Hadrian. Yet fashions change slowly. Several years after the reinstatement of the Canterbury school, Aldhelm was to complain: 'Why, I ask, is Ireland, whither assemble the thronging students by the fleet-load, exalted with a sort of ineffable privilege?' (p. 163). Apparently English students flocked to Ireland not only to learn, but the brightest among them must have been invited to teach there as well, as Aldhelm devotes a long plea to Heahfrith to pursue his vocation in his own country: ' "Keep them [*scil.* the waters] to thyself alone neither let strangers be partakers with thee" [Prov. V. 15–17]'.

Aldhelm's letter—a *tour de force*—goes beyond an attempt to establish equality of the English to the Irish in educational matters. Rather it does not hesitate to claim superiority for the English. Theodore excels the Irish in all the subtleties of the Paschal computus. And, as we noted earlier, Aldhelm—thanks to his training by Hadrian in Latin metrics—surpasses the *soi-disant* poets of Ireland who are capable only of accentual poetry. Finally, the convoluted sentences and bombastic vocabulary, sustained throughout the whole of the letter, are clearly intended to show that the English are not second-best to the Irish in *copia verborum*.[19]

Letter VI: Anonymous Student to Aldhelm

This letter is preserved only in the Codex Vindobonensis. Ehwald assigns the authorship to an Irishman presumably on the basis of the words 'because you [*scil.* Aldhelm] were nourished by a certain holy man of our race'. Clearly the author was not English, but we cannot take the words of themselves as evidence that he was Irish. It is possible that the 'certain holy man' referred to Hadrian, thereby making the writer Italian or African (see above, p. 6). It is at least a possibility that the student learned of Aldhelm's eloquence during the abbot's stay in Rome—an event mentioned in the letter.

Against that speculation can be raised objections based on proximity and style. It seems far less likely that an Italian would journey the great distance to England to improve his Latinity than that an Irishman would cross the channel, or—in the more plausible case—come to Malmesbury from some Irish settlement in England or Scotland. If William of Malmesbury is to be trusted, we know of other Irishmen in England who submitted their writings to Aldhelm for his criticism.[20] We hear nothing of Italians (or Africans) studying in England in this period. (In any case, our author is not writing *from* his home country, as he speaks of sending 'messengers and horses' to Aldhelm to collect a book). Moreover, at least one passage smacks of *Hibernitas*, namely, *ne haec fastidium in tua mente creet*, which is reminiscent of a formula in the *Hisperica Famina*: 'Caetera non explico famine scemata,/ne doctoreis suscitauero fastidium castris' (A 529–30). On the whole, then, the evidence seems to favour Irish authorship. The 'certain holy man of our race' *might* refer to Máeldub, but one must remain cautious about such equations. Aldhelm himself is curiously silent about the mentor so often alleged for him.[21]

The dating of the letter scarcely admits of a solution. If *vario flore litterarum* is intended to refer to either or both versions of the *De Virginitate*,[22] then the letter was written after the publication of that (those) work(s). Unfortunately, as has been argued above (p. 14), there is no sure way of dating the treatises. The mention of the journey to Rome—though invaluable for establishing the authenticity of the alleged deed—is of no help here, since there are reasons for doubting William's claim that Aldhelm went to Rome during the papacy of Sergius.[23] It is perhaps most probable that the letter was directed to Aldhelm while he was still abbot and teacher at Malmesbury, but there is really nothing to prevent us from believing that Aldhelm continued to write and teach during his episcopacy.

Letter VII: Æthilwald to Aldhelm
Letter XI: Aldhelm to Æthilwald

Letter VII is preserved only by the Codex Vindobonensis; Letter XI, only in William. Ehwald here, at Letter XI, and again in the preface to the *Carmina Rhythmica* (p. 522), identifies Æthilwald with Æthilbald, king of the Mercians (716–57). The identification rests upon no firmer evidence than that King Æthilbald received a letter from Boniface warning him of youthful excesses in a fashion reminiscent of the letter sent by Aldhelm to his student on the same subject.[24] However, the identification is impossible on the grounds that -w- and -b- are not interchangeable in Old English. All that we know with certainty about this Æthilwald is that he was the author of some of the *Carmina*

Rhythmica (Nos. ii–v), printed by Ehwald (pp. 528–37). The poem addressed to Wihtfrith entitled 'De Transmarini Itineris Peregrinatione', which is mentioned in Letter VII, is preserved in the Codex Vindobonensis and printed by Ehwald (pp. 528–33).[25]

Letter VII, to Aldhelm, cannot be dated with any certainty. The inscription shows only that Aldhelm was not yet bishop. Letter XI, from Aldhelm, *might just* fall into the episcopacy, if the phrase *extremus servorum Dei* is to be taken as the equivalent of the episcopal formula *servus servorum Dei*. At the time of composition of Æthilwald's letter the relationship between the two men has been of some duration, since the disciple claims that his mentor has brought him 'from the very cradles of tenderest infancy . . . as far as vigorous adolescence'. Even allowing for hyperbole (gleaned, no doubt, from Aldhelm's own hoard of metaphors), Æthilwald's formative years (or portions of them) were spent under Aldhelm's tutelage. The probability, then, is that the letter was written after the mid-point of Aldhelm's abbacy. Since Aldhelm's letter to Æthilwald is not a direct reply to Letter VII, one can neither establish the order of the letters nor the time elapsed between their composition.

Ethilwald's letter is interesting, not only because it attests Aldhelm's reputation as a teacher, but because it also shows the thoroughness with which Æthilwald had mastered the intricacies of Aldhelm's style. Thus began in Aldhelm's lifetime the fondness for a type of preciousness that characterized much of Anglo-Latin prose for three centuries: long and convoluted sentences, love of superlatives and much pleonasm, fondness for grecisms (*epimenia, sofia*), archaism (*pedetemptim, vorsu*), abstractions used concretely (*numerositatibus*), and words used in novel senses (*caraxare* < χαράσσω, 'to write').

Letter VIII: To Sigegyth

This letter is found only in the Codex Vindobonensis. Sigegyth is not one of the nuns whom Aldhelm addressed by name in his preface to the prose *De Virginitate*. She is apparently known only from this letter. The inscription of the letter shows clearly that it is to be dated to the abbacy. The simpler Latin style found here and in Letter IV would appear to characterize Aldhelm's 'official' correspondence (above, p. 143).

Letter IX: Cellanus to Aldhelm

Letter X: Aldhelm to Cellanus

This fascinating correspondence is preserved only in the fragments quoted by William. It is a great pity that we no longer possess copies of the originals. The brevity of William's selections makes the correspondence difficult to assess. Cellanus's use of the term *archimandrita* reveals that the letter must be assigned to the abbacy, probably in the latter half, when Aldhelm's literary fame would have been well established.

Cellanus was an Irish monk of *Perrona*, or Péronne, situated in Picardy on the Somme. Péronne was the foundation of Eorcenwald; its church became the resting place of St Fursa (*HE* III. 19) and became known as *Perrona Scottorum* on account of the numbers of Irish monks who flocked there. It lasted until 880, when it was destroyed by the Vikings. Certain Latin verses have been ascribed to this Cellanus.[26]

An ambiguity in Cellanus's Latin presents a problem in the interpretation of the inscription. What is the meaning of *reperienti in oris (Saxonum), quod nonnulli cum laboribus et sudoribus in alieno aere vix lucrantur?* Bolton translates—quite plausibly—'discoverer in the land of the Saxons of that which some in foreign parts hardly obtain by labour and effort' (*Anglo-Latin Literature I*, p. 99). But the phrase could just as well mean 'discovering on the shores of the Saxons *that* some scarcely benefit', etc. If taken that way, might not Cellanus's remark be a reference to the letter to Heahfrith, which might already have begun to be circulated with Aldhelm's compositions? If so, Cellanus's phrase could be taken as a gibe.

Gibe or not, it is clear that Cellanus holds Aldhelm in high esteem. Copies of Aldhelm's books (probably the two books of the *De Virginitate*; see above, p. 14) had reached northeastern France within the author's own lifetime and had been deemed praiseworthy by the Irish scholarly community. The letter also provides evidence, followed by William (p. 344), that Aldhelm wrote *sermones* ('discourses' or 'sermons'?), which have not survived.

Aldhelm's reply, with its allusion to himself as *tantillum homunculum* and his reference to Péronne as *famoso et florigero* may strike one as ironic. Compare the similar praise in similar words heaped upon Ireland and its scholars in the letter to Heahfrith (p. 161), which is later revoked! Despite the paucity of our fragments, there is some evidence to suggest that the exchange of letters constituted yet another episode in the literary war between Aldhelm and Irish scholars towards the end of the seventh century.

Letter XII: To the Abbots of Wilfrid

This letter is preserved only by William and is an excerpt. There probably was a lengthy inscription in Aldhelmian fashion; the letter may have been considerably longer. William has preserved the introduction to the piece (compare the letter to Geraint for length and structure).

For the student of English ecclesiastical history, this fragment must be the most interesting of all the remains of Aldhelm's correspondence, for it plunges our subject into the thick of seventh-century ecclesiastical politics. The act of affiliation with Wilfrid's cause may have led to adverse consequences for Aldhelm, as Wilfrid was easily the most hated and feared man of his day in the English Church.[27] Wilfrid's career is well documented: a *Vita S. Wilfridi* by 'Eddius' Stephanus, his younger contemporary, and two rather long chapters by Bede (*HE* IV. 13 and V. 19). It requires little recounting here. On the negative side, we need only mention Wilfrid's difficulty in regaining his see upon his return from Gaul where he had sought episcopal consecration; his expulsion from Northumbria and his see by Ecgfrith, with the apparent co-operation of Theodore; his stormy relations with Aldfrith and a second expulsion from Northumbria; his lack of success at the Synod of Austerfield; the failure of his journeys to Rome to improve his situation at home. In the end, Wilfrid was reduced from virtual complete control of the Northumbrian Church to abbacy of his two earliest acquisitions: Ripon and Hexham. Yet despite Wilfrid's trials and setbacks, he scored several outstanding successes in his career. He brought England firmly into the orbit of the Roman party at Whitby; he missionized Frisia and—on another occasion—Sussex; he built and decorated churches and monasteries.

What was Aldhelm's connection to this powerful and complex figure and why did he intervene on his behalf? We can only guess, as Aldhelm's career is poorly documented, apart from the testimony of the letters. We have no record of a meeting of the two churchmen. But it must be remembered that the two were not far apart in age;[28] they were both passionate partisans of the Roman Church and hostile to Celtic influences; they were both proud men—Wilfrid in the political sphere, Aldhelm in the world of learning. Neither displayed much taste for compromise.

When did Aldhelm's defence of Wilfrid take place? Historians have argued for each of the three occasions when Wilfrid set out to seek aid in Rome (677, 691 and 702)—each occurring after an expulsion or political setback. Ehwald makes a case for a period in Aldhelm's episcopacy, on the ground that Aldhelm would not have wished to offend Theodore in 677, or Aldfrith on the other two occasions. But that theory can safely be rejected, since in the year of Aldhelm's episcopacy (706), the quarrel ensuing between Wilfrid and Berhtwald (and the other bishops) after the Synod of Austerfield had been patched up, and we have no further news of Wilfrid (notwithstanding his miracles) from that time until his death in 709. Nor can we assign the letter to the period following immediately after Austerfield (702), since the council, though depriving Wilfrid of episcopal office, did not impose exile, but required that he confine himself to Ripon ('Eddius', *Vita S. Wilfridi*, c.XLVII). Aldhelm's letter states specifically that Wilfrid is to go into exile.

What of 691, when Aldfrith banished Wilfrid from Northumbria over territorial and jurisdictional disputes ('Eddius', c.XLV)? But in this case Aldfrith did not—or could not—strip Wilfrid of ecclesiastical rank. Such an act could have been attempted only by an archbishop (and there was a vacancy at Canterbury between 690 and 692), or by a synod, of which we have no record. It therefore seems most likely that Aldhelm wrote in 677, the year of the outbreak of the troubles between Wilfrid and his clergy and the combined forces of Ecgfrith and Theodore. The mention of 'transmarine country' in Aldhelm's letter also accords well with the first expulsion, since Wilfrid, according to 'Eddius' (c. XXVI), chose to go to Frisia, whereas in 691 he sought solace in Mercia, and in 702 was not banished.

Letter XIII: To Wynberht

This excerpt is preserved only by William. Its genuineness has been doubted (cf. Ehwald, p. 502). If genuine, it dates to the episcopacy, as the writer uses the episcopal formula *servus servorum Dei.* Wynberht may be identical with the man of that name who was abbot of *Nhutscelle* (probably Nursling, Hants.) and who was the teacher of Boniface.

THE LETTERS OF ALDHELM

LETTER 1: TO LEUTHERE [?]¹

[p. 475] To the most reverend Lord (Leuthere), venerable for every effort in virtue and, after God, my special patron, (Aldhelm), humble servant of your Holiness, (wishes) salvation in the Lord.

[p. 476] I declare, O most blessed bishop, that I decided some time ago, if the course of events and the swift mutations of time permitted, to celebrate joyfully in the same place the approaching feast of our Lord's longed-for birth, in the company of the brethren, and afterwards, if life is our companion, to enjoy the affable presence of your Goodness. But because we were delayed by various obstacles (and) hindrances, as the bearer of the present (letters) will propound more fully in oral delivery, we could not achieve that aim; therefore, I beg you, grant me pardon on account of that hardship.

Nor should these small intervals of time be prolonged in the midst of study (and) reading by him, who, kindled with keen sagacity for the study of Roman laws, will examine the laws to the marrow and will scrutinize all the secrets of the jurisconsults to their innermost recesses, and what is much more involved and complicated than these, to wit, *[p. 477]* to distinguish among the hundred types of metres² according to their divisions of feet, and to survey the musical modulations of song along the straight path of syllables: the more the inextricable obscurity of this subject is put forward to studious readers, the smaller the number of scholars becomes.

But the narrow confines of the epistle do not permit me to deliberate on these topics along a broad course of verbiage, that is, as to how the hidden ornaments of this metrical art are grouped according to letters, words, feet, poetic figures, verses, accents, and rhythms; also, as to how the affective part of the sevenfold discipline varies, that is, *acefalos, lagaros, procilios,* along with the rest;³ which verses are measured as

152

monoscemi, which *pentascemi*, which *decascemi* according to a definite counting of feet, and how catalectic or brachicatalectic or hypercatalectic verses are estimated according to skilful argument. These matters, in my opinion, and matters like them, will be able in no wise to be apprehended in a brief interval of time or in an instantaneous stroke.

What should be said about the method of calculation, since intense disputation of computation has bent the neck of (my) mind so much that I regarded all my past labour of study (as being) of little value, when I thought all along that I knew the secret compartments of that study, and, to cite the phrase of blessed Jerome, as the opportunity has presented itself: 'Shall I begin again to be a student, who thought myself learned?' [*Praef. ad versionem Danielis*, PL IX, 1354]. And so finally, sustained by heavenly grace, I learned the most difficult proofs of the subject and the reckonings of calculations, which they call fractions, through persistent study. Furthermore, with regard to the zodiac, the circle of the twelve signs that rotates at the peak of heaven, I think one should be silent lest an obscure and profound subject, which requires a lengthy kind of explanation of its matter, [p. 478] be defamed and cheapened, should it be explicated by a paltry train of interpretation, especially since the skill of the astrological art and the complex reckoning of the horoscope require the laborious investigation of the expert.[4]

Therefore, dearest father, we have touched on these matters carefully and cautiously, not (because we are) enticed by the garrulous chatter of verbosity, but that you might know that so many hidden matters of subjects cannot be accurately understood without the application of frequent and extended concentration. Greet in Christ the entire throng of my companions from the youngest to the eldest, whom I beseech and adjure through the goodness of Christ, to pour forth prayers to the Lord for me who am oppressed by the weight of sin and the burden of guilt.

LETTER II: TO HADRIAN

[p. 478] To the most reverend father Hadrian, venerable teacher of my rough ineloquence,[5] Aldhelm, servant of the family of Christ and suppliant fosterchild of your Goodness, (wishes) salvation.

I confess, my dearest friend—whom I embrace with the grace of pure love—that after I was separated from your intimate fellowship on leaving Kent almost three years ago, my inconsiderable self yearned until now with burning desire for your company, so that I meditated for a long time, just as in prayer, how I might accomplish this purpose, if the course of events and vicissitudes of the times permitted; and had not various obstacles (and) hindrances held me back—I was especially prevented by a debilitating illness in the body that burned my wasting limbs to the marrow, on account of which I was previously forced to return home, when I was with you the second time after the elementary instruction . . .

LETTER III: TO WIHTFRITH

[p. 479] To Master Wihtfrith, who is to be cherished venerably and to be venerated pleasurably, Aldhelm, humble servant in Christ, (sends his wishes for) eternal salvation.

It has come to my attention from the reports of newsmongers regarding the intentions of your Charity, that you have decided to undertake, with the Lord as your pilot, a journey across the sea, since you have been inflamed by a keenness for study. And therefore, as you sail towards the hoped-for port of Ireland, while life is your companion, read (these) most sacrosanct admonitions, having rejected the fabrications of the (worldly) philosophers.[6] I think it absurd to spurn the inextricable rule of the New and the Ancient Document [i.e. the New and the Old Testament] and undertake a journey through the slippery paths of a country full of brambles, that is to say, through the troublesome meanderings of the (worldly) philosophers; or surely, (it is absurd) to drink thirstily from briny and muddy waters, in which a dark throng of toads swarms in abundance and where croaks the strident chatter of frogs, when there are clear waters flowing from glassy pools.

What, pray, I beseech you eagerly, is the benefit to the sanctity of the orthodox faith to expend energy by reading and studying the foul pollution of base Proserpina, which I shrink from mentioning in plain speech; or to revere, through celebration in study, Hermione, the wanton offspring of Menelaus and Helen, who, as the ancient texts report, was engaged for a while by right of dowry to Orestes, then, having changed her mind, married Neoptolemus; or to record—in the heroic style of epic—the high priests of the *Luperci*, who revel in the fashion of those cultists that sacrifice to Priapus ... which were destroyed and vanished into the earth, when a serpent once was raised at the end of a rod and presented to the gaze of the Hebrew assembly [Num. XXXI. 8ff], that is, when the nourishing staff of the Gibbet was affixed with the death of Death?

154

Moreover, I, compelled by this foul report, beg your Discipleship, genuflecting, as it were, with arched knee and bent leg, that you in no wise go near the whores or the trumpery of bawdy houses,[8] *[p. 480]* where lurk pretentious prostitutes with luxury as their pander, who are adorned with the flashing burnish of leg-bands and with smooth arm bracelets, just as ornamented chariots are adorned with metal bosses; but rather, having spurned the exalted summit of the banquet hall, where patricians and praetors hold sway, let your fortunate Fraternity enjoy happily and contentedly the shelter of the lowly hovel, and, rather than the dusky purple of a graceful mantle, let it employ a common cloak and the inelegant covering of the sheepskin—as befits a disciple of Christ—against the freezing blasts of winter that arise in the once-neglected region of the North.[9]

LETTER IV: TO GERAINT

[p. 480] To the most glorious King Geraint, the lord who guides the sceptre of the western kingdom, whom I embrace with fraternal charity—as He who scrutinizes my heart and inwards is witness—and likewise to all *[p. 481]* the bishops of God abiding throughout Devon,[10] Aldhelm, performing the office of abbot without distinction of merits, (sends his wishes for) the salvation (that we) hope for in the Lord.

Recently when I was present at an episcopal council, where, out of almost the entirety of Britain an innumerable company of the bishops of God came together, having assembled for this purpose expressly, that out of concern for the churches and the salvation of souls, the decrees of the canons and the statues of the (Church) Fathers might be discussed by all and be maintained in common, with Christ offering his protection—when these matters were duly accomplished, the entire episcopal council compelled my insignificant self with like precept and similar sentiment to direct epistolary letters to the presence of your Loyalty, and, through the style of writing, to intimate their fatherly request and wholesome suggestion, that is, respecting the unity of the Catholic Church and the harmony of the Christian religion, without which an indifferent faith grows sluggish and future gain is exhausted. For what profit the emoluments of good works, if they are performed outside the Catholic Church, even if someone should meticulously carry out the rules of practice of a rigid life according to monastic discipline, or with fixed purpose decline the companionship of mortals

155

and pass a life of contemplative retirement away in some squalid wilderness? Therefore, that your Wisdom may be able to grasp more surely to what purposes my Mediocrity has directed these writings to you, I shall explain (them) briefly and succinctly.

[p. 482] For indeed we have heard and received report from the relation of diverse rumours that your bishops are not at all in harmony with the rule of the Catholic Faith according to the precepts of Scripture, and, on account of their animosities and verbal assaults, a grave schism and cruel scandal may arise in the Church of Christ, which the maxim of the Psalmist detests that says. 'Much peace have they that love thy law and to them there is no stumbling block' [Ps. CXVII. 165]. For truly, obedient harmony in religious matters unites with charity, just as harsh strife contaminates it. For the Psalmist enjoins the unity of brotherhood upon the followers of truth, saying: 'God who maketh men of one manner to dwell in a house' [Ps. LXVII. 7]. This house, according to allegory, is understood to be the Church, spread throughout all (four) points of the world. For indeed, heretics and schismatics, foreign to the society of the Church, sprouting up in the world and like, so to speak, the dreadful seed of darnels sown in the midst of a fertile crop, defile the harvest of the Lord by their contentious arguments. But the Apostolic Trumpet [i.e. St. Paul] curbs the disgrace of altercation of this sort: 'But if any man seems to be contentious', he says, 'we have no such custom nor does the Church of God' [I Cor. XI. 16], 'which does not have spot or wrinkle' [Ephes. V. 27]. Indeed, the evangelical oracles proclaim that peace is the mother of Catholics and the authoress of the children of God: 'Blessed are the peace-makers, for they shall be called the children of God' [Matth. V. 9]. Hence, when our Lord and Saviour came down from the highest summit of heaven in order to erase 'the handwriting of the decree that was against us' [Coloss. II. 14], and to reconcile the world through mediating peace, the angelic melody sang out: 'Glory to God in the highest and on earth peace to men of good will' [Luc. II. 14]; and the Psalmist: 'Let peace be in thy strength and abundance in thy towers' [Ps. CXXI. 7].

Finally, a rumour hostile to the faith of the Church has bruited it about far and wide that there are in your province certain bishops and clerics who obstinately refuse the tonsure of St Peter, Prince of the Apostles, and persist in recalcitrantly defending themselves with the exculpating apology that they imitate the tonsure of their founders and predecessors, whom they argue with grandiloquent assertions to have been illumined by divine grace. And if these should be concerned to learn from us who was the first to employ this manner of shaving or tonsure, they fall dumb, either not knowing the truth or concealing

156

the falsehood. However, we have learned that the author of (this mode of) tonsure, in the opinion of many, was Simon, the founder of the magical art. 'The Struggle of the Apostles' [cf. Act. VIII. 14–24] and the ten books of Clement [i.e. Ps.-Clement, *Recognitiones*][11] give witness to what sort and how great was the deception of necromancy that he fraudulently devised against the blessed Peter.[12] We, I say, bearing witness to our tonsure of truth *[p. 483]* according to the inviolable authority of Scripture, assert that the Apostle Peter chose this mode for various reasons: in the first place, that he might wear the form and likeness of Christ upon his head, since (Christ) was cruelly crowned with sharp points of thorns by the cursed race of Jews before he suffered the gibbet of the cross for our redemption; secondly, that the priests of the Old Testament and the New might be distinguished by habit and tonsure; lastly, that the same Apostle and his successors and followers in his footsteps might bear derision and mocking laughter from the Roman people, whose custom it was to sell both the enemy and their mercenaries 'under the crown' after conquering an army.[13] Moreover, in the Old Testament the sign of the tonsure took its beginning from the Nazarenes, that is, from the saints, unless I am mistaken; for it is a royal and priestly indication of origin. Indeed the tiara among the ancients was set upon the head of priests; it was round, made of twisted fine linen, and was in the shape of a half sphere, and this is signified in the shaved part of the head. A crown, however, is a circular golden perimeter which girds the head of kings. And so each sign is expressed on the head of clerics, in the words of Peter: 'But you are a chosen generation, a kingly priesthood' [I Petr. II. 9]. This method of tonsuring and shaving is a sign that vices are trimmed back and that we are shorn of the hair of our flesh as though of crimes.[14]

There is, however, another crueller bane to our souls, that in the most holy celebration of Easter[15] they [i.e. Geraint's bishops] do not follow the rule of the three-hundred-eighteen Fathers, who at the Council of Nicaea ordained with prudent perception that a nineteen-year cycle, divided into parts of eight years and eleven, is to be traversed along a straight course until the end of the world, and who bequeathed a sequence of computation and a boundary of paschal calculation from the fifteenth moon to the twenty-first, and they deemed it against law and right and (also) illicit either to anticipate the limit or to exceed it. Furthermore, those people following the nineteen-year computation of Anatolius or the rule of Sulpicius Severus—who described a course of eighty-four years—observe the paschal solemnity on the fourteenth moon along with the Jews, since neither follows the bishops of the Roman Church in their perfect

method of computation; but they also declared that the paschal computus of Victorius,[16] which observes a cycle of five-hundred-thirty-two
years, should not be followed in future. For there was a certain type of
heretic among the Orientals that was called *Tessereskaidecaditae*, that is
'fourteeners', *[p. 484]* because they celebrate the feast of Easter on the
fourteenth moon along with Jews, who blaspheme Christ and trample
the pearls of the Gospel in the manner of swine [Matth. VII. 6], and for
that reason they are regarded as alien to the blessed society of the
orthodox, (and are) unfortunately reckoned among the assemblies of
the schismatics, whom I recall the blessed Augustine mentioned in a
book written on ninety heresies [*De Haeresibus*, c. XXIX].

How very different from the Catholic Faith and what a departure
from the evangelical tradition it is that bishops of Dyfed,[17] on the
other side of the strait of the River Severn, glorying in the private
purity of their own way of life, detest our communion to such a great
extent that they disdain equally to celebrate the divine offices in
church with us and to take courses of food at table for the sake of
charity.[18] Rather they cast the scraps of their dinners and the remains
of their feasts to be devoured by the jaws of ravenous dogs and filthy
pigs, and they order the vessels and flagons [i.e. those used in common
with clergy of the Roman Church] to be purified and purged with
grains of sandy gravel, or with the dusky cinders of ash. No greeting of
peace is offered, no kiss of affectionate brotherhood is bestowed according to the words of the Apostle: 'Salute one another with an holy
kiss' [Rom. XVI. 16]. Nor is loment[19] or water and towel set out for
the hands nor basin appointed for washing the feet, although the
Saviour, girded in a garment of muslin, when he washed the feet of
the disciples gave us a precedent for imitation, saying: 'As I have done
to you, so you do also' [Ioan. XIII. 15]. But indeed, should any of us, I
mean Catholics, go to them for the purpose of habitation, they do not
deign to admit us to the company of their brotherhood until we have
been compelled to spend the space of forty days in penance; and in this
they unfortunately imitate the heretics, who liked to call themselves
cathari, that is, 'pure ones'. With 'alas, alas' rather than with 'bravo'
and with tearful voices and lamenting sobs do I think one ought to
groan mournfully over such great errors; and they are known to do all
this contrary to the teachings of the Gospel (and) according to the
hollow traditions of the Pharisees, as Christ truly said: 'Woe to you,
scribes and Pharisees, (Hypocrites); because you make clean the outside of the cup and of the dish' [Matth. XXIII. 25].[20] For the Lord is
said to have attended banquets with publicans and sinners, so that the
true healer might prepare the medicines of divine *[p. 485]* love and
the poultice of heavenly mercy for the festering wounds of souls.

158

Wherefore, he did not at all despise the company of sinners after the fashion of Pharisees, but rather, he mercifully renewed with his accustomed clemency that sinner [i.e. Mary Magdalene] who dolefully lamented the sins of her polluted life and who washed the feet of the Lord with outpoured floods of tears and wiped them with the loose and flowing curls of her hair, when he said: 'Many sins are forgiven her, because she has loved much' [Luc. VII. 47].

Since these things are so, we humbly entreat and adjure your Brotherhood with hopeful prayers and bended knees, on account of the common destiny of our fatherland and the companionship of the angelic host, that you no longer detest with swollen pride of heart and with scornful breast the doctrine and decrees of blessed Peter, and that you in no wise haughtily spurn the tradition of the Roman Church, employing tyrannous obstinacy, for the sake of the ancient statutes of your predecessors. For truly, Peter, when he confessed the Son of God with holy voice, merited to hear: 'Thou art Peter; and upon this rock I will build my Church; and the gates of hell shall not prevail against it, and I will give thee the keys of the kingdom of heaven' as far as 'loosed also in heaven' [Matth. XVI. 18–19]. If then the keys to the kingdom of heaven were given by Christ to Peter, concerning whom the poet said:[21]

Aetherial key-bearer, who opens the gateway to the heavens,

who shall go rejoicing through the gate of heavenly paradise that scorns the principal statutes of his Church and condemns the commands of his teaching? And if through blessed election and special privilege he merited to receive the power of binding and the authority of loosing in heaven as well as on earth, who that renounces the rule of the paschal celebration and the mode of the Roman tonsure could believe in any way that he ought not to be inextricably bound with powerful bonds rather than mercifully released?

But what if by chance some wily student of books and clever interpreter of the Scriptures should defend himself with such a shield of excuse and buckler of apology, saying: 'I venerate with sincere faith the teaching of each Document [i.e. the Old and the New Testament], and I confess with believing heart the single essence, sole substance, and the threefold subsistence of Persons of the Holy Trinity.[22] [p. 486] And I shall preach with full voice among the people the mystery of the Lord's Incarnation, his suffering on the cross, and the glory of his resurrection; and I shall earnestly proclaim the Last Judgement of the living and the dead, when disparate payment will be weighed out to each and every one on the most just scales of judgement according to the diversity of their merits; (and) I shall be numbered together and included amongst the community of Catholics, according to the privilege of this faith, without any unhappy hindrance'. But I shall strive to shake and break and bring tumbling to the ground with the ballista of apostolic castigation the bulwark of this excuse, beneath which they trust to conceal themselves. For verily James, the son of the aunt of our Lord, said: 'Thou believest that there is one God' [Iac. II. 19], and because he was speaking in irony to the twelve tribes abiding in dispersion,[23] he added immediately: 'Thou dost well; the devils also believe and tremble', because 'faith without works is dead' [Iac. II. 20]. Surely the Catholic Faith and the harmony of brotherly love walk inseparably with even steps, as the great preacher and vessel of election [i.e. St. Paul] elegantly attests: 'And if I should have prophecy and should know all mysteries, if I should have all faith so that I could remove mountains ... and if I should deliver my body to be burned, and have not charity, it profiteth me nothing' [I Cor. XIII. 23].

And so that all may be concluded in the summary of a brief sentence: he who does not follow the teaching and rule of St Peter boasts vainly and idly about his Catholic Faith. For certainly the foundation of the Church and the firmament of the Faith established in the first instance in Christ, and subsequently in Peter, shall in no wise shake or waver before the onrushing blasts of storms, and so the Apostle teaches: 'For other foundation no man can lay except that which is laid, which is Jesus Christ' [I Cor. III. 11]. Moreover, Truth has thus made inviolable for Peter the privilege of the Church: 'Thou art Peter and upon this rock I will build my Church' [Matth. XVI. 18].

LETTER V: TO HEAHFRITH[24]

/p. 488/ Aldhelm, meagre in the Lord, wishes eternal salvation to Master Heahfrith (who is) to be extolled for his venerable renown and greatly honoured according to the merits of the saints.

Principally, with particularly pious and paternal privilege, publicly proferring beneath the pole panegyric and poems promiscuously to the Procreator of all princes and praetors, let us raise a hymn in measured rhythms with a loud blending of voices and with song of melodious music, especially because He who thrust into Tartarus of terrible torture the ghastly three-tongued serpent who vomits torrents of rank and virulent poisons through the ages deigned in like measure to send to earth the offspring begotten of holy parturition in order to obliterate from the earth the criminal offence of first matter and the record of the first men on account of their inextricable sin; and (because), where

160

once the crude pillars of the same foul snake and the stag were worshipped with coarse stupidity in profane shrines,[25] in their place dwellings for students, not to mention holy houses of prayer, are constructed skilfully by the talents of the architect.

I confess, fellow of fraternal companionship and inhabitant of a noble community, that, after we learned from the reports of talebearers that your Ambrosia [i.e. your Wisdom], returning hither from the wintry regions of the north-west part of the island of Ireland—where it encamped for a course of thrice-two years sucking the teat of wisdom—embraced the shore of British territory safe and sound, straightway, as a flaming and burning love required, we offered our inexpressible thanks to the High-throned in Heaven, exulting with palms extended on either side, especially because the Holy Judge /p. 490/ deigned to lead you back—an exile visiting the venerable brotherhood of your paternal country[26]—across the blue of the sea and the enormous rocks of the tides and the spuming eruptions of the water, with your ashen boat[27] ploughing the billowy brine and the captain rejoicing, so that now, in turn, supported abundantly by succouring favour from on high, you may confidently pursue and achieve your destined vocation as a teacher, repatriating after your residence in a foreign country, where, nourished for a long time in the first cradles of learning,[28] you grew up to the age of young manhood.

Likewise I do not hesitate in the least to disclose from the depths of my heart to your propitious Blessedness that this [i.e. your return] has come about especially for the increase of joy among deacons and priests, nay rather, for the glory of the name of the Lord, because—rumour aside—by the proclamation of those dwelling on Irish soil, on whose companionship you relied for a little while, was our hearing shaken, as if by a kind of bellow of thunder issuing from a clashing of clouds, and common opinion bruited it abroad through so many and such large measures of the land of learning and to the parishes and provinces that the wandering hither and thither and back and forth of those traversing the abysses of the sea on ship-path[29] is as busy as a kind of kindred swarm of bees skilfully manufacturing (their) nectar. For just as the honey-flowing swarm (of bees)—when the mist of night departs in its course and Titan [i.e. the sun] emerges from the sea up to the peak of heaven—clothed in yellow vestments carries its burden through the flowering tops of blooming lindens to the graceful honey-combs, in like fashion, if I am not mistaken, a mass of ravenous scholars and an avid throng of sagacious students,[30] the residue from the rich fields of Holy Writ, thirstily seize and swallow not only the grammatical and geometrical arts—to say nothing of the twice-three scaffolds of the art of physics—but also, the fourfold honeyed oracles of allegorical or rather tropological disputation of opaque problems in aetherial mysteries,[31] conceal and store them away to be conserved until death with perpetual meditation in the beehives of learning, from the catalogue of which an excellent report has bruited it that your Sagacity emerged burdened with booty and drenched and overflowing with floods of the sacred torrent.

Wherefore I entreat your kindly Discipleship, as one bowing and genuflecting with sobs and with earnest prayers, that a forgetful memory not pass over the fact that Pacificus, [i.e. Solomon][32] endowed with ambrosia [i.e. wisdom] from heaven, having been chosen by his father according to the law of succession, exercising rule over the empire of the Israelite people for twice-four *lustra* of time [i.e. about forty years], being filled with the Holy Spirit, spoke, saying: 'Drink water out of thy own cistern and the streams of thy own well; let thy fountains be conveyed abroad and in the streets divide thy waters; keep them to thyself alone neither let strangers be partakers with thee' [Prov. V. 15-17]. Wherefore, since you are imbued through persistent effort with this holy food of orthodox teaching, open your throat and moisten the thirsting fields of the mind, so that the seed of heavenly ecstasy, sown by the sweat of the Creator, may swell and blossom in the living and fertile furrows of the orthodox without hindrance of parching drought, and that the thickly sown crop at length come richly to fruition by the will of God.

Therefore, such a resolutely suppliant prayer seems to have adduced these things, because some are known to be endowed with heavenly wisdom and unusually replete with hidden light; nevertheless, what they have attained by receiving from the spontaneous generosity of heaven and the bountiful bequest of God, without benefit of their own merits, they in no wise publish fully by unlocking the treasury of knowledge, but dole out bit by bit to the ravenous! For according to the example of evangelical authority, to no purpose is the burning wick secretly hidden in the dark recess of the loathsome urn [Matth. V. 15] which was supposed to shine to all */p. 492/* from the end of a candlestick with limpid light; and in vain are the profits of the talent barricaded and concealed in subterranean sands [Matth. XXV. 18], which should have been spent for the plentiful pieces of the changers of money, lest perchance the slothful man, numb, so to speak, with sluggishness, after having received the talent of his masters, be thrust headlong into the utmost filth of prisons; but rather—let us rejoice!—let him merit from the Holy Creator to enter into joy. Whence for this reason, the prophetic psalmwriter expiating his guilty conscience of sin, commencing with sacred presage, declared: 'I have not hid thy justice,' etc. [Ps. XXXIX. 11].

162

But I, wretched little man, meditating upon these matters as I wrote, was forthwith troubled and trembled with a twofold anxiety. Why, I ask, is Ireland, whither assemble the thronging students by the fleet-load, exalted with a sort of ineffable privilege, as if here in the fertile soil of Britain, teachers who are citizens of Greece and Rome cannot be found, who are able to unlock and unravel the murky mysteries of the heavenly library to the scholars who are eager to study them? Although the aforesaid opulent and verdant country of Ireland is adorned, so to speak, with a browsing crowd of scholars, just as the hinges of heaven are decorated with stellar flashings of twinkling stars, yet nonetheless, Britain, although situated in almost the outer limit of the western world, possesses, for example, the luculent likeness, as it were, of the flaming sun and the moon, that is, Theodore, who discharges the duties of the pontificate and was from the very beginnings of his apprenticeship mature in the flower [p. 493] of the arts of learning,[33] and his colleague of the same sodality, Hadrian, equally endowed with ineffably pure urbanity. And boldly fighting in the open against the worthless and despised seducer of falseness, with a balanced view of the truth, shall I pronounce judgement: although Theodore[34] who pilots the helm of the high priesthood, be hemmed in by a mass of Irish students, like a savage wild boar checked by a snarling pack of hounds, with the filed tooth of the grammarian—nimbly and with no loss of time—he disbands the rebel phalanxes; and just as the warlike bowman in the midst of battle is hemmed in by a dense formation of enemy legions, then, when his bow is tensed by his powerful hands and arms and arrows are drawn from the quiver, that is, from the obscure and acute syllogisms of chronography,[35] the throng, swollen with the arrogance[36] of pride, their shield-wall having been shattered, turn their backs and flee headlong to the dark recesses of their caves, while the victor exults.

Nor by asserting such things, should I be accused by someone of insulting Irish savants—whose bejewelled honeycomb of doctrine your Wisdom has somewhat over-employed—especially as I meant to busy myself with building and forging in good humour the reputation of our own (scholars), not with heaping derisive and scornful abuse on yours! But rather, after the fashion of jesters and buffoons, who speak with rash wit (and) mockery, and with the excuse of fraternal affection, was my raillery put forward. If indeed, with the support of prating ignorance, a text can be shamelessly proved to have prompted it, as the versifier said:

In the words of Glengus, a fleeing rhetor
                is worthy of enslavement.[37]
        Let not the writer fear the sport of abusive
                tongues.
        Thus they always hope to pluck the pages of poets,
        As the hairy goat chews the grapes with his teeth.
        Nonetheless, they don't emend a letter of the
                reeling bard.[38]

LETTER VI: ANONYMOUS STUDENT TO ALDHELM

To the holy and most wise Lord Aldhelm, very dear indeed in Christ, [a person of unknown name] (wishes) salvation in God eternal.

As I am not unaware that you are distinguished in native ability and for your Roman eloquence, and for various flowers of letters, [39] even those in the Greek fashion, I prefer to learn from your lips than to drink from some other turbid master. Know this especially in advance: that I beseech you confidently to receive and instruct me on this account, since the brightness of wisdom, as it has been said, flashes in you more than in many learned men, and (since) you are aware that the minds of foreign travellers are eager to learn wisdom (from you), because you were a visitor at Rome, and especially because you were nourished by a certain holy man of our race. Let these suffice for the sake of brevity, because, if you should attend to them humbly and with charity, you will understand no less through a few words than through many.

I also candidly declare this to you: I desire to read a certain book which I do not have, and that is for a period no longer than two weeks; moreover, I mention this brief period, not because I do not have more need of it, but so that this request may not cause annoyance to your mind. I shall obtain a messenger and horses, I imagine. Moreover, in this harvest time I shall hope for a favourable response from you. May Divine Grace deign to preserve your Blessedness who prays for us.

LETTER VII: ÆTHILWALD TO ALDHELM

[p. 495] To the most holy Abbot Aldhelm, bound to me by the inextricable bonds of glowing charity, as observance requires, Æthilwald, humble fosterchild of your loving Paternity, (wishes) the perpetual well-being of salvation in the Lord.

In the course of the summer time, when this (our) most pitiable country was being sadly ravaged by the successive mounting of large and savage attacks and by baneful hatred, I used to tarry and sojourn with you in the pursuit of learning. At that time, although I was unworthy, the venerable sagacity of your Blessedness, being imbued, I believe, with almost all praiseworthy writings, both of secular (literature) produced with the fluency of verbal eloquence,[40] as well as of the spiritual corpus, abundantly lucubrated in the style of ecclesiastical teaching, revealed and made perfectly plain to me—once the veil of thick stupidity had been snatched away—the arcane studies of the liberal arts, insofar as they are closed off to every ignorant mind by the opaque secrets of their mysteries. Once these feasts of exuberant genius had been ravenously absorbed in their entirety [p. 496] by the gluttonous jaws of (my) thirsty intelligence, a most generous fare of happy token began abundantly to refresh the still lean pallor of my hebetude, promising by its teaching, freely to imbue me with every means to the study I desired, by which (your Wisdom) might most easily recognise as its own the efforts of my Mediocrity, which are sufficiently earnest. Wherefore, my dearest preceptor of pure instruction, we deem it worthwhile that you put to the test the faith of these words with good effect and with no hardship to yourself, prompted by such oracles of Holy Writ: 'My son, if you be surety for thy friend, thou hast engaged fast thy hand to a stranger; thou art ensnared with the words of thy mouth' [Prov. VI. 12].

I also say: if you in no wise recall that you are entangled and enveloped in the ample network of a proferred promise, nevertheless, since you brought me forward from the very cradles of tenderest infancy, by nourishing, loving, and gradually restoring me with the more delicate foods of knowledge as far as vigorous adolescence, it is judged seemly by all men of sound intelligence that you feed one already nourished with the pablum suited to a younger condition with a more solid food of even deeper learning, and, even though my most humble entreaty of submissive devotion aspires with importuning insistence, do not hesitate to lay out banquets for my full satisfaction, (and) even though you regard me as of little worth, do not refuse at a fitting time to enrich in some measure the adoptive child of your Sublimity with all the abundant wealth of your paternal Wisdom, lest at some time the malicious bands of (your) rash rivals triumphantly congratulate (themselves) with the rough laughter of (their) desired reproach, if they discover offspring disinherited of the opulent wealth of paternal wisdom and suffering the penury of savage ignorance; and not unfittingly could that Roboam, of the noble stock of King Solomon—a man most famous as much for the surpassing size of his laudable wisdom as for his rich abundance of goods—who [i.e.

Roboam], because he was of ignoble birth, sadly had no part of almost all of the fund of his father's felicity,[41] be compared to me. Come, then, at last: resolve now to fulfil my hopes and, being roused, complete the benefit of the generous instruction that you undertook, with the knowledge that you will doubtless obtain from it the greater glory of your eternal reward, with the assent of the Lord, who said: 'But he that shall persevere unto the end, he shall be saved' [Matth. X. 22].

Moreover, we have appended to this letter from our humble self three poems of melodius euphony arranged into two types: the first of which is plainly measured out in the dactylic hexameter and the metrical rule of the heroic poem, I think, and divided into the *formulae* of seventy equal verses,[42] with the help of Fortune, or—to speak more truly—with the guiding approval of divine dispensation; the third, wrought not according to the measure of feet, but written swiftly and with ploughing pen, with eight syllables arranged in any one verse, *[p. 497]* and one and the same letter adapted to the equal courses of the lines,[43] I have dedicated and dispatched to you, O wisest father; the middle (poem), regarding the pilgrimage of transmarine journeys, likewise composed of quite similar lines of verses and syllables, I sent without delay to my and your colleague, Wihtfrith. Hence, I thought it necessary that these matters be laid before the gaze of the venerable eyes of your Blessedness, as seemed fitting in the judgement of our humble self, so that I might first lay before and expose to you, as to a father, all the meagre output of my compositions, so that, approved by the credible and rational judgement of your Sublimity and brought to the criterion of (your) fairness, it might henceforward be acceptable to all the masses of readers. Farewell in Christ.

LETTER VIII: TO SIGEGYTH

To Sister Sigegyth, most beloved and most loving and venerable to me for the sincere emotion of (her) charity, Aldhelm, a suppliant, unworthily enjoying the title of abbot, (wishes) salvation in the Lord.

Let your kindness be aware that I petitioned the bishop regarding the baptism of the sister, and he gave leave for that religious person to be baptized, although in a private and confidential manner.[44] I greet you earnestly, O Sigegyth, from the deepest chamber of my heart, and I entreat you with hopeful prayers that you do not cease to occupy your mind with continual meditation on the Scriptures, that you may fulfil the words of the Psalmist, when he said: 'And on his law he shall meditate day and night' [Ps. I. 2], and the same Psalmist avers this

166

again, saying: 'How sweet are thy words to my palate!' [Ps. CXVIII. 103]. I suppliantly beseech all the sisters in Christ that they be mindful of my prayers, because the Apostle says: 'For the continual prayer of a just man availeth much' [Iac. V. 16]. Farewell, ten times, nay a hundred times and a thousand times beloved, and may God cause you to fare well!

LETTER IX: CELLANUS[45] TO ALDHELM

[p. 498] To the Lord Abbot Aldhelm, enriched by learned pursuits and adorned by sweet lucubrations, admirably discovering on the shores of the Saxons what some scarcely obtain, through labour and sweat, in a foreign clime,[46] Cellanus, born on the Isle of Ireland, an exile concealed in the farthermost corner of the territory of the Franks, the lowest and (most) worthless servant of Christ in a famous settlement, (wishes) salvation in the whole and wholesome Trinity.

The encomiastic report of your Latinity has reached the ears of our Poverty as though by winged flight, nor does the hearing of able scholars reject it: and it is noted, without twisting of nostrils or the pretence of stink, for the brilliant beauty of its Roman eloquence. And although we have not had the privilege of hearing you in the flesh, nonetheless we have read your books, which are well constructed and balanced, and adorned with the charms of various flowers;[47] but if you would refresh the sad little heart of the pilgrim, [p. 499] send us a few little sermons[48] from those most beautiful lips of yours—from whose most pure source sweet rivulets, when dispersed, may restore the minds of many—to the place where Master Furseus rests in holy and incorrupt body.[49]

LETTER X: TO CELLANUS

(Aldhelm ... to Cellanus ... Salvation)
I am astonished that the Diligence of your fraternal Wisdom, (emanating) from the famous and flourishing country of the Franks, should address me, such a very insignificant personage,[50] born of the race of Saxon stock and fostered in tender cradles beneath the Arctic sky ...

To Æthilwald, son and likewise disciple most dear to me, Aldhelm, the least of the servants of God (wishes) salvation.

Just as I have been concerned to warn you about certain matters on various occasions when actually present, so now also I am not reluctant to exhort you by letter, though absent, relying on my paternal authority according to (the will of) God. Therefore we act in this way, because the 'charity of Christ' as the Apostle said, 'presseth us' [II Cor. IV. 14]. And so, my dearest son, even though you are at the age of young manhood, nevertheless, do not in any wise expose yourself too much to the most deceptive enticements of this world, whether in daily drinking parties and banquets, /p. 500/ which are shamefully excessive in their so frequent and prolix practice, or in riding about aimlessly, which is blameworthy, or in any of the other execrable pleasures of corporeal indulgence. Always remember what has been written: 'Youth and pleasure are vain' [Eccles. XI. 10]. Further, do not at all submit to an excessive and ardent love of money and to all the ostentation of the glory of this world, which is always hateful to God, remembering that phrase: 'For what shall it profit a man if he gain the whole world and lose his soul?' [Marc. VII. 36]—'The son of man shall come in the glory of his Father with his angels: and then he will render to every man according to his works, [Matth. XVI. 27].[51]

But rather, my dearest (friend), be always attentive to divine readings and sacred discourse. Moreover, should you labour to know anything of secular letters, do it only for this reason: that since in the divine law the entire structure of words stands in complete accord with the rules of the art of grammar, the more fully you have learned beforehand the most diverse rules of that art according to which it is composed, the more easily will you understand the deepest and holiest meanings of the same divine discourse (in the course of) your reading. Moreover, do not fail to keep this letter perpetually among the other books that you are reading, so that by oft-repeated perusal of it you may be admonished to fulfil those things which are written in it according to my office. Farewell.

LETTER XII: TO THE ABBOTS OF WILFRID

(Aldhelm to the Abbots of Wilfrid, Greeting)
Recently a raging and tempestuous disturbance—as you learned from experience—has shaken the foundations of the Church in the manner

of a gigantic earthquake, the noise of which [p. 501] has resounded far and wide like a thunderclap through the various regions of the land. Wherefore, I beg of you, sons of the same tribe, with bended knee and hopeful prayer, to be in no wise scandalized by the deceit of this disturbance, lest anyone of you grow sluggish in a faith of lazy inactivity, since the necessity of event requires that you along with your own bishop, who has been deprived of the honour of his office, be expelled from your native land and go to any transmarine country in the wide world that is suitable. What harsh or cruel burden in existence, I ask, would separate you and hold you apart from that bishop, who like a wet-nurse gently caressed you, his beloved fosterchildren, warming you in the folds of his arms and nourishing you in the bosom of charity, and who brought you forward in his paternal love by rearing, teaching, and castigating you from your very first exposure to the rudiments (of education) and from your early childhood and tender years up to the flower of your maturity? Examine carefully, I beseech you, the order of creation and the nature divinely planted within it, so that by comparing the very least things, you may comprehend with Christ's help the unchanging pattern of life. (See) how swarms of bees eagerly emerge from their hives, yearning for nectar, when warm heat descends from the sky, and, when their leader departs, the cohorts thronging in swift flight heap up to the aether their winter shelters of close-packed dwellings, excepting only the female servants of their former homes who are left behind for the propagation of future offspring! Behold, I say, even more marvellous to note: should their king, protected by dense swarms of companions when he goes out of the winter quarters with his throng and explores the hollow wood of logs, [p. 502] be entangled in a sprinkling of sand-grains or hindered by a sudden shower falling in drops from the waterfall of heaven, and return to his beloved honeycomb and former home, straightway the entire army bursts out of its wonted dwellings and goes with rejoicing to the confines of former cells. If, then, a creature in such wise lacking reason, which the fixed laws of nature govern without written prescriptions, obeys the precept of its leader in the recurring course of time, answer, I ask you, whether they ought not be reproached with an infamy of dreadful abomination, who, although endowed with grace granted by the septiform Spirit, break rein from their devoted obedience in frantic fashion? Hear, then, why I assemble arguments of various kinds and hasten with strident pen to stir the depths of your breast.

Now then, if worldly men, exiles from divine teaching, were to desert a devoted master, whom they embraced in prosperity, but once the opulence of the good times began to diminish and the adversity of bad fortune began its onslaught, they preferred the secure peace of their dear country to the burdens of a banished master, are they not deemed worthy of the scorn of scathing laughter and the noise of mockery from all? What, then, will be said of you, if you cast into solitary exile the bishop who nourished and raised you? ...

LETTER XIII: TO WYNBERHT

To Lord Wynberht, most beloved in the Lord of Lords, Aldhelm, servant of the servants of God, (wishes) salvation in the cornerstone of the two testaments, cut from the highest peaks of mountains, which overwhelmed the statue made of four kinds of metals that signify the four kingdoms of men and destroyed it from its golden head down to the legs [Dan. II. 34, 45].

[p. 503] We have appointed a bearer of letters to the presence of your Goodness who will make known to you more fully in person the imminent cause of our necessity, that is, regarding the land which Baldred, the venerable atheling, offered for our possession at an agreed price, a becoming place and especially suitable for the catching of fish. Wherefore, since it [i.e. the land] seems to have been granted and conferred under the authority of your king, we strenuously petition that we may obtain and firmly hold the same tract of land through the patronage of your Beneficence, lest we be cheated of the same holding by force, because often the laws of justice are fickle.

APPENDIX I: CHANGES TO EHWALD'S TEXT

Epistola ad Acircium

    p. 67. 23 for *defusarum* read *diffusarum*
    p. 68. 6 for *ramnorum* read *ramorum*
    p. 68. 9 for *obumbratae* read *obumbrata*; no lacuna
    p. 69. 12 for *septinarius calculus* read *septinarios calculos*
    p. 203. 18 after *alimoniam*: supply some such word as *spernens*

De Virginitate (prose)

    p. 234. 5 for *flagrantis* read *fragrantis*[1]
    p. 237. 21 for *flagrantia* read *fragrantia*
    p. 238. 1 for *qui* read *quae*
    p. 255. 15 replace question mark with full stop
    p. 272. 16 replace full stop with question mark after *percrebruit*
    p. 278. 4–5 for *praepararent* read *praepararerant*
    p. 279. 9 for *flagrantem* read *fragrantem*
    p. 281. 14 for *vel* read *in*
    p. 283. 6 for *flagrantiam* read *fragrantiam*
    p. 299. 14 for *lumina* read *limina*
    p. 307. 20 for *flagrantia* read *fragrantia*
    p. 308. 3 for *ista* read *istae*
    p. 317. 4 for *Abra* read *abra*

The Letters

    p. 477. 12 for *tantae* read *tanta*
    p. 477. 13 for *desperatio* read *disputatio*
    p. 478. 3 for *cursim* read *curiose* (-im?)
    p. 478. 9 for *reverentissimo* read *reverendissimo*

p. 479. 13 place dash after *enucleate*
p. 479. 19 for *pabuli* read *patibuli*[2]
p. 483. 18 for *decursurum* read *discursum* (*iri?*)
p. 484. 22 for *ingeminandum* read *ingemiscendum*
p. 485. 20 for *dementer* read *clementer*
p. 491. 12 for *iugi* read *iugique*
p. 491. 21 for *nequaquam* read *nequiquam*
p. 492. 16 for *potiatur* read *potitur*
p. 494. 1 omit *fiat* (see discussion, p. 202, n. 37)
p. 494. 15 for *significant* read *sufficiant*
p. 498. 12 for *reficere vis* read *refici⟨a⟩s* (*reficis* MS)
p. 503. 5 omit *terra*

APPENDIX II: TWO 'ALDHELMIAN' CHARTERS

Ehwald printed in his edition five charters which, in his estimation, deserved to be received into the canon of Aldhelm's works (*quae inter opera Aldhelmi reciperentur*).[1] In spite of Ehwald's opinion, no modern student of Anglo-Saxon diplomatic would consider any of the five as authentic.[2] Nevertheless, two of these charters have an especial claim to the attention of students of Aldhelm: they are written in a Latin style which is unmistakeably 'Aldhelmian'. For this reason, enthusiastic attempts have been made to claim the charters for Aldhelm, notably by Hahn[3] and Bönhoff,[4] and Ehwald similarly chose to believe that these two charters were indeed drafted by Aldhelm.[5] It is true that the charters in question bear a striking resemblance to Aldhelm's other prose works, but as A. S. Cook demonstrated with reference to the first of these (the donation by Leuthere),[6] the resemblance derives from the fact that these charters are each a confection of phrases from Aldhelm's other works carefully stitched together. Accordingly, although these charters might perhaps preserve some authentic basis,[7] their present form derives from the industry of a later imitator, not from Aldhelm himself.

I. *Leuthere, bishop of the West Saxons, to Aldhelm: grant of land at Malmesbury for a monastery (A.D. 675):*

[p. 507] ... For often it is wont to happen, that when the warm autumnal heat departs, wintry blasts of raging winds follow in turn upon their receding course, by which the boisterous blue of the sea and the vast waters of the ocean are battered this way and that [p. 508], so that no one sailing by ship-path may pass without danger, when the raging wind is ripping sails, so indeed, when the pompous vainglory of this world has been laid low, and now the end of the same is close at hand, the fluctuating storms of the age appear to press upon us clear

173

proof that truly and without any ambiguous reservation those prophecies of the Lord are at last in our days proved to be fulfilled, wherein he fixed those events by heavenly oracle, saying: 'Behold the fig and the other trees' and so on [Luc. XXI. 19]. Moreover, amidst the turbulent tempests of this world, the rudders of the scriptures should be turned and the equipment and the instruments of the entire ship should be made ready, so that, after having spurned the garrulous song of the Sirens, it may be conducted safely to the port of its homeland.

Wherefore I, Leuthere, bishop by the grace of God, steering the rudders of the pontificate of Wessex, have been entreated by the abbots, who, according to the law of our province are known to preside over the cloistered throng of monks with pastoral concern, that I deign to confer and bestow upon Aldhelm the priest that land whose name is Malmesbury, for the living of life according to monastic rule, in which place he was educated from his early childhood and from his earliest training in the study of the liberal arts and spent his life nourished in the bosom of Holy Mother Church, and for this reason especially, fraternal charity is seen to instigate this petition. Wherefore, assenting to the entreaties of the aforesaid abbots, impelled by fraternal petition, I willingly concede the same land, of which we made mention above, both to himself and to his successors who follow the pattern of the holy rule, so that, with the removal of the strife of conflicting disputes, they may serve God into future posterity, in continual quiet and perpetual peace, without impediment. But lest by chance an occasion of conflict should arise in future, I strengthen and confirm (the pact) by imposing this condition upon the matter: that no one indeed of succeeding bishops or kings, through the employment of tyrannical power, may forcibly assail this charter of our bequest, obstinately asserting that it seemed to have been removed and separated from the power of the episcopate. Wherefore, let it be known and promulgated against rivals that it was much more fitting [p. 509] to me to have added enhancement to the pontifical church than to have taken it away by force. Finally, that the grant of the aforesaid donation be more secure and endure perpetually, we have ordered the aforesaid abbots to subscribe with their own hands. But should anyone strive to annul these writings and decrees of our decision, let him know that he will render account before the tribunal of Christ.

Acted publicly at the river Bladon, 24 August, in the year of the incarnation 675.

+ I, Leuthere, though an unworthy bishop, at the behest of the monks, have subscribed this charter of endowment.

+ I, Cyniberht, abbot, have subscribed.
+ I, Hæddi, abbot, have subscribed.
+ I, Hiddi, priest, have subscribed.
+ I, Wynberht, priest, have subscribed.
+ I, Hedda, have subscribed.

II. *Cenfrith*, comes[8] *of the Mercians, to Aldhelm, abbot: grant of land at Wootton Bassett, Wiltshire (A.D. 680):*

*[*p. 509*]* The insolent fortune of the deceptive world, not lovable for the milk-white beauty of imperishable lilies, but hateful for the galling bitterness of woeful corruption, lacerates the children in the vale of tears *[*p. 510*]* with the venemous rendings of the putrid flesh; and although it is attractive to wretches by its pleasantness, nevertheless, it [i.e. the vale of tears] slopes downwards to the depths of Acherontean Cocytus, unless the offspring of the High Thunderer comes to their aid. And therefore, because that ruinous fortune in foreasking us vanishes in smoke, one should hasten with all one's effort to those beautiful fields of indescribable joy, where the hymning voices of angelic jubilation and the mellifluous aromas of blossoming roses are sensed as indescribable sweets by the noses of the good and the blessed and as delights without end by the ears of the blissful.

Enticed by the desire for such blessedness, I, Cenfrith, *comes* of the Mercians, with the consent of King Æthelred, have bestowed a certain small part of land, in the amount of ten *cassati* in the place which is called Wootton Bassett (Wiltshire), upon the venerable abbot Aldhelm, for the service of God and St Peter, in perpetual legitimacy.

In the year of the Incarnation 680, the eighth indiction.

+ Theodore, archbishop.
+ Æthelred, king of the Mercians.
+ Berhtwald, *subregulus.*
+ Cenfrith, *patricius.*
+ Sexwulf, bishop of Lichfield.
+ Bosel, bishop of Worcester.

APPENDIX III: CHECK-LIST OF SOURCES OF ALDHELM'S EXEMPLARY VIRGINS

For the convenience of readers who have no immediate access to Ehwald's edition of Aldhelm, we append a list of the principal sources from which Aldhelm drew the exemplary material for the *De Virginitate*; the list is based almost entirely on Ehwald's own annotation. Also for the sake of convenience, references are given where possible to standard collections such as the *Acta Sanctorum* and Migne's *Patrologia Latina*, even where more modern editions are available.

1. Elijah: III Reg. XVIII. 45; IV Reg. I. 9–II. 11.
2. Elisha: IV Reg. II. 2–24, XIII. 21.
3. Jeremiah: Ier. I. 5 *et passim*.
4. Daniel: Dan. I. 8–10, II. 32–4, III. 1–19, IV. 7, VIII. 5–24, IX. 24.
5. The Three Youths (Shadrach, Meshach, Abednego): Dan. III. 12–30.
6. John the Baptist: Matth. III. 1–16; Marc. VI. 16–29.
7. John the Evangelist: Isidore, *De Ortu et Obitu Patrum*, c. lxxii (PL LXXXIII, cols. 151–2).
8. Didymus (Thomas): source unknown (see p. 194 below).
9. Paul: Phil. III. 5; II Cor. XI. 24–5, XII. 2 *et passim*.
10. Luke: Isidore, *De Ortu et Obitu Patrum*, c. lxxxii (PL LXXXIII, col. 154).
11. Clement: *Liber Pontificalis*, c. iv (ed. T. Mommsen, Monumenta Germaniae Historica. Gesta Pontificum Romanorum I (Berlin, 1898), p. 7).
12. Silvester: *Gesta Silvestri*. There is no modern edition of the *Gesta Silvestri*; cf. the Bollandists' *Bibliotheca Hagiographica Latina* (Brussels, 1898–9), vol. II, pp. 1119–20.
13. Ambrose: Paulinus, *Vita S. Ambrosii* (PL XIV, cols. 27–46).
14. Martin: Sulpicius Severus, *Vita S. Martini* (PL XX, cols. 159–76).

15. Gregory of Nazianzus: Rufinus, *Eusebii Historiarum Continuatio* II. ix (PL XXI, cols. 517–21).

16. Basil: Rufinus, *Eusebii Historiarum Continuatio* II. ix (PL XXI, cols. 517–21); Jerome, *De Viris Illustribus*, c. cxvi (PL XXIII, col. 707); Cassian, *De Institutis Coenobiorum* VI. xix (PL XLIX, col. 289).

17. Felix: *Acta Sanctorum, .xxiv. Octobris*, vol. VI, pp. 625–8.

18. Antony: Rufinus, *Eusebii Historiarum Continuatio* I. viii (PL XXI, cols. 477–8); Jerome, *De Viris Illustribus*, c.lxxxviii (PL XXIII, col. 693). It is not certain that Aldhelm used Evagrius's translation of Athanasius's *Vita S. Antonii*, even though he mentions it.

19. Paul the Hermit: Jerome, *Vita S. Pauli* (PL XXIII, cols. 17–28).

20. Hilarion: Jerome, *Vita S. Hilarionis* (PL XXIII, cols. 29–54).

21. John the Hermit: Rufinus, *Historia Monachorum*, c. i (PL XXI, cols. 393–405).

22. Benedict: Gregory the Great, *Dialogi* II. i-xxxviii (PL LXVI, cols. 126–204).

23. Malchus: Jerome, *Vita S. Malchi* (PL XXIII, cols. 53–60).

24. Narcissus: Eusebius, *Ecclesiastica Historia* VI. vii–ix, translated by Rufinus (ed. E. Schwarts and T. Mommsen, *Eusebius Werke. Die griechischen christlichen Schriftsteller* (Leipzig, 1903), pp. 537–43).

25. Athanasius: Rufinus, *Eusebii Historiarum Continuatio* I. xiv–xviii (PL XXI, cols. 486–91).

26. Babilas: *Acta Sanctorum, .xxiv. Ianuarii*, vol. II, pp. 569–73.

27. Cosmas and Damianus: *Acta Sanctorum, .xxvii. Septembris*, vol. VII, pp. 469–74.

28. Chrysanthus and Daria: *Acta Sanctorum, .xxv. Octobris*, vol. XI, pp. 469–84.

29. Julian: *Acta Sanctorum, .ix. Ianuarii*, vol. I, pp. 575–87.

30. Amos of Nitria: Rufinus, *Historia Monachorum*, c. xxx (PL XXI, cols. 455–7).

31. Apollonius: Rufinus, *Historia Monachorum*, c. vii (PL XXI, cols. 410–20).

32. Caecilia: *Acta Sanctorum, .xiv. Aprilis*, vol. II, pp. 203–8.

33. Agatha: *Acta Sanctorum, .v. Februarii*, vol. I, pp. 615–18.

34. Lucia: L. Surius, *De Probatis Sanctorum Historiis* (Cologne, 1575), vol. VI, pp. 892–4.

35. Justina: *Acta Sanctorum, .xxvi. Septembris*, vol. VII, pp. 217–19.

36. Eugenia: pseudo-Rufinus, *Vita S. Eugeniae* (PL XXI, cols. 1105–22).

37. Agnes: *Acta Sanctorum, .xxi. Ianuarii*, vol. II, pp. 351–4; PL XVII, cols. 735–42.

38. Thecla and Eulalia: source unknown; cf. *Acta Sanctorum, .xxiii. Septembris*, vol. VI, pp. 546–68.
39. Scholastica: Gregory the Great, *Dialogi* II. xxxiii (PL LXVI, cols. 194–6).
40. Christina: *Acta Sanctorum, .xxiv. Iulii*, vol. V, pp. 524–8.
41. Dorothea: *Acta Sanctorum, .vi. Februarii*, vol. I, pp. 773–6.
42. Constantina: source unknown; cf. *Acta Sanctorum, .xviii. Februarii*, vol. III, pp. 67–71.
43. Eustochium: Jerome, *Ep.* xxii (PL XXII, cols. 394–425).
44. Demetrias: Pelagius, *Epistola ad Demetriadem* (PL XXX, cols. 15–45).
45. Chionia, Irene and Agape: *Acta Sanctorum, .iii. Aprilis*, vol. I, pp. 248–50.
46. Rufina and Secunda: *Acta Sanctorum, .x. Iulii*, vol. III, pp. 30–1.
47. Victoria: *Analecta Bollandiana* II (1883), pp. 157–60; cf. L. Surius, *De Probatis Sanctorum Historiis* (Cologne, 1575), vol. VI, pp. 942–3.
48. Anatolia: *Acta Sanctorum, .ix. Iulii*, vol. II, pp. 676–80.

FOOTNOTES

GENERAL INTRODUCTION (pp. 1–4)

1 *Historia Ecclesiastica* V.18 (ed. B. Colgrave and R. A. B. Mynors [Oxford, 1969], p. 514; ed. C. Plummer, *Venerabilis Baedae Opera Historica*. 2 vols. [Oxford, 1896], I, p. 321). References to Bede throughout are to book and chapter number in the Colgrave-Mynors edition. The translation here is our own; subsequent citations of Bede (in English) are from the Colgrave-Mynors edition.

2 For arguments that the first of the *Carmina Rhythmica* printed by Ehwald (pp. 523–8) is by Aldhelm, see above, pp. 16–18. Full reference to Ehwald's edition of Aldhelm is given in n. 24, p. 181 below.

3 The poems of Æthilwald are printed by Ehwald, pp. 528–37. See discussion of the poems by W. Meyer, *Gesammelte Abhandlungen zur mittellateinische Rythmik*. 3 vols. (Berlin, 1936), III, pp. 328–46; I. Schröbler, 'Zu den Carmina Rhythmica in der Wiener HS. der Bonifatius-Briefe', *Beiträge zur Geschichte der deutschen Sprache und Literatur* LXXIX (1957), pp. 1–42; and F. W. Schulze, 'Reimkonstruktionen im Offa-Preislied Æthilwalds', *Zeitschrift für deutsches Altertum* XCII (1963), pp. 8–31. On the identity of this Æthilwald, see above p. 147.

4 Cf. Boniface, *Epp.* IX and X (ed. M. Tangl, *Die Briefe des heiligen Bonifatius und Lullus*. Monumenta Germaniae Historica. Epistolae Selectae I [Berlin, 1916], pp. 6 and 15); Lul, *Ep.* CXL (ed. Tangl, *op. cit.*, p. 280), and Berhtgyth, *Epp.* CXLVII and CXLVIII (*ibid.*, pp. 285–6).

5 Ed. Ehwald, pp. 3–32.

6 E.g. the verses which constitute the epitaph of Bugga, abbess of a double monastery at Withington, Gloucestershire, printed by M. Lapidge, 'Some Remnants of Bede's Lost *Liber Epigrammatum*', *English Historical Review* XC (1975), pp. 798–820, esp. pp. 815–7.

7 All these Latin riddles, together with Aldhelm's own *Enigmata*, have been collected and printed with translations and cross-referencing by F. Glorie, *Collectiones Aenigmatum Merovingicae Aetatis*. 2 vols. Corpus Christianorum, Series Latina CXXXIII–CXXIIIA (Turnhout, 1968).

8 The Old English riddles of the Exeter Book are edited with extensive commentary by F. Tupper, *The Riddles of the Exeter Book* (Boston, 1910); with facing translation by W. S. Mackie, *The Exeter Book Part II*. Early English Text Society (Oxford, 1934); and critically by G. P. Krapp and E. V. K. Dobbie, *The Anglo-Saxon Poetic Records*. 6 vols. (New York, 1936), III. A convenient edition of the 'Leiden Riddle' is found in A. H. Smith, *Three Northumbrian Poems* (London, 1933).

9 Aldhelm's influence may easily be gauged by consulting the verbal parallels noted by M. Tangl in his edition of the Bonifatian correspondence (see n. 4 above) together with parallels in this correspondence noted by Ehwald in the apparatus to his edition of the prose *De Virginitate* (*passim*); even a cursory consultation will indicate the inaccuracy of Stenton's judgment (*Anglo-Saxon England*, 3rd edn., p. 183): that the quality of Boniface's writing 'owes nothing to Aldhelm's example'.

[10] Lul's correspondence is printed with that of Boniface and others by Tangl (*op. cit.*, n. 4 above).

[11] B. Colgrave, ed., *Felix's Life of St Guthlac* (Cambridge, 1959).

[12] Ed. W. Levison, Monumenta Germaniae Historica. Scriptores rerum Germanicarum (Hannover, 1905), pp. 1–57.

[13] Hygeburg, *Vita Germanuum Willibaldi et Wynnebaldi*, ed. O. Holder-Egger. Monumenta Germaniae Historica. Scriptores XV.1 (Hannover, 1887), pp. 80–117. See now E. Gottschaller, *Hugeburc von Heidenheim.* Münchener Beiträge zur Mediävistik XII (Munich, 1973).

[14] This conjecture is made by Ehwald, pp. 211–12. On the origin of Codex Vindobonensis 751 see the remarks of F. Unterkircher in his introduction to the facsimile edition, Codices Selecti Phototypice Impressi XXIV (Graz, 1971), p. 9.

[15] E.g. MSS London, British Library, Royal 15.A.XVI and Oxford, Bodleian Library, Rawlinson C. 697.

[16] Nearly all surviving Aldhelm manuscripts have been richly glossed (see L. Goossens, *The Old English Glosses of MS. Brussels, Royal Library 1650* [Brussels, 1974], pp. 16–27). Because Aldhelm was studied so intensively in England, many Aldhelm manuscripts contain glosses in Old English, and these glosses have occupied the attention of Old English philologists (see Bibliography, Section B, above). Latin glosses to Aldhelm have been studied less enthusiastically.

[17] Cf. F. C. Robinson, 'Syntactical Glosses in Latin Manuscripts of Anglo-Saxon Provenance', *Speculum* XLVIII (1973), pp. 443–75, and the remarks of Ehwald, p. 215.

[18] M. Lapidge, 'The Hermeneutic Style in Tenth-Century Anglo-Latin Literature', *Anglo-Saxon England* IV (1975), pp. 67–111.

[19] *Gesta Pontificum*, ed. N. E. S. A. Hamilton. Rolls Series (London, 1870), p. 330: 'Moreover, excepting what Bede says about him in his *Historia Ecclesiastica*, Aldhelm has always been held in less esteem than he deserves; he has always—as a result of our countrymen's indolence—been hidden in disreputable obscurity'.

[20] W. B. Wildman, *Life of S. Ealdhelm* (London, 1905), and G. F. Browne, *St Aldhelm* (London, 1903) which contains discussion of the remains of Aldhelm's churches.

[21] E.g. J. Fowler, *St Aldhelm* (Sherborne, 1947), and M. R. James, *Two Ancient English Scholars* (Glasgow, 1931).

[22] E. S. Duckett, *Anglo-Saxon Saints and Scholars* (New York, 1937), pp. 3–97.

[23] W. F. Bolton, *A History of Anglo-Latin Literature I: 597–740* (Princeton, 1967), pp. 68–100. Two examples of error: on p. 76 Bolton tells us that Bugga, whose church is the subject of the third *carmen ecclesiasticum*, was the daughter of King Cædwalla, whereas the second line of the poem calls her 'Centwini filia regis'; on p. 89 he remarks that '*pontificalis curae* could as easily apply to the duties of an abbot as those of a bishop' (which is certainly not true)—but in any case Aldhelm wrote *pastoralis curae*, not *pontificalis curae* (Ehwald, p. 320). Cf. also the review of Bolton's book by M. Winterbottom in *Medium Ævum* XXXVIII (1969), pp. 299–300.

[24] R. Ehwald, *Aldhelmi Opera*. Monumenta Germaniae Historica. Auctores Antiquissimi XV (Berlin, 1919).

ALDHELM'S LIFE (pp. 5–10)

[1] *The Anglo-Saxon Chronicle*, tr. D. Whitelock, D. C. Douglas and S. I. Tucker (London, 1961), p. 26 (s.a. 709). On the tenuous nature of our evidence for Aldhelm's life see also A. S. Cook, 'Sources for the Biography of Aldhelm', *Transactions of the Connecticut Academy of Arts and Sciences* XXVIII (1927), pp. 273–93.

[2] The dates of Faricius's *vita* are fixed by the fact that he mentions the translation of Aldhelm's remains by Warin, which occurred in 1080, and that he left Malmesbury to become abbot of Abingdon in 1100; one assumes that he will have written his *vita* of a Malmesbury saint while still there.

[3] Ed. N. E. S. A. Hamilton. Rolls Series (London, 1870). All citations from William of Malmesbury refer to page numbers of Hamilton's edition. On William and his sources see H. Farmer, 'William of Malmesbury's Life and Works', *Journal of Ecclesiastical History* XIII (1962), pp. 39–54, and D. Whitelock, 'William of Malmesbury on the Works of King Alfred', in *Medieval Literature and Civilization. Studies in Memory of G. N. Garmonsway*, ed. D. A. Pearsall and R. A. Waldron (London, 1969), pp. 78–93, esp. pp 90–91.

[4] E.g. the story related by Faricius and repeated by William concerning Aldhelm's apparition in a dream to Ecgwine, bishop of Worcester. Ecgwine rushed to Doulting (Somerset) where Aldhelm had died at the time of the apparition, and transported his body with ceremony back to Malmesbury. It can be shown that this story is a fiction invented by Dominic of Evesham to magnify Ecgwine, the founder of Evesham; see M. Lapidge, 'The Medieval Hagiography of St Ecgwine', *Vale of Evesham Historical Society Research Papers* VI (1977), pp. 77–93.

[5] Cf. William's own statement: 'Nam annos aetatis ejus (*scil.* Aldhelmi) nulla scriptura misit in calculum; sed est conjectura non fallax grandaevum fuisse sanctum . . .' (p. 385).

[6] The name *Kenten* looks suspiciously like a corrupt and misunderstood form of the name *Centwine*, a well-attested predecessor of Ine as king of the West Saxons.

[7] See A. S. Cook, 'Hadrian of Africa, Italy, and England', *Philological Quarterly* II (1923), pp. 241–58, and R. L. Poole, 'Monasterium Niridanum', *English Historical Review* XXXVI (1921), pp. 540–5.

[8] It is possible that William's only knowledge of Máeldub's existence derived simply from etymological interpretation of the name *Malmesbury*. Bede in fact refers to Malmesbury as *urbs Maildubi* (V.18), whence one might easily conjecture that the founder of the *urbs* was someone called *Maildub*. In early documents the town is also called *Meldunum* and *Meldunesburg*, and perhaps we ought as readily to speculate about an eponymous Irish founder called

Máeldúin! See the detailed discussion by Plummer, *Venerabilis Baedae Opera Historica*, II, pp. 310–11, and the conjectures by Browne, *St Aldhelm*, pp. 72–6.

9   E.g. *The Annals of the Kingdom of Ireland by the Four Masters*, ed. J. O'Donovan. 7 vols. (Dublin, 1856), s.a. 622, 681, 695 and 890; *The Martyrology of Donegal*, ed. J. O'Donovan, J. H. Todd and W. Reeves (Dublin, 1864), pp. 68, 264, 278, 340 and 346; and the *Martyrology of Oengus the Culdee*, ed. W. Stokes. Henry Bradshaw Society XXIX (London, 1905), pp. 78, 90 and 224. Recently, I tentatively advanced the identification of the alleged teacher of Aldhelm with the last-mentioned Máeldub of the *Martyrology of Oengus* ('Some Conjectures on the Origins and Tradition of the Hisperic Poem *Rubisca*', *Ériu* XXV (1974), pp. 85–6). However, the links are tenuous, and I am sceptical of any final solution, given the available evidence [M.H.].

10 *St Aldhelm*, pp. 46–8.

11 We know that Aldhelm's reading was vast, and that he spent only about two (interrupted) years at Canterbury. He must have had access to a very considerable library before he arrived there. Many difficulties would appear to be solved by a hypothesis that Aldhelm received his early education in Rome where books were certainly available (thus the reference in Letter VI), rather than in the woods of Wessex. Nevertheless, it is doubtful, if Aldhelm had gone to Rome for his education, that he would have complained to Leuthere about the poverty of his education in computus!

12 'Aldhelm's Prose Style and its Origins', *Anglo-Saxon England* VI (1977), pp. 39–76.

13 I previously referred to Aldhelm as a 'Hisperic' writer (*Hisperica Famina* I, p. 36). I now concur wholeheartedly with M.L. that Aldhelm's style cannot be labelled thus, although I still think it likely on the basis of the verbal parallels adduced by Grosjean (*Celtica* III (1956), pp. 65–7) that Aldhelm had read some version(s) of the *H.F.* and that we can continue to use Aldhelm as the *terminus ante* for the date of those works [M.H.].

14 Ehwald, p. 494.1. For evidence that Virgilius Maro Grammaticus was an Irishman, see the study by M. Herren, 'Some New Light on the Life of Virgilius Maro Grammaticus', *Proceedings of the Royal Irish Academy* LXXVIII C (1978), forthcoming.

15 Ed. M. C. Diaz y Diaz, *Liber de Ordine Creaturarum. Un anónimo irlandés del siglo VII* (Santiago de Compostela, 1972), p. 37.

16 P. Grosjean, 'Confusa Caligo', *Celtica* III (1956), pp. 65–7.

17 Cf. the interesting but insupportable conjectures of A. S. Cook, 'Theodore of Tarsus and Gislenus of Athens', *Philological Quarterly* II (1923), pp. 1–25.

18 Ehwald, pp. 544–6; cf. M. Manitius, *Sitzungsber. d. österr. Akad. d. Wiss.* CXII (Vienna, 1886), pp. 535–614.

19 These works include: a brief poem in octosyllables (quoted by Bolton, *A History of Anglo-Latin Literature I*, p. 62, and mistranslated); a Penitential which may be based on Theodore's teaching but which is transmitted to us at third-hand (ed. A. W. Haddan and W. Stubbs, *Councils and Ecclesiastical Documents relating to Great Britain and Ireland.* 3 vols. (Oxford, 1869), III, pp.

173–204); and a series of fascinating biblical glosses which have not yet been printed (see B. Bischoff, 'Wendepunkte in der Geschichte der lateinischen Exegese im Frühmittelalter', in *Mittelalterliche Studien.* 2 vols. [Stuttgart, 1966], I, pp. 206–9).

20 Bede's statement therefore corroborates that of Aldhelm in Letter I (see above, p. 152–3.

21 It is worth noting that Aldhelm occasionally reproduces a Greek word in a mutilated form (e.g. he spells Greek *dipsas* as *gypsa*), which might suggest that he derived the word from a glossary rather than from first-hand knowledge.

22 See Ehwald's remarks, p. 94, as well as his general discussion, pp. xii–xiii.

23 The three Hebrew words which Aldhelm cites in c. XXI of his prose *De Virginitate* (*mane, techel, phares*) derive from the Vulgate (Dan. V. 24–8); cf. Ehwald, p. xiii.

24 William states (p. 385) that Aldhelm died in the thirty-fourth year after he had been made an abbot by bishop Leuthere (709 − 34 = 675). The source of William's information is not specified, and he himself tampered with this date in the autograph manuscript of the *Gesta Pontificum* (Oxford, Magdalen College, MS. 172).

25 The one trustworthy fact concerning the date of the prose *De Virginitate* is that it was written before Aldhelm became bishop in 706 (see above, p. 10); the 'ecclesiastical administration' must therefore refer to his duties as abbot. Some part of Aldhelm's ecclesiastical administration is reflected in surviving charters to which he subscribed as witness. Two such charters are believed to be genuine (they are not among those printed by Ehwald); they are printed together with their witness-lists by W. deG. Birch, *Cartularium Saxonicum.* 3 vols. (London, 1885–99), Nos. 72 and 78. Bibliography pertaining to these charters is given by P. H. Sawyer, *Anglo-Saxon Charters: An Annotated List and Bibliography* (London, 1968), Nos. 235 and 45 respectively. Birch No. 72 (= Sawyer, No. 235) is translated by D. Whitelock, *English Historical Documents I: c. 500–1042* (London, 1955), p. 445. A number of other charters bear Aldhelm's name as witness, but they are all considered to be spurious; Birch Nos. 25 (Sawyer 227), 61 (Sawyer 236), 62 (Sawyer 237), 108 (Sawyer 245), 109 (Sawyer 246), 113 (Sawyer 248), 118 (Sawyer 1175) and 124 (Sawyer 79).

26 William states specifically that the church was *juxta fluvium qui vocatur From* (p. 346); modern scholars often state that the church in question was *at* Frome (Somerset). But there were several rivers called *Frome* in Anglo-Saxon times; and since there are no remains of an Anglo-Saxon church at the present-day village of Frome, it is perhaps worth looking elsewhere for the location of Aldhelm's church. One river Frome debouches at Wareham (Dorset), and at Wareham there is evidence of the existence of two pre-conquest churches which are now largely destroyed (see H. M. and J. Taylor, *Anglo-Saxon Architecture.* 2 vols. (Cambridge, 1965), II, pp. 634–9). Furthermore, William of Malmesbury states elsewhere (pp. 363–4) that Aldhelm had built a church at *Werham*, and it is possibly this church which was *juxta fluvium ... From*, not one at the village of Frome.

27 The church of St Laurence at Bradford-on-Avon is one of the most complete and beautiful Anglo-Saxon churches still standing. In the opinion of
the Taylors, 'its main fabric is indeed the work of Aldhelm's period, early
in the eighth century' (*Anglo-Saxon Architecture*, I, p. 87). The question of the
date of this church, however, is a complicated one, and not everyone is persuaded that the church as it stands dates from Aldhelm's time. See further
H. M. Taylor, 'The Anglo-Saxon Chapel at Bradford-on-Avon',
Archaeological Journal CXXX (1973), pp. 141–71 (as well as the comments
by Lord Fletcher quoted on pp. 170–1 of this article).

28 See D. Knowles, *The Monastic Order in England*. 2nd edn. (Cambridge,
1966), pp. 576–7; cf. the remarks of W. Levison, *England and the Continent
in the Eighth Century* (Oxford, 1946, repr. 1973), pp. 22–6.

29 The dates of Aldfrith's death and Osred's accession are discussed in detail
by K. Harrison, *The Framework of Anglo-Saxon History to A.D. 900*
(Cambridge, 1976), pp. 85–91.

30 On traces of an Anglo-Saxon church still visible at Sherborne, see H. M.
and J. Taylor, *Anglo-Saxon Architecture*, II, pp. 540–3. On the territory
of Aldhelm's diocese, see F. P. Magoun, 'Aldhelm's Diocese of Sherborne
be westan wuda', *Harvard Theological Review* XXXII (1939), pp. 103–14.

31 From Bede's information, both the compiler of the *Anglo-Saxon Chronicle*
entry and William compute that Aldhelm died in 709, but this date is
not entirely reliable because it takes no account of the fact that Aldfrith
died very late in 705 (14 December).

THE WRITINGS OF ALDHELM (pp. 11–19)

1 See M. Lapidge, 'Some Remnants of Bede's Lost *Liber Epigrammatum*',
English Historical Review XC (1975), pp. 798–820 (esp. Nos. 6, 7, 8 and 10);
cf. L. Wallach, 'The Urbana Anglo-Saxon Sylloge of Latin Inscriptions', in
*Poetry and Poetics from Ancient Greece to the Renaissance: Studies in Honor of James
Hutton*, ed. G. M. Kirkwood. Cornell Studies in Classical Philology XXX-
VIII (Ithaca, N.Y., 1975), pp. 134–51, and the discussion of these two ar-
ticles by D. Schaller, 'Bemerkungen zur Inschriften-Sylloge von Urbana',
Mittellateinisches Jahrbuch XII (1977), pp. 9–21.

2 Ed. E. Dümmler, Monumenta Germaniae Historica. Poetae Latini Aevi
Carolini I (Berlin, 1881), pp. 304–44.

3 See M. Lapidge, 'Aldhelm's Latin Poetry and Old English Verse', *Comparative Literature* XXXI (1979), forthcoming.

4 See discussion by M. Roger, *L'enseignement des lettres classiques*, pp. 350–83.

5 Ed. T. Gaisford, *Scriptores Latini Rei Metricae* (Oxford, 1837), pp. 577–85.

6 Ed. C. B. Kendall, in *Bedae Venerabilis Opera I: Opera Didascalica*, ed. C. W.
Jones. Corpus Christianorum, Series Latina CXXIIIA (Turnhout, 1975),
pp. 59–141. See also R. B. Palmer, 'Bede as Text-Book Writer: A Study of
his *De Arte Metrica*', *Speculum* XXXIV (1959), pp. 573–84.

7 Cf. Aldhelm's metrical preface to the *Enigmata*: 'Munera nunc largire,

rudis quo pandere rerum/Versibus enigmata queam clandistina fatu' (Ehwald, p. 97).

8 A translation of the *Carmen de Virginitate* is being prepared by Professor James L. Rosier.

9 Ed. J. Huemer, *Corpus Scriptorum Ecclesiasticorum Latinorum* X (Vienna, 1885).

10 E.g. among male virgins Thomas and Malchus are omitted from the poetic part, whereas Gervasius and Protasius are added; among female virgins, Felicitas and Anastasia are omitted from the poetic part.

11 Bede's metrical *Vita Cuthberti* is edited by W. Jaager, *Bedas metrische Vita S. Cuthberti*, Palaestra CXCVIII (Leipzig, 1935); the prose work is edited by B. Colgrave, *Two Lives of St Cuthbert* (Cambridge, 1940), which edition also includes the text of the anonymous *vita* of Cuthbert. The poetic and prose lives of Bede have not been printed together for over one hundred years.

12 The poetic and prose parts of Alcuin's *Vita S. Willibrordi* are printed together by P. Jaffé, *Monumenta Alcuiniana*. Bibliotheca Rerum Germanicarum VI (Berlin, 1873), pp. 35–79.

13 *Carmen de Virginitate*, lines 2855, 2844, 2845 and 2843 respectively.

14 *Ep.* LXXI (ed. Tangl, p 144): 'Similiter obsecro, ut mihi Aldhelmi episcopi aliqua opuscula seu prosarum seu metrorum aut rithmicorum dirigere digneris ad consolationem peregrinationis meae'. The letter is dated by Tangl to 745 × 746; Dealwine is otherwise unknown. Scholars agree that the octosyllables quoted by Aldhelm in c. VII of the *De Virginitate* (above, p. 64) are by Aldhelm himself.

15 Most recently by Bolton, *A History of Anglo-Latin Literature I*, p. 188.

16 Cf. Unterkircher, *Sancti Bonifacii Epistolae*, p. 24.

17 H. Bradley, 'On Some Poems Ascribed to Aldhelm', *English Historical Review* XV (1900), pp. 291–2. Bradley's position is adopted by Bolton, *op. cit.*, p. 189.

18 He was in good company: cf. L. Traube, *Karolingische Dichtungen* (Berlin, 1888), pp. 130–5.

19 It might seem strange that the first poem in a series would be inscribed *carmen aliter*; but we have no means of proving that the first poem in the manuscript as it survives was indeed the first poem of the series. The first rhythmical poem begins a new quire (at f. 40[r]), and although written by the one scribe, this quire has no organic connection with the ordered sequence of Bonifatian correspondence contained in the previous five quires. Since there are no quire signatures in the present quires, it must remain a possibility that a quire has been lost before f. 40[r] and that this lost quire may have contained other rhythmical poems. Concerning the use of *aliter* to mark the beginning of a new poem: it is noteworthy that *aliter* is similarly used to mark the beginnings of new poems in the famous Codex Salmasius, a nearly contemporary manuscript (s.viii[ex]) containing an anthology of Late Latin poetry, now preserved in Paris (BN lat. 10318: *CLA* V.593). The Codex Salmasius is edited in facsimile by H. Omont, *Anthologie des poètes latins dite de Saumaise* (Paris, 1903).

20 *English Historical Review* XV (1900), p. 292.

[21] It occurs, for example, in the *Liber Vitae* of Durham, ed. H. Sweet, *The Oldest English Texts*. E.E.T.S. (London, 1885), index, s.v. 'Helmgils'.

[22] Cf. A. Campbell, *Old English Grammar* (Oxford, 1959), pp. 185–6.

[23] The identity of this Helmgils requires investigation. It is tempting to think that the addressee of Aldhelm's poem was Hæmgils, abbot of nearby Glastonbury (678–*c*. 704) and a contemporary of Aldhelm. However, this identification is difficult to affirm on philological grounds: the first element of the abbot's name, *Hæm-*, is not equivalent to *Helm-*, and Aldhelm must have known this (*Hæm-* is probably from *ham-* with i-affection caused by the element *-gils*; cf. Campbell, *Old English Grammar*, p. 83). Could Aldhelm's poem originally have read *casa . . . obses* (= *hæm* + *gils*), whence *casa* was replaced by *casses* in the light of *cassem priscum* in poem No. IV?

[24] Unterkircher, *Sancti Bonifacii Epistolae*, p. 25.

[25] Ehwald, p. 509; H. Hahn, *Bonifaz und Lul* (Leipzig, 1883), pp. 8 and 84; B. Bönhoff, *Aldhelm von Malmesbury* (Dresden, 1894), pp. 59–60.

[26] Cf. H. P. R. Finberg, *The Early Charters of Wessex* (Leicester, 1964), Nos. 181 and 182 (these two charters are 'available in later . . . copies, thought to embody the substance of the original, but having some material, probably spurious, substituted or interpolated'). Many scholars would be even more sceptical than Finberg.

[27] See bibliography on the charters by P. H. Sawyer, *Anglo-Saxon Charters*, Nos. 1166 and 1245; cf. A. S. Cook. 'A Putative Charter to Aldhelm', in *Studies . . . in Honor of Frederick Klaeber*, pp. 254–7.

[28] 'Eine anglo-lateinische Ubersetzung aus dem Griechischen um 700', *Zeitschrift für deutsches Altertum* LXXV (1938), pp. 105–11.

[29] Ed. M. Haupt, *Opuscula* (Leipzig, 1876), II, pp. 218–52.

[30] It was suggested by S. Backx ('Sur la date et l'origine du De Monstris, belluis et serpentibus', *Latomus* III (1939), p. 61) that the work probably originated in Anglo-Saxon England in the second half of the seventh century. Subsequently, E. Faral ('La queue de poisson des sirènes', *Romania* LXXIV (1953), pp. 466–70) has suggested that Aldhelm was the author. Recently, L. G. Whitbread has reviewed the evidence and come again to the conclusion that Aldhelm was the author of the *Liber Monstrorum*: 'The *Liber Monstrorum* and *Beowulf*', *Mediaeval Studies* XXXVI (1974), pp. 434–71, esp. pp. 455–8.

TRANSLATORS' NOTES (pp. 20–1)

[1] 'Aldhelm's Prose Style and its Origins', *Anglo-Saxon England* VI (1977), pp. 39–76.

[2] See the remarks concerning *hypallage* by A. Campbell, in his edition of Æthelwulf's *De Abbatibus* (Oxford, 1967), p. xxxix.

[3] A check list of these sources (for the *De Virginitate* alone) is provided in Appendix III, above.

1 See Ehwald's discussion, pp. 35–41. The *Epistola and Acircium* is transmitted entire in but half a dozen manuscripts, whereas there are more than four times that number containing the *Enigmata* alone.

2 William lists them as separate works (pp. 343–4).

3 J. H. Pitman, *The Riddles of Aldhelm* (New Haven, 1925); also F. Glorie, *Collectiones Aenigmatum Merovingicae Aetatis.* Corpus Christianorum, Series Latina CXXXIII–CXXXIIIA. 2 vols. (Turnhout, 1968), I, 359–540. The latter reprints Ehwald's text together with Pitman's translation.

4 The attribution to Isidore has been denied by B. Bischoff, 'Eine verschollene Einteilung der Wissenschaften', in *Mittelalterliche Studien.* 2 vols. (Stuttgart 1967), II, pp. 273–88, and by M. C. Diaz y Diaz, 'Arts libéraux et écrivains espagnols et insulaires', in *Arts libéraux et philosophie au moyen age* (Montreal/Paris, 1969), pp. 37–46, who writes: 'En effet, la paternité isidorienne n'a pas été suffisament prouvee' (p. 41).

5 Ed. among the works of Isidore in *Patrologia Latina* LXXXIII, cols. 179–200. A new edition is being prepared by C. Leonardi; see his remarks in *Bullettino dell'Istituto storico italiano per il medio evo* LXVIII (1956), pp. 203–31.

6 See R. E. McNally, *Der irische Liber de numeris* (Munich, 1957). The *Liber de Numeris* is partially edited in *Patrologia Latina* LXXXIII, cols. 1293–1302; a new edition by Fr McNally is in progress.

7 If the work is pseudonymous, the probability that it was Irish is very great. By the middle of the seventh century, or very shortly afterwards, there already existed pseudo-Isidorian works of Irish provenance such as the *De Ortu et Obitu Patrum* and the *Liber de Ordine Creaturarum.* Genuine Isidorian works were known in Ireland earlier than they were in England, although we cannot now preclude the possibility that Isidore's works reached England directly from Spain. For the dissemination of Isidore's works, see B. Bischoff, 'Die europäische Verbreitung der Werke Isidors von Sevilla', in *Mittelalterliche Studien*, II, pp. 171–87; M. Herren, 'On the Earliest Irish Acquaintance with Isidore of Seville' in the forthcoming proceedings of the International Visigothic Colloquium held in Dublin, May, 1975. For possible stylistic connections between Spain and England, see the observations of M. Winterbottom in *Anglo-Saxon England* VI (1977), pp. 65–8. Professor Bischoff has also pointed to a probable direct connection between Julian of Toledo and Hadrian of Canterbury (*Settimane di studio del Centro italiano di studi sull'alto medioevo* XXII (1975), p. 299).

8 Aldfrith's learning was attested by numerous sources of both English and Irish provenance; see Plummer's excellent note, *Baedae Opera Historica*, II, pp. 263–4, and note Aldhelm's own remark, above, p. 46.

9 Plummer, *Baedae Opera Historica*, II, p. 263.

10 Prose *Vita S. Cuthberti*, c. XXIV (ed. B. Colgrave, *Two Lives of St Cuthbert* [Cambridge, 1940], p. 236).

The EPISTOLA AD ACIRCIUM (pp. 34–47)

[1] The name *Acircius* means 'from the North' (*a + circius*); cf. above, p. 32.

[2] Translating *clientelae*. *Cliens* and *clientela* in some passages in Aldhelm denote a relationship of dependency, as they do in 'normal Latin'. Elsewhere, however, they point to a relationship of equality. Here the word may refer to Aldfrith's spiritual dependence upon Aldhelm, his godfather. See above, p. 32 and below, p. 197, n. 3.

[3] A *lustrum* is the equivalent of five *lunar* years, as Aldhelm himself shows, above, p. 40. I have retained the Latin *lustrum*, as there is no satisfactory modern English rendering of that word.

[4] The Latin of this passage is especially obtuse, but Aldhelm appears to be saying that his intellectual and artistic development is grounded in spirituality, expressly in the sacraments. *Nostrae necessitudinis* should not be construed with *primordia*, since, as it becomes clear (p. 45), there is no improvement in the relationship between the two men; rather the reverse is implied.

[5] The notion that the world would last seven thousand years from the time of the creation to the end of the millennium of rest that was to follow the Six Ages is repeated by Bede in the *Chronicon* appended to his *De Temporum Ratione*, c. LXVII (ed. T. Mommsen, MGH. Auct. Antiq. XIII. 2 [Berlin, 1895], p. 322). See C. W. Jones's introduction to *Bedae Opera de Temporibus* (Cambridge, Mass., 1943), pp. 133–5 and esp. p. 345; F. E. Robbins, *The Hexaemeral Literature* (Chicago, 1912), p. 27; and R. E. McNally, *The Bible in the Early Middle Ages* (Westminister, Maryland, 1959), pp. 43–4.

[6] Modern editions of the Vulgate give *coenacula et tristega*.

[7] See Jerome's *Praefatio in Librum Iob* (*Patrologia Latina* XXVIII, cols. 1140–1).

[8] The phrase *nequaquam pars ultima profetantium* could mean alternatively 'Isaias, by no means the least of the prophets', but this is less likely; cf. Ehwald, p. 66.18: *Zacharias . . . in ordine vaticinantium undecimus*. Thus we have an example of Aldhelmian irony, as Isaias appears first in the prophetic canon.

[9] *Qui* must refer to Elias, but the author of the miracles mentioned is Eliseus, who received 'the double spirit' of Elias after he was taken up into heaven (IV Reg. II. 9–13).

[10] The name *Solomon* (or *Salomon*) is derived from Hebrew *shālōm*, 'peace'. See Jerome's *Libri Interpretationis Hebraicorum Nominum* (ed. L. Lagarde, Corpus Christianorum, Series Latina LXXII [Turnhout, 1959], pp. 57–161), pp. 138 and 148: 'Salomon. pacificus'; cf. Isidore, *Etymologiae* VII. vi. 65. Jerome elsewhere calls him 'Salomon pacificus et amabilis Domini' (*Ep.* LIII). Cf. Aldhelm's Letter to Heahfrith, p. 162.

[11] The four rivers of Paradise, described in Genesis II. 10–14, are applied typologically to the four Evangelists; cf. *De Virginitate*, c. VII (above p. 64).

[12] Translating *frena*. It is difficult to imagine the smashing of reins; the more likely translation is 'ties' or 'bands' in the sense of 'restraining forms'; cf. *Oxford Latin Dictionary*, s.v. 'frenum'.

¹³ Scotomatic: one with dim vision.

13 Scotomatic: one with dim vision.
14 A probable allusion to the infancy Gospels, such as to the story of Jesus's 'teaching' of carpentry to Joseph. See the 'Gospel of Thomas' (in M. R. James, *The Apocryphal New Testament* [Oxford, 1924], pp. 52 and 57).
15 Aldhelm seems especially fond of this line; see the Letter to Geraint, p. 159.
16 For the prophecy of Gabriel, see Daniel IX. 22–7 in the Vulgate version. A week is traditionally understood as a week of years.
17 For the Hebrew calendar, see Jones, *Bedae Opera de Temporibus*, pp. 7–8.
18 Jones's note on Bede's *De Temporum Ratione* ((*op. cit.*, p. 344) applies equally well to Aldhelm and is worth quoting: 'The Messianic tradition Bede followed comes from Julius Africanus (*circ.* 220), the most skilled of early Christian chronographers, whose interpretation was repeated by Eusebius in his Chronicle (ed. Fotheringham, pp. 196, 242–3, 256–7) and in *Demonstratio Evang.* VIII, 2 ff. . . . But Bede's immediate source was Jerome's *In Danielem*, c. IX (PL XXV, cols. 541–3 [see now F. Glorie's edition in Corpus Christianorum, Series Latina LXXVA (Turnhout, 1964)]), where a clear and complete exposition of Africanus's doctrine is given together with other theories'.
19 I have not as yet discovered a precise reference to a seven-volume Bible prior to Aldhelm. Cassiodorus divided the Bible into nine actual volumes (Octateuch, Kings, Prophets, the Psalter, Solomon, Hagiographa, Gospels, Epistles of the Apostles, Acts and Apocalypse). In England, in Aldhelm's day, the pandect was already established. Could Aldhelm have been thinking of theoretical divisions rather than physical ones? Even so, the popular division of the Bible as represented by Isidore (*Etym.* VI. i–ii) gives only six: the Laws, the Prophets, the Hagiographa, non-canonical writings, the Gospels, and the writings of the Apostles.
20 The seven ages are: (1) from the creation to the flood; (2) from the flood to Abraham; (3) from Abraham to Samuel and Saul; (4) from David to the captivity; (5) from the captivity to Christ; (6) from Christ to the present. The seventh age is the millennium of rest that will follow the end of the world; cf. p. 188, n. 5.
21 The steps to the priesthood are: (1) porter, (2) reader, (3) exorcist, (4) acolyte, (5) sub-deacon, (6) deacon. The seventh rank is the priesthood itself which includes the episcopacy.
22 Arator was a sixth-century Christian poet, author of the hexameter poem *De Actibus Apostolorum* (ed. A. P. McKinlay, Corpus Scriptorum Ecclesiasticorum Latinorum LXXII (Vienna, 1951)). Arator also indulged in the mystical interpretation of numbers.
23 The Nicolaites were apparently guilty of moral laxity. They are labelled as fornicators in the Apocalypse of John (II. 14–15, Douay numbering). Eusebius (*Hist. Eccl.* XXIX. 4) quotes an anecdote recorded by Clement of Alexandria to the effect that the sect practised sexual promiscuity, whereas their founder, Nicolaus, was chaste. See A. von Harnack, 'The Sects of the Nicolaitans and Nicolaus the Deacon in Jerusalem', *Journal of Religion* II (1923), pp. 413–22.

24 Aldhelm compresses the details of the two dreams of Pharaoh (Gen. XLI. 2–4 and 5–7) into a single sentence.

25 The decalogue is traditionally divided between the three commandments respecting man's duty to God and the seven respecting his duty to his neighbour. See V. F. Hopper, *Medieval Number Symbolism* (New York, 1938), p. 85.

26 The Lord's Prayer consists of seven petitions, though not of seven biblical verses.

27 This canon of the *artes* appears to follow Isidore or pseudo-Isidore, *Liber Numerorum*, c. XLIV (*Patrologia Latina* LXXXIII, col. 182). See B. Bischoff, 'Eine verschollene Einteilung der Wissenschaften', in *Mittelalterliche Studien*, II, pp. 273–88, and M. Diaz y Diaz, 'Arts libéraux et écrivains espagnols et insulaires', in *Arts libéraux et philosophie au moyen âge* (Montreal/Paris, 1969), pp. 37–46.

28 See Isidore, *Etym.* III. lxvii and *De Natura Rerum*, c. XXXIII. 3.

29 Yoke and the Cart: *Ursa Major* or 'The Big Dipper'.

30 For the probable source of these etymologies, see Isidore, *Etym.* III. lxxi. 13 and *De Natura Rerum*, c. XXVI. 6.

31 The term *stella* included the planets; cf. Isidore, *Etym.* III. lxvii.

32 See Isidore, *Etym.* V. xxxi. 6–9.

33 i.e. the seven *volumina* of the Scriptures and the seven commandments respecting behaviour to one's neighbour.

34 The last two verses are Aldhelm's own; compare the pastiche at the end of the Letter to Heahfrith, p. 164.

35 Though Paul himself mentions the 'third heaven' (II Cor. XII. 2), Aldhelm's reference is probably to the *Visio Pauli* or 'Apocalypse of Paul', an apocryphal work which was widely read in the middle ages. This work is edited by T. Silverstein, *Visio S. Pauli: The History of The Apocalypse in Latin together with Nine Texts* (London, 1935); the Latin version is translated by M. R. James, *The Apocryphal New Testament* (Oxford, 1924), pp. 525–55, and a translation of the 'Revelation of Paul' based on Tischendorf's Greek text can be found in A. Roberts and J. Donaldson, *Apocryphal Gospels, Acts and Revelations*. Ante-Nicene Christian Library XVI (Edinburgh, 1870). Aldhelm alludes to the *Visio Pauli* again at *De Virginitate*, c. XXIV (p. 81).

36 See Isidore, *Etym.* II. xxi. 4.

37 Aldhelm is at his most inscrutable here, but I gather his meaning to be this: if God can in a sense violate his own nature and establish a *corporeal* relation with a mortal, it is incumbent upon man to follow that example by establishing a *spiritual* relation with his fellows.

38 Translating *domesticae familiaritatis*. Aldhelm alludes to the spiritual kinship of godfather and godson, not to blood relationship.

39 The Pelasgian tongue, i.e. the Greek language. Aldhelm's knowledge of the history of Greek literature was not profound. Hesiod most certainly wrote a work on farming and the seasons entitled *Works and Days*; but no agricultural treatise was composed by Homer and I know of no tradition ascribing one to him.

[40] This was Theodosius II, emperor of the East, 408–450. He was the instigator of the great codification of Roman law known as the Codex Theodosianus. The tradition that he was a calligrapher was based on two poems printed in the *Anthologia Latina* (ex. A. Riese [Leipzig, 1894], Nos. 724 and 783.

[41] The tradition that Theodosius transcribed the grammar of Priscian is certainly false, since the emperor was dead in 450, whereas the grammarian was not active until the early sixth century. It is probable that Aldhelm had seen a manuscript of Priscian which contained the *subscriptio* of Flavius Theodorus ('Fl. Theodorus Dionysii v.s. memorialis s. scrinii epistolarum et adiutor v.m. quaestoris s. palatii scripsi artem Prisciani eloquentissimi grammatici doctoris mei manu mea in urbe Roma Constantinopoli . . .'), and that he misread *Theodorus* as *Theodosius*.

INTRODUCTION TO ALDHELM'S PROSE DE VIRGINITATE (pp. 51–8)

[1] See D. Whitelock, *Some Anglo-Saxon Bishops of London* (London, 1974), pp. 5–10.

[2] On the foundation of Barking and its early charters, see C. R. Hart, *The Early Charters of Eastern England* (Leicester, 1966), pp. 117–45; cf. also Plummer, *Venerabilis Baedae Opera Historica*, II, p. 218.

[3] The date is from [Florence] of Worcester (first half of twelfth century); see Plummer, *op. cit.*, II, p. 219.

[4] *Ep.* X (ed. Tangl, pp. 8–15); tr. E. Emerton, *The Letters of St Boniface* (New York, 1940), pp. 25–31.

[5] On double monasteries see F. M. Stenton, *Anglo-Saxon England.* 3rd edn. (Oxford, 1971), pp. 161–2; see further M. Bateson, 'Origin and Early History of Double Monasteries', *Transactions of the Royal Historical Society* XIII (1899), pp. 137–98, S. Hilpisch, *Die Doppelklöster: Entstehung und Organisation.* Beiträge zur Geschichte des alten Mönchtums und des Benediktinerordens XV (Munster, 1928), and more recently J. Godfrey, 'The Place of the Double Monastery in the Anglo-Saxon Minster System', in *Famulus Christi: Essays in Commemoration of . . . the Venerable Bede*, ed. G. Bonner (London, 1976), pp. 344–50.

[6] *The Anglo-Saxon Chronicle*, tr. D. Whitelock, D. C. Douglas and S. I. Tucker (London, 1961), p. 27.

[7] The identity can never be finally proved, of course; but I think that the very tendentious argumentation of the *De Virginitate* concerning women who have abandoned marriages must indicate that the identity is highly probable.

[8] Most of the works are printed in Migne's *Patrologia Latina*: Cyprian, *De Habitu Virginum* (IV, cols. 440–64); Augustine, *De Sancta Virginitate* (XL, cols. 397–427); Ambrose, *De Virginibus ad Marcellinam* (XVI, cols. 187–232), *De Virginitate* (*ibid.*, cols. 265–302), *De Institutione Virginis* (*ibid.*, cols. 305–34), and *Exhortatio Virginitatis* (*ibid.*, cols. 335–64). Tertullian's treatise, *De Velandis Virginibus*, is available in a more recent edition, ed. E. Dekkers, Corpus

Christianorum, Series Latina II (Turnhout, 1954), pp. 1209–26. Jerome's 'treatise' is in fact one of his Letters (No. XXII) addressed to one Eustochium: ed. and tr. F. A. Wright, Loeb Classical Library (London/Cambridge, Mass., 1963), pp. 52–159. Alcimus Avitus's poem *De Virginitate* (or better, perhaps, *De Consolatoria Castitatis Laude*) is edited by R. Peiper, MGH. Auct. Antiq. VI. 2 (Berlin, 1883), pp. 274–94. Venantius Fortunatus's poem *De Virginitate* is edited by F. Leo, MGH. Auct. Antiq. IV. 1 (Berlin, 1881), pp. 181–91. There is some discussion of patristic works on virginity in M. Bernards, *Speculum Virginum: Geistigkeit und Seelenleben der Frau im Hochmittelalter* (Cologne/Graz, 1955), pp. 33–6. Early texts relating to the ecclesiastical status of virgins have been collected by J. Mayer, *Monumenta de viduis diaconissis virginibusque tractantia*, Florilegium Patristicum XLII (Bonn, 1938); see also F. de B. Vizmanos, *Las virgines cristianas en la Iglesia primitiva: estudio historico y antologia patristica* (Madrid, 1949).

9 On the traditional aspects of Aldhelm's conception of virginity, see M. Byrne, *The Tradition of the Nun in Medieval England* (Washington, 1932), pp. 25–43.

10 St Paul's conception of woman and marriage is treated by P. Tischleder, *Wesen und Stellung der Frau nach de Lehre des heiligen Paulus* (Münster, 1930), and by G. Delling, *Paulus' Stellung zu Frau und Ehe*, Beiträge zur Wissenschaft vom Alten und Neuen Testament IV. 5 (Stuttgart, 1931).

11 Jerome, Letter XXII to Eustochium, c. 20 (ed. F. A. Wright, Loeb Classical Library, p. 94).

12 *PL* XL, col. 403: 'non enim licet dimittere uxorem, nisi ex causa fornicationis'.

13 *PL* XVI, cols. 195–6.

14 *Bedae Venerabilis Opera III: Opera Homiletica*, ed. D. Hurst, Corpus Christianorum, Series Latina CXXII (Turnhout, 1955), p. 92: 'reliquit uxorem et filios non quidem uxorem acceptam et filios ex ea natos sed uxorem prorsus accipere ex qua filios habere posset castitatis amore contempsit mallens ad illa centum quadraginta quattuor milia electorum pertinere qui cantant canticum nouum ante sedem agni . . .'; cf. Aldhelm, *De Virginitate*, c. VII.

15 The poem is edited by F. J. H. Jenkinson, *Hisperica Famina* (Cambridge, 1908), p. 33; I have silently altered and emended the text which I translate here. I hope to publish a full discussion of this poem elsewhere.

16 A. W. Haddan and W. Stubbs, *Councils and Ecclesiastical Documents Relating to Great Britain and Ireland*. 3 vols. (Oxford, 1869), III, p. 199: 'Mulieri non licet virum dimittere licet sit fornicator, nisi forte pro monasterio. Basilius hoc judicavit'.

17 See discussion by M. Bernards, *Speculum Virginum*, pp. 40–4, and by J. Bugge, *Virginitas: An Essay in the History of a Medieval Ideal* (The Hague, 1975), pp. 67–8.

18 Ambrose, *De Virginibus ad Marcellinam*, I. x. 60 (*PL* XVI, col. 205); Jerome, *Comm. in evang. Matth.*, 2 (*PL* XXVI, col. 92); Augustine, *De Sancta Virginitate*, c. XLV (*PL* XL, col. 423).

19 Ehwald (p. 248) suggested that Aldhelm was indebted to a certain *Passio S.*

Victoriae (printed *Analecta Bollandiana* II (1883), pp. 157–60) for this novel conception. However, discussion in the *Passio S. Victoriae* is far too cursory to have provided Aldhelm with the depth of meaning with which he invests his revised tripartite division, nor is it improbable that the *Passio* was based on Aldhelm rather than vice versa.

20 How successfully Cuthburg pursued her career of chastity is another matter. Among the Bonifatian correspondence in Codex Vindobonensis 751 is an anonymous letter from a monk to another unknown monk which describes a vision of heaven and hell much like Dryhthelm's (*HE* V.12) or that of the monk of Much Wenlock (Boniface, *Ep.* X). From an internal reference to 'Ethilbealdum . . . quondam regalem tyrannum' the letter can be dated to some time after 757, the year of Æthelbald's death. In his vision the anonymous monk saw Cuthburg and another lady called Wialan, both of whom had once enjoyed queenly authority, immersed in penitential pits ('in ipsis poenalibus puteis Cuthburgam simulque Wialan quondam reginali potestate fruentes demersas'), where they were being tormented for their carnal sins (*Ep.* CXV, ed. Tangl, p. 248). If this is the Cuthburg who had been married to Aldfrith of Northumbria and who later became abbess of Womborne, she seems to have failed (at least according to the judgment of a later age) in her striving after perfection—in spite of Aldhelm's admonitions. Once again, however, the identity cannot be proved absolutely.

21 The bee as a type of virginity is a well-known literary topos which has its origin in Latin tradition in Vergil's *Georgics* (IV.197–202). I am afraid I cannot agree with E. S. Duckett (*Anglo-Saxon Saints and Scholars*, p. 62) that Aldhelm's use of the simile indicates that bees were kept at Malmesbury.

22 It is also noteworthy that, among Aldhelm's catalogue of virgins, there is a number of couples—such as Chrysanthus and Daria (c. XXXV)—who strive together to attain to the perfection of virginity.

23 On this passage as evidence for contemporary Anglo-Saxon dress, see R. I. Page, *Life in Anglo-Saxon England* (London, 1970), pp. 166–9.

24 Aldhelm does not display a profound knowledge of the poems of Paulinus of Nola as he does of (say) Caelius Sedulius; nonetheless, he quotes a line of Paulinus of Nola in his metrical treatise (Ehwald, p.96. 16), and must presumably have known the poems at first hand. It is interesting to note that Bede subsequently produced a prose *Vita S. Felicis* from the accounts of that saint contained in various of Paulinus of Nola's poems.

The Prose DE VIRGINITATE (pp. 59–132)

1 Of these nuns only Hildelith may be identified with virtual certainty: she is also known from the pages of Bede's *Historia Ecclesiastica* (see above, p. 51); and from the identification of Hildelith the identification of the monastery in question (Barking) may be determined. The identification of Cuthburg with the erstwhile wife of King Aldfrith of Northumbria is reasonably certain. It is often stated by modern commentators that

Aldhelm was related to Cuthburg, but the Latin of the preface will not admit of such an interpretation: only Osburg (otherwise unknown) is stated by Aldhelm to be a relative. The other nuns addressed by Aldhelm are not known elsewhere. It is worth remarking that the names of the four nuns which are given in Latin—Justina, Scholastica, Eulalia and Thecla—are names of martyrs whose stories are subsequently recorded by Aldhelm in the *De Virginitate*.

2 It is not possible to identify this council, but there is perhaps some reason to believe that it was that at Hertford in 672 (see above, p. 141).

3 The letters from Barking addressed to Aldhelm have not survived.

4 The author of this rhythmical poem was probably Aldhelm himself (cf. Ehwald, pp. 520–1), who was fond of quoting his own verse: see *De Virginitate*, c. LV (above, p. 124), and Letter V (above, p. 164).

5 The Vulgate text reads *circumdata varietate* [Ps. XLIV. 10], whereas Aldhelm reads *circumamicta*; possibly Aldhelm, quoting from memory, conflated the Psalmist's words with those describing the vision of the throne of God in the *Apocalypse*, where the twenty-four elders are *circumamicti vestibus albis* [Apoc. IV. 4].

6 The *Acts of the Apostles* refer to Paul/Saul as the *vas electionis* [IX. 16]

7 Cf. Gen. III 24: 'And he cast out Adam; and placed before the paradise of pleasure Cherubims, and a flaming sword, turning every way, to keep the way of the tree of life'.

8 The exact meaning and derivation of the word *indruticans* is unknown. It is glossed in English MSS. as *ticgende* ('palpitating') and as *luxurians* (cf. Goosens, *The Old English Glosses of MS. Brussels, Royal Library 1650*, p. 230). Pheifer (*Old English Glosses in the Epinal-Erfurt Glossary*, p. 92) suggests that Aldhelm may simply have Latinized OE *drutian*, 'to swell', in the sense of 'behave insolently'. To my knowledge, there is no other example of Aldhelm Latinizing an OE word; see further Lindsay, *The Corpus, Epinal, Erfurt and Leiden Glossaries*, p. 21.

9 Apoc. XVII. 3: 'And I saw a woman sitting upon a scarlet coloured beast, full of names of blasphemy, having seven heads and ten horns'.

10 The volume in question would seem to be the *Passio S. Victoriae* (ed. *Analecta Bollandiana* II (1883), pp. 157–60), where a similar three-fold distinction is briefly enunciated. The application and elaboration of the idea, however, are Aldhelm's.

11 It is not quite clear why the 'urn of death' should be double (*gemina*)—possibly because it is both the urn of fate from which one's final lot is drawn, as well as a burial-urn.

12 Ehwald confessed himself unable to find the source of this quotation (*frustrum quaesivi*), and after a protracted search, I am obliged to agree with him. Nothing nearly resembling the quotation is found in the extant Greek versions of the *Acta Thomae* (cf. only the words of Thomas to Mygdonia, tr. M. R. James, *The Apocryphal New Testament*, corr. edn. [Oxford, 1953], p. 403), and we have no reason to assume that Aldhelm was citing such a version. Similarly, *Acta Thomae* constitute Book IX of pseudo-Abdias, *Historia Apostolica* (ed. J. A. Fabricius, *Codex Apocryphus Novi Testamenti* [Hamburg,

1703], vol. II, pp. 687–736), a sixth- or seventh-century Latin text which appears to have been known in the British Isles; but I have searched in vain through pseudo-Abdias for Aldhelm's quotation. However, from a fragment of the docetic Acts of Thomas, which was written in Ireland in the third quarter of the seventh century—hence contemporary with Aldhelm—we may surmise the existence of other apocryphal texts relating to Thomas which have not survived (cf. D. N. Dumville, 'Biblical Apocrypha and the Early Irish: A Preliminary Investigation', *Proceedings of the Royal Irish Academy* LXXIII C (1973), pp. 299–338, esp. p. 329). Aldhelm may have been quoting from some such lost text of the *Acta Thomae*.

13 It would appear that Aldhelm misread the *Second Epistle to the Corinthians* at this point: St Paul says merely, 'thrice I suffered shipwreck, a night and a day I was in the depth of the sea' (*ter naufragium feci, nocte et die in profundo maris fui* [II Cor. XI. 25]). Aldhelm unaccountably alters *in profundo maris* to *in fundo maris profundo* (p. 256. 6).

14 Aldhelm is not so much interested in praying to the classical gods (*superi*) to avert such a monster from England, as to reveal his facility in adapting a line from Vergil: *di talem terris avertite pestem* [*Aen.* III. 620].

15 The Vulgate text here reads *matresfamilias* (mistresses of families': Douay); Aldhelm altered this to *patresfamilias* to suit the context of the parents' exhortation to Julian.

16 This geographical error is not of Aldhelm's devising, but is found in several manuscripts of his source at this point, the *Acta Iuliani et Basilissae* (see above, p. 177.

17 Both here and in c. XXII Aldhelm seems to have conceived of an obelisk as a quadrate pillar surmounted by a sphere—unlike modern obelisks which do not normally have a sphere set on their top. Whether or not Aldhelm ever saw such an obelisk is beside the point; he may have gleaned some notion of their shape from Isidore, *Etym.* XVIII. xxxi: 'Summo obolisco superpositum est quoddam auratum in modum flammae formatum, quoniam sol plurimum in se caloris atque ignis habet'. That is to say, the sphere on top of the obelisk was intended to represent the sun.

18 The words *et cadent in terram* which are added here to the quotation from Isaias [XIX. 1] are found neither in the Vetus Latina nor in the Vulgate. Aldhelm copied them directly from Rufinus (*Historia Monachorum*, c. vii), but where Rufinus found them is unknown.

19 This is not the customary meaning of *legatarius*, but must be the way Aldhelm intended the word to be understood, to judge from Rufinus, Aldhelm's immediate source for this anecdote: 'omni auxilio frustrati legatos ad hominem Dei mittunt pollicentes, ut, si eos resolvat his vinculis, pariter quoque erroris in eis vincula dissolveret' [*Historia Monachorum*, c. vii: PL XXI, col. 414].

20 The meaning of this passage is not clear. It is of course anachronistic to associate Caecilia with the music of the organ at so early a period: she is not otherwise associated with the organ before the fourteenth century. What is in dispute is what meaning Aldhelm intended *organica harmonia* to bear: it is not out of the question that he conceived one instrument to be playing,

even though he himself had never seen such an instrument. On the other hand, *organica musica* is that which is produced by wind instruments (cf. Isidore, *Etym.* III. xix: 'organica, quae ex flatu consistit'); perhaps the one hundred and fifteen *voces sonorum* were produced by one hundred and fifteen woodwind players. Unfortunately, to my knowledge, this detail is not preserved in any printed version of the *Acta Caeciliae* which may have served as Aldhelm's source.

21 *Acta Sanctorum Aprilis*, vol. II, p. 204.

22 Paschasius the consul was not Lucia's suitor; but since Aldhelm's source did not give the name of the suitor, some ambiguity here was inevitable.

23 In his Addenda to the edition (after p. XXIV), Ehwald noted the view of von Winterfeld, that *vel trudere* ('or thrust') should be removed from the text; presumably the words originated as a gloss on *trahere* and were subsequently incorporated into the text.

24 This account of Cyprian is almost entirely apocryphal: he was an orator, not a sorcerer; he was converted by one Caecilian, an aged presbyter; he was martyred in 260 under Valerian, not under Claudius II (268–70). It was perhaps Jerome's statement (*Comm. in Ion.*, c. iii), that in his youth he was an *adsertor idolatriae*, that gave rise to the conception of him as a sorcerer.

25 On the six (or seven) stages of baptism, see Isidore, *De Ecclesiaticis Officiis* II. xxv. 4 (PL LXXXIII, col. 821).

26 Until fairly recently, the *Epistola ad Demetriadem* was considered to be the work of Jerome, and it is printed among his works by Migne. However, modern scholarship has demonstrated that the author of the letter is in fact Pelagius, the arch-enemy of both Jerome and Augustine (cf. G. de Plinval, *Pélage, ses écrits, sa vie et sa réforme* [Lausanne, 1943], pp. 26 and 245–51). Aldhelm would no doubt have been horrified to find that the *volumen prolixa et lepida sermonum serie* was by Pelagius.

27 Aldhelm's *Tribulanum municipium* is ancient *Trebula Mutuesca*, now Monteleone, some thirty miles from Rome in the Sabine hills.

28 Aldhelm, apparently quoting from memory, seems to have conflated more than one biblical passage here. Ehwald draws attention to II Reg. XXI. 17 ('iam non egrederis nobiscum in bellum, ne extinguas lucernam Israel'). More relevant are two passages not mentioned by Ehwald: the eternal succession of David's seed is promised in Psalm. LXXXVIII. 3–4, and the phrase *extinguere scintillam* is used of a line perishing by a female suppliant to Joab (II Reg. XIV. 7). A similar divine commandment is recorded at III Reg. XI. 11–12.

29 The word Aldhelm uses of Lot's relationship to Abraham, *fratruelis*, is specific and means 'cousin'; in the Vulgate, Lot is the son of Abraham's brother (*filium fratris sui*: Gen. XII. 5).

30 On Aldhelm's use of Cyprian in this passage, see R. B. Domra, 'Notes on Cyprian's *De Habitu Virginum*, its Source and Influence', *Traditio* IV (1946), pp. 399–407.

31 MSS. of Vergil invariably read *mutabit* here, which is consonant with the other future tenses in the quoted passage; some MSS. of Aldhelm, however,

read *mutavit*, and this reading was printed by Ehwald: presumably Ehwald thought that Aldhelm was quoting Vergil from a corrupt exemplar.

32 The phrase *et composuit se in rapinam virorum*, upon which Aldhelm bases his claim that the adornment of women is the depredation of men, is not found in the Vulgate. It is, however, found in a Vetus Latina version (*Biblorum Sacrorum Latinae Versiones Antiquae*, ed. P. Sabatier [Rheims, 1743], vol. I, p. 772), from which Aldhelm was apparently quoting.

INTRODUCTION TO THE LETTERS OF ALDHELM (pp. 136–51)

1 W. Levison, *England and the Continent in the Eighth Century* (Oxford, 1946), p. 238, n. 6.
2 A. S. Cook, 'Aldhelm's Rude Infancy', *Philological Quarterly* VII (1928), pp. 115–9.
3 In the glossaries one finds such definitions of *cliens* as *amicus minor* and *amicus inferior*, hence 'companion' (*Corpus Glossariorum Latinorum*, ed. G. Goetz. 7 vols. [Leipzig, 1888–1923], VI, s.v. 'cliens'). In the British Isles, the word became part of monastic usage, perhaps in the sense *sodalis*; see the index to Ehwald and the *Hisperica Famina* (ed. Herren) at A 296: *conclientibus* = 'companions'.
4 See Plummer's note to *HE* IV. 4 (*Baedae Opera Historica*, II, pp. 210–11), and more recently the discussion by N. K. Chadwick, 'Bede, St Colmán and the Irish Abbey of Mayo', in *Celt and Saxon*, ed. N. K. Chadwick (Cambridge, 1964), pp. 186–205.
5 The arguments that have raged over the state of classical learning in sixth- and seventh-century Ireland cannot be adequately summarized here. Much hinges on two problems surrounding St Columbanus (=Columba the Younger, *ob.* 615): (1) the authenticity of several poems attributed to him that show acquaintance with classical literature (some are in classical metres); (2) the extent to which his training in Ireland can account for the classical allusions in those works accorded as genuine. Although extravagant claims are no longer made for either Columbanus's classical education or for Irish humanism in general, the closest adherent to the view championing Irish classical learning is Ludwig Bieler; see his 'The Island of Scholars', *Revue de moyen âge latin* VIII (1952), pp. 227–34, and *Ireland, Harbinger of the Middle Ages* (London, 1963). The most sceptical investigator of these questions is J. W. Smit, *Studies on the Language and Style of Columba the Younger (Columbanus)* (Amsterdam, 1971).
6 Herren, *Hisperica Famina I*, pp. 24–6; J. F. Kenney, *Sources for the Early History of Ireland I: Ecclesiastical*, rev. L. Bieler (New York, 1966), pp. 286–7. For a parody of a Vergilian line by Virgilius Maro Grammaticus, see E. Ernault, *De Virgilio Marone Grammatico Tolosano* (Paris, 1886), p. 24.
7 Professor Carney's views are summarized by W. B. Stanford, 'Towards a History of Classical Influences in Ireland', *Proceedings of the Royal Irish Academy* LXX C (1970), 15–91, at p. 33.
8 *Ibid.*, pp. 33–8.

9 H. Hahn, *Bonifaz und Lul* (Leipzig, 1883), p. 39.
10 Faricius, *Vita S. Aldhelmi*, c. II (ed. J. A. Giles, *Vita Quorundum Anglo-Saxonum*, p. 131), reports a council of the West Saxons, convoked in 705, to deal with the British schism. According to Faricius, that council asked Aldhelm to address a letter to the Britons. But Faricius would seem to have had no other authority than Bede, since he refers to Aldhelm as 'still a priest' (as does Bede) and makes the synod a local one. As we have observed, Aldhelm's own words contradict such an interpretation.
11 Some authorities have accepted the identification without question; e.g. F. M. Stenton, *Anglo-Saxon England*. 3rd edn. (Oxford, 1971), p. 64.
12 Ehwald (p. 493) was undoubtedly right to bracket the words *beatae memoriae* placed before Theodore's name, as Aldhelm has just made it abundantly clear (p. 492) that Theodore is still alive and active.
13 See above, p. 182, n. 14.
14 For a full discussion of Aldhelm's adaptation, see the note to the translation, p. 202 below.
15 A. S. Cook 'Who was the Ehfrid of Aldhelm's Letter?', *Speculum* II (1927), pp. 363–73.
16 See K. Hughes, 'Evidence for Contacts Between the Churches of the Irish and English', in *England before the Conquest: Studies presented to Dorothy Whitelock*, ed. P. Clemoes and K. Hughes (Cambridge, 1971), pp. 51–3, as well as the study by N. K. Chadwick cited above n. 4.
17 Aldhelm's Letter to Wihtfrith, above p. 154; *Hisperica Famina* A 1–357 (ed. Herren) and the editor's remarks on pp. 33–5; Bede, *HE* III. 27 and IV. 4. The so-called First Synod of Patrick (ed. L. Bieler in *The Irish Penitentials*. Scriptores Latini Hiberniae V (Dublin, 1963), pp. 54–9) contains this canon: 'Clericus vagus non sit in plebe' (No. 3).
18 J. N. Hillgarth, 'Visigothic Spain and Early Christian Ireland', *Proceedings of the Royal Irish Academy* LXII C (1962), pp. 167–94; D. N. Dumville, 'Biblical Apocrypha and the Early Irish: A Preliminary Investigation', *Proceedings of the Royal Irish Academy* LXXIII C (1973), pp. 299–338, esp. pp. 330ff.
19 P. Grosjean, 'Confusa Caligo', *Celtica* III (1956), p. 64.
20 'Pretereo Scottos, tunc maxime doctos, qui idem fecisse noscuntur. Quorum aliquos non obscurae litteraturae nominare possem, maxime Artwilum regis Scottiae filium. Hic quicquid litterariae artis elaborat, quod non adeo exile erat, Aldelmi committebat arbitrio, ut perfecti ingenii lima eraderetur scabredo Scottica' (pp. 336–7).
21 See above, p. 9.
22 See above, p. 14.
23 See above, p. 101 and n. 28.
24 See Ehwald's preface to the *Carmina Rhythmica*, pp. 522–3. The possibility that Æthilwald could be identical with King Æthilbald has been peremptorily disposed of by I. Schröbler, 'Zu den Carmina Rhythmica in der Wiener Handschrift der Bonifatiusbriefe', *Beiträge zur Geschichte der deutschen Sprache und Literatur* LXXIX (1957), pp. 1–42, esp. pp. 1–8.
25 It has been suggested that this Æthilwald is identical with the Æthilwald

who later became bishop of Lindisfarne (724–40) and who is known to be the author of some acrostic verses; see D. N. Dumville, 'Liturgical Drama and Panegyric Responsory from the Eighth Century? A Re-examination of the Origin and Contents of the Ninth-Century Section of the Book of Cerne', *Journal of Theological Studies* XXIII (1972), pp. 374–406, at p. 399, n. 1.

26 For the authenticity of various poems assigned to Cellanus, see L. Traube, 'Perrona Scottorum', *Sitzungsberichte d. phil.-hist. Cl. d. k. bayer. Akad. d. Wiss. zu München, 1900* (Munich, 1901), pp. 469–538; see also Kenney, *Sources*, p. 507, and M. Lapidge, 'Some Remnants of Bede's Lost *Liber Epigrammatum*', *English Historical Review* XC (1975), pp. 798–820, esp. pp. 804–5.

27 If Aldhelm championed Wilfrid in 677, we could expect him to have incurred the disfavour not only of Theodore, but also of Ecgfrith. The restoration of Wilfrid to his see by Aldfrith in 686 might have thawed out relations between Aldhelm and Northumbria and—it is tempting to think—have occasioned the *Epistola ad Acircium*.

28 For the chronology of Wilfrid, see Plummer, *Baedae Opera Historica*, II, p. 316.

THE LETTERS OF ALDHELM (pp. 152–70)

1 For the identity of the recipient of this letter, see Ehwald's thorough discussion, p. 475, and above, p. 137.

2 'Hundred types of metres': a reference to the *De Centum Metris* of Servius; cf. H. Keil, *Grammatici Latini.* 7 vols. (Leipzig, 1848–80), IV, pp. 456–67.

3 Aldhelm discusses these in the *De Metris et Enigmatibus ac Pedum Regulis* (=*Epistola ad Acircium*), Ehwald, pp. 94–5; that section of the *Epistola ad Acircium* is not translated in the present volume.

4 Aldhelm lists astrology as one of the seven liberal arts (in addition to astronomy) in both the *Epistola ad Acircium*, c. III (above p. 42) and in the *De Virginitate*, c. XXXV (above, p. 96). See the paper by M. L. W. Laistner, 'The Western Church and Astrology', reprinted in his *Intellectual Heritage of the Early Middle Ages* (Ithaca, N.Y., 1957), pp. 57–82. Aldhelm expresses a much more negative view towards astrology in the *Epistola ad Acircium*, p. 43.

5 Translating *infantiae* in its most basic sense; see also above, p. 138 and n. 2.

6 Philosophers, i.e. 'men of learning'. In Aldhelm's writings and in his period generally, the terms *philosophus* and *philosophia* were not used in the specialized sense employed by ancient writers and by writers of the later middle ages. 'Philosophy' was rather the sum of learning as expressed in the seven liberal arts; see now P. O. Kristeller, 'The Historical Position of Johannes Scottus Eriugena', in *Latin Script and Letters A.D. 400–900: Festschrift presented to Ludwig Bieler*, ed. J. J. O'Meara and B. Naumann (Leiden, 1976), p. 158.

7 Translating *parasitorum*; elsewhere Aldhelm uses the word to mean

'follower', 'adherent', e.g. at *De Virginitate*, c. XXXV (Ehwald, p. 279.19).

8 Aldhelm may have been somewhat shaky in his knowledge of prostitution in Ireland.There seems to have been ample opportunity in that country for sexual relations outside marriage, and prostitutes composed one of the classes of women named in the laws, but there is no other evidence for the existence of bawdy houses *per se*; see the articles by R. Thurneysen and N. Power in *Studies in Early Irish Law*, ed. D. A. Binchy (Dublin, 1936), pp. 1–80 and 81–108.

9 Aldhelm hints only that Wihtfrith's place of sojourn is in the *climate septentrionali*. This could mean virtually anywhere in the northern part of Ireland or even Iona. In the letter to Heahfrith, however, Aldhelm provides a clue that Heahfrith has just come from Mayo, or spent some time there; see above, p. 139, n. 4.

10 Translating *Domnonia*, i.e. modern Devon and Cornwall.

11 This work was known to the English through the Latin translation of Rufinus; see J. D. A. Ogilvy, *Books Known to the English 597–1066* (Cambridge, Mass., 1967), p. 116.

12 Aldhelm's attribution of the 'tonsure-heresy' to Simon may derive ultimately from Eusebius's statement that 'Simon was the prime author of every heresy' (*Hist. Eccl.* XIII. 1); Aldhelm will have known Eusebius in Rufinus's translation.

13 The custom is mentioned by Aulus Gellius, *Noctes Atticae* VI. iv. 3.

14 'Hair ... crimes': a word-play on *crinibus* and *criminibus*.

15 For a detailed discussion of the paschal controversy, see C. W. Jones, *Bedae Opera de Temporibus*, pp. 6–112; more succinct accounts may be found in Plummer, *Baedae Opera Historica*, II, pp. 348–54, and Kenney, *Sources for the Early History of Ireland*, pp. 210–13. There is a more recent discussion by K. Harrison, *The Framework of Anglo-Saxon History to A.D. 900* (Cambridge, 1976), pp. 30–51.

16 The *Cursus Paschalis Annorum DXXXII* by Victorius of Aquitaine is ed. T. Mommsen, MGH. Auct. Antiq. IX, pp. 667–743.

17 Translating *Demetia*, i.e. south-western Wales; Aldhelm's diatribe crosses the Severn to include the clergy of that district.

18 The same complaint was voiced earlier by Laurentius, Mellitus and Justus in their letter addressed *fratribus episcopis uel abbatibus per universam Scottiam* (partially preserved by Bede, *HE* II.4).

19 Translating *lomentum*, i.e. some type of washing agent, possibly nitre or soda; cf. *Corpus Glossariorum Latinorum* V.544 and 602. The classical meaning of *lomentum*, 'a cosmetic made of bean-meal and rice' could hardly apply here.

20 Aldhelm omits *hypocritae* given after *Pharisaei* in modern editions of the Vulgate.

21 The poet is Aldhelm himself; the line is repeated in the *Carm. Eccles.* I. 6 and IV. i. 2 (Ehwald, pp. 11 and 19); in the prose *De Virginitate*, c. LV (Ehwald, p. 314); and in the *Epistola ad Acircium* (Ehwald, p. 68).

22 This formula, which distinguishes between *substantia* and *subsistentia*, is somewhat different from that of the Council of Hatfield (679): 'Patrem et

Filium et Spiritum Sanctum trinitatem in unitate consubstantialem et un-
itatem in trinitate, hoc est unum Deum in tribus subsistentiis, uel personis
consubstantialibus' (Bede, *HE* IV. 17; cf. Plummer's note, *Baedae Opera
Historica*, II, p. 232). We need not therefore suppose that Aldhelm was in-
corporating in his letter a formula of the Council of Hatfield, as Hahn
(*Bonifaz und Lul*, p. 39) and Ehwald, following him, supposed.

23 The 'Catholic Epistle of St James' is addressed specifically to the 'twelve
tribes which are scattered abroad' (Iac. I. 1), i.e. the Jews of the Diaspora.

24 On the identity of Heahfrith, see above, p. 145.

25 Mynors and Colgrave's note is worth repeating here: 'Our knowledge of
Old English heathenism is comparatively limited and Bede is our most important source of information about what is always referred to as "devil
worship". The three most important passages on the subject are the letter
from Gregory to Mellitus (I. 30), the account of Edwin's conversion (II.
13), and a chapter in Bede's *De Temporum Ratione* entitled *De Mensibus
Anglorum*' (*Bede's Ecclesiastical History of the English People*, p. 107). The present passage in Aldhelm ought henceforth to be added to these passages in
Bede.

26 See above, p. 145.

27 Translating *circili carina*. *Circilis* is apparently an adjectival form combining
Greek χερχίς, 'aspen' with the Latin ending -*ilis*. The English must have
understood *circilis* 'of aspen' as 'of ash', for we find the Latin–Old English
gloss *circilis: æsc uel nauis* (see J. D. Pheifer, *Old English Glosses in the Epinal-
Erfurt Glossary* [Oxford, 1974], p. 11), which possibly arose because *æsc* in
Old English means both the tree and things made of the tree, especially the
spear and the boat.

28 Translating *tirocinii*. Aldhelm sometimes uses the term *tirocinium* in connection with education, so I have used the term 'learning' here; cf. *Epistola ad
Acircium*, Ehwald, p. 62.15 *(matura rudimentorum tirocinia)* and p. 69.14 *(ab ipso
tirocinio rudimentorum)*.

29 Translating *navigero calle*, possibly an attempt by Aldhelm to render an Old
English kenning into Latin.

30 After *conglobatio lectorum* there follows the gloss in a number of manuscripts:
tunning tat fried (or *tunning tatfrid*). Ehwald, p. 490, reports an explanation of
the gloss as *cunning tatfrid*, i.e. *experientia Tatfrithi*. Someone named Tatfrith,
who was appointed to the see of the Hwicce, is mentioned by Bede (*HE* IV.
23). It is possible, however, that the gloss may be a corruption of *Tunna et
Tatfrith*: someone called Tunna is also mentioned by Bede as being abbot of
the unidentified *Tunnacæstir*, c. 680 (*HE* IV. 22). If that conjecture is
right, then Tunna and Tatfrith are mentioned by the glossator as two
examples of Anglo-Saxon students who studied in Ireland.

31 This would indicate that Irish biblical scholars in the latter part of the
seventh century engaged in the traditional 'Alexandrine' method of
biblical interpretation as well as the Antiochene type that was so popular in
Ireland. See M. L. W. Laistner, 'Antiochene Exegesis in Western Europe
during the Middle Ages', *Harvard Theological Review* XL (1947), pp. 19–31;
for Ireland in particular see B. Bischoff, 'Wendepunkte in der Geschichte

der lateinischen Exegese im Frühmittelalter', reprinted in his *Mittelalterliche Studien*, I, pp. 205–73, and now translated in *Biblical Studies: The Medieval Irish Contribution*, ed. M. McNamara (Dublin, 1976), pp. 74–160.

32 *Pacificus*, i.e. Solomon; cf. p. 188, n. 10.

33 Translating *philosophicae artis*; cf. p. 199, n. 6.

?4 Ehwald has rightly bracketed the words *beatae memoriae* that occur after the name of Theodore, as Aldhelm has just spoken of Theodore as very much alive.

35 Syllogisms of chronography, i.e. the intricacies of the reckoning of the Paschal cycle.

36 Translating *tyfo*, from *typhus*, a grecism (τῦφος) meaning 'arrogance' or 'vanity'; cf. *Carmen de Virginitate*, 2713 and 2753.

37 This line has been much discussed, e.g. by P. Lejay, *Revue de philologie* XIX (1895), p. 6of., and by L. Traube, *Hermes* XXIV (1889), pp. 647–9. Lejay's reworking of the line, cited by Ehwald (p. 494) does not seem possible. I am inclined to think that the line should be printed as a couplet containing two seven-syllable verses:

> Dignus fante Glingio
> gurgo fugax fambulo.

Without begging the question of the metre, *fiat* can be excised on grounds of sense. Moreover, there is some slight textual evidence for the deletion: the erasure of *fante* in Salisbury Cathedral, MS. 38 (s. x²), indicates that the line was regarded as suspect. In any case, the line is to be scanned rhythmically, not metrically. *Gurgo* is glossed by *garrulus* (*Corpus Glossariorum Latinorum*, V. 299), and I have treated it here as a noun. *Fambulo* is not to be taken for *bambulo* (as does Ehwald), but rather as a variant spelling for *famulo*. Thus *dignus ... fambulo* means 'worthy of a slave', or, as I have translated, 'worthy of enslavement'. 'Glengus' is one of the bogus sources of Virgilius Maro Grammaticus. The borrowing clearly shows Aldhelm's knowledge of the latter writer, who wrote: 'ne in illud Glengi incedam, quod cuidam conflictum fugienti dicere fidenter ausus est, "gurgo", inquit, "fugax fambulo dignus est" ' (ed. Huemer, p. 121). Traube, *op. cit.*, p. 649, showed long ago the aptness of the quotation: if Heahfrith left England to teach elsewhere, he would earn the label *gurgo fugax*. In my opinion, there were other reasons for Aldhelm's citation: (1) he uses an Irish writer to make his satire on the Irish; (2) he contrasts a common Hiberno-Latin verse type with his own metrical hexameters. For the Irish origin of Virgilius, see my 'Some New Light on the Life of Virgilius Maro Grammaticus', *Proceedings of the Royal Irish Academy* LXXVIII C (1978), forthcoming.

38 The last four lines of the pastiche are found also in Aldhelm's *Carmen de Virginitate*; see Ehwald, p. 494, and above, p. 144.

39 'Various flowers of letters': probably a reference to the *De Virginitate*; see above, p. 147.

40 Translating *litterariae verbositatis*. *Verbositas* does not appear to be pejorative in this context.

41 Roboam: canonical books tell us only that Roboam was the son of Solomon by Naama, an Ammonitess (III Reg. XIV. 21 and II Paral. XII. 13).

42 Translating 'et in LXX coaequantium vorsuum formulas'. This is intriguing: does Æthilwald here refer to some types of iso-syllabic hexameter?

43 The poems mentioned in this letter are extant in the same manuscript (Codex Vindobonensis 751). They are printed by Ehwald as Nos. ii and iv of the *Carmina Rhythmica* (pp. 528–33 and 534–4).

44 See Plummer's enlightening note (*Baedae Opera Historica*, II, pp. 276–7) on the dubious practice of re-baptism in England at this period. The fact that the practice was not widely condoned explains the unnamed bishop's desire for secrecy in the matter.

45 For Cellanus, see above, p. 149.

46 The Latin is ambiguous and could also mean: '. . . discovering on the shores of the Saxons *that* some scarcely benefit through labour and sweat in a foreign clime'; see above, p. 149.

47 Translating *deliciis florum*: again, probably a reference to either or both versions of the *De Virginitate*. See Letter VI, p. 164, n. 39, and the introduction, p. 147.

48 That Aldhelm wrote sermons (or 'discourses'?) is also attested by William of Malmesbury (p. 344); but William may have derived his information from this letter of Cellanus.

49 Furseus's resting place was Péronne in Picardy. A full account of his life is given by Bede, *HE* III. 19.

50 Translating *tantillum homunculum*: the phrase smacks of sarcasm as does the reference to *famoso et florigero Francorum rure*.

51 The text quoted here (Douay), which follows standard modern editions of the Vulgate, is not what Aldhelm wrote. Our author has: *in gloria sua et sanctorum angelorum*, which gives a quite different sense.

APPENDIX I (pp. 171–2)

1 The variation between *l* and *r* is common in medieval orthography, and it is quite possible that Aldhelm himself did not distinguish between *flagro* and *fragro* in writing. However, because this particular orthographical variation in Aldhelm manuscripts is not noted by Strecker (in Ehwald, pp. 756–65), and because modern readers might wish to distinguish between (say) 'fragrant ambrosia' and 'flagrant (i.e. burning) incense', we have noted—at the risk of pedantry—those places where one or the other variant is required.

2 We are indebted to Dr Michael Winterbottom for this conjecture.

APPENDIX II (pp. 173-5)

1 Ehwald, p. 507.
2 See the bibliography pertaining to the first three charters printed by Ehwald in P. H. Sawyer, *Anglo-Saxon Charters. An Annotated List and Bibliography* (London, 1968), Nos. 230 (King Cædwalla to bishop Wilfrid, of land at Pagham, etc. = Ehwald, No. III, pp. 510–12), 1166 (Cenfrith, *comes* of the Mercians to Aldhelm, of land at Wootton Bassett = Ehwald, No. II, pp. 609–10), and 1245 (bishop Leuthere to Aldhelm, of land at Malmesbury = Ehwald, No. I, pp. 507–9). The other two charters printed by Ehwald (a confirmation of privileges by Pope Sergius I for Malmesbury (no. IV) and confirmation by King Ine concerning abbatial succession at Malmesbury (No. V)), are patently spurious.
3 *Bonifaz und Lul*, pp. 8 and 84.
4 *Aldhelm von Malmesbury*, pp. 59–60; .cf. M. Roger, *L'enseignement des lettres classiques*, p. 291.
5 Ehwald, p. 509: 'charta (*scil.* Ehwald No. II) ab Aldhelmo videtur esse concepta'.
6 'A Putative Charter to Aldhelm', in *Studies in English Philology. A Miscellany in Honor of Frederick Klaeber*, pp. 254–7.
7 As H. P. R. Finberg wished to believe: *The Early Charters of Wessex* (Leicester, 1964), Nos. 181 and 182 (p. 69).
8 On the difficulties of translating this term in Anglo-Saxon contexts see H. M. Chadwick, *Studies on Anglo-Saxon Institutions* (Cambridge, 1905), pp. 318–27.

INDEX OF NAMES

205

Constantius, father of Constantine, 115
Cosmas and Damianus, 95–6
Cuthburg, queen of Aldfrith, 15, 52, 54, 56, 59, 193
Cyniberht, abbot, 175
Cyprian, St, 52, 109–10, 125–6, 196

Dalila, 123
Damianus: see Cosmas
Daniel, 77–8, 89, 103, 123
Daniel, bishop of Winchester, 2
Daria, St, 97–9, 193
David, 37, 57, 70, 122–3
Dealwine, 2, 16, 18, 185
Decius, Roman emperor, 119
Demetrias, 115–6
Devon (*Domnonia*), 141, 142, 155
Diana (goddess), 121
Didymus (Thomas), 81, 185
Diocletian, Roman emperor, 95, 99, 107, 109, 117, 118
Diomedes, grammarian, 13, 31
Dominic of Evesham, 181
Domitian, Roman emperor, 64
Donatus, grammarian, 31
Dorothea, St, 113–5
Doulting, Somerset, 10, 181
Dryhthelm, 54
Dulcitius, 117–8
Dyfed (*Demetia*), 142, 158

Eadburg, abbess of Thanet, 2, 51
Eadfrith, bishop of Lindisfarne, 145
Eanflæd, abbess of Whitby, 52
Ebroin, 138
Ecgberht, Northumbrian priest, 145
Ecgburg, correspondent of St Boniface, 2
Ecgfrith, king of Northumbria, 32, 52, 150, 151, 199
Ecgwine, bishop of Worcester, 181
Echfrith, abbot of Glastonbury (?), 145
'Eddius' Stephanus, 144, 150, 151
Edwin, king of Northumbria, 52

Eleazar, 36
Elias (Elijah), 35, 76, 106, 188
Eliseus (Elisha), 40, 76
Ely, monastery at, 51, 52
Emath, 36
Eorcenwald, bishop of London, 51, 149
Epicurus, 110
Epidaurus (Dalmatia), 88, 89
Esau, 40
Etna, Mt, 107
Eugenia, St, 110–11
Eugenius, 120
Eulalia, St, 113
Eulalia, nun at Barking, 59
Eusebius of Caesarea, historian, 86, 90, 93
Eusebius (Hwætberht) of Jarrow, 1
Eustochium, 53, 115–16
Eutyches, heresy of (Monophysitism), 141
Evagrius, 87
Ezechiel, 79, 81

Farisius, biographer of Aldhelm, 5, 6, 9, 181, 198
Felicity, St, 108, 185
Felix, author of the *Vita S. Guthlaci*, 2
Felix, bishop, 87
Felix, St, of Nola, 57
Frisia, 150
Frome, river, 9, 183
Fursa, St, 149, 167

Gabriel, 40
Gallicanus, 115
Gallienus, Roman emperor, 118
Geraint, king of *Domnonia*: Aldhelm's letter to: 5, 9, 11, 140–3, 150, 155–60
Gervasius, 185
Gideon, 39
Gilboa, Mt, 69
Gilgal, 76
Gilling, monastery at, 52
Glengus, 144, 164, 202

210